Patsy Walker, A.K.A. HELLCAT!

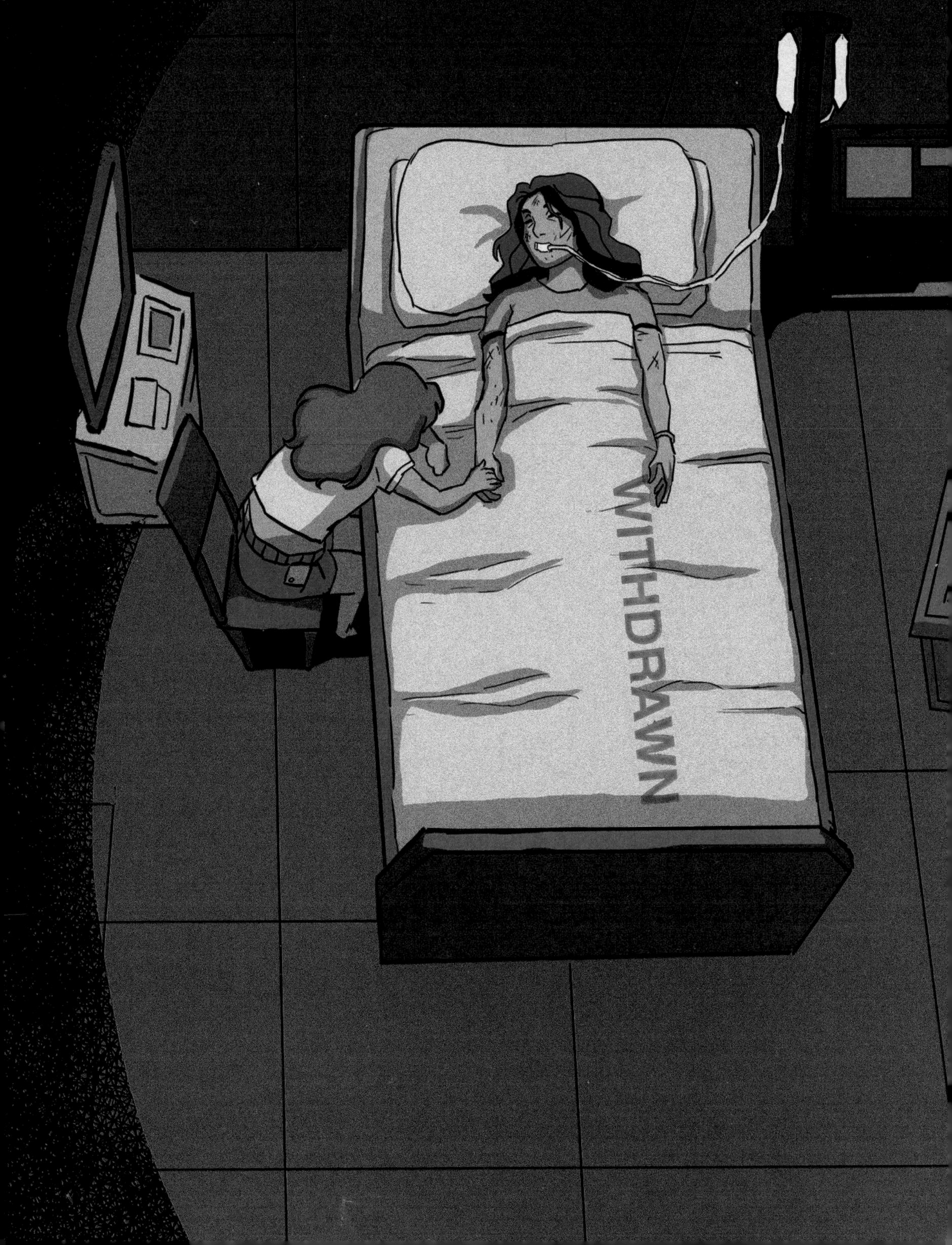

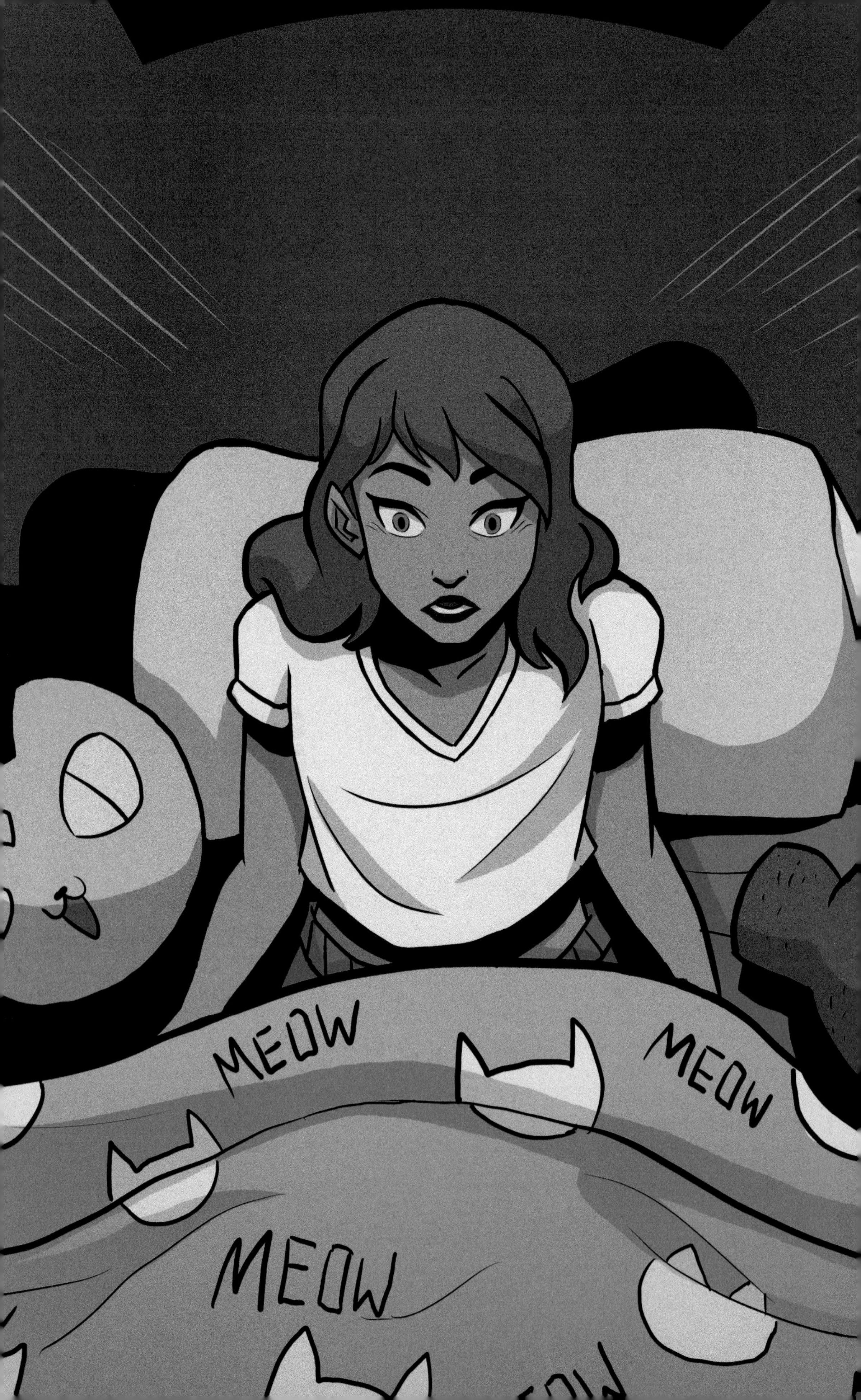
MEOW
MEOW
MEOW

Patsy Walker, A.K.A. HELLCAT!

Don't Stop Me-Ow

Kate Leth
WRITER

Brittney L. Williams
ARTIST

Megan Wilson (#7, #9-10) &
Rachelle Rosenberg (#8, #11-12)
COLOR ARTISTS

VC's Clayton Cowles
LETTERER

Brittney L. Williams COVER ART

Chris Robinson &
Kathleen Wisneski
ASSISTANT EDITORS

Wil Moss &
Jake Thomas
EDITORS

Tom Brevoort
EXECUTIVE EDITOR

Jennifer Grünwald
COLLECTION EDITOR

Kateri Woody
ASSOCIATE MANAGING EDITOR

Sarah Brunstad
ASSOCIATE EDITOR

Mark D. Beazley
EDITOR, SPECIAL PROJECTS

Jeff Youngquist
VP PRODUCTION & SPECIAL PROJECTS

David Gabriel
SVP PRINT, SALES & MARKETING

Jay Bowen
BOOK DESIGNER

Axel Alonso
EDITOR IN CHIEF

Joe Quesada
CHIEF CREATIVE OFFICER

Dan Buckley
PUBLISHER

Alan Fine
EXECUTIVE PRODUCER

PATSY WALKER, A.K.A. HELLCAT! VOL. 2: DON'T STOP ME-OW. Contains material originally published in magazine form as PATSY WALKER, A.K.A. HELLCAT! #7-12. First printing 2016. ISBN# 978-1-302-90036-6. Published by MARVEL WORLDWIDE, INC., a subsidiary of MARVEL ENTERTAINMENT, LLC. OFFICE OF PUBLICATION: 135 West 50th Street, New York, NY 10020. **Printed in the U.S.A.** ALAN FINE, President, Marvel Entertainment; DAN BUCKLEY, President, TV, Publishing & Brand Management; JOE QUESADA, Chief Creative Officer; TOM BREVOORT, SVP of Publishing; DAVID BOGART, SVP of Business Affairs & Operations, Publishing & Partnership; C.B. CEBULSKI, VP of Brand Management & Development, Asia; DAVID GABRIEL, SVP of Sales & Marketing, Publishing; JEFF YOUNGQUIST, VP of Production & Special Projects; DAN CARR, Executive Director of Publishing Technology; ALEX MORALES, Director of Publishing Operations; SUSAN CRESPI, Production Manager; STAN LEE, Chairman Emeritus. For information regarding advertising in Marvel Comics or on Marvel.com, please contact Vit DeBellis, Integrated Sales Manager, at vdebellis@marvel.com. For Marvel subscription inquiries, please call 888-511-5480. **Manufactured between 10/28/2016 and 12/5/2016 by QUAD/GRAPHICS WASECA, WASECA, MN, USA.**

10 9 8 7 6 5 4 3 2 1

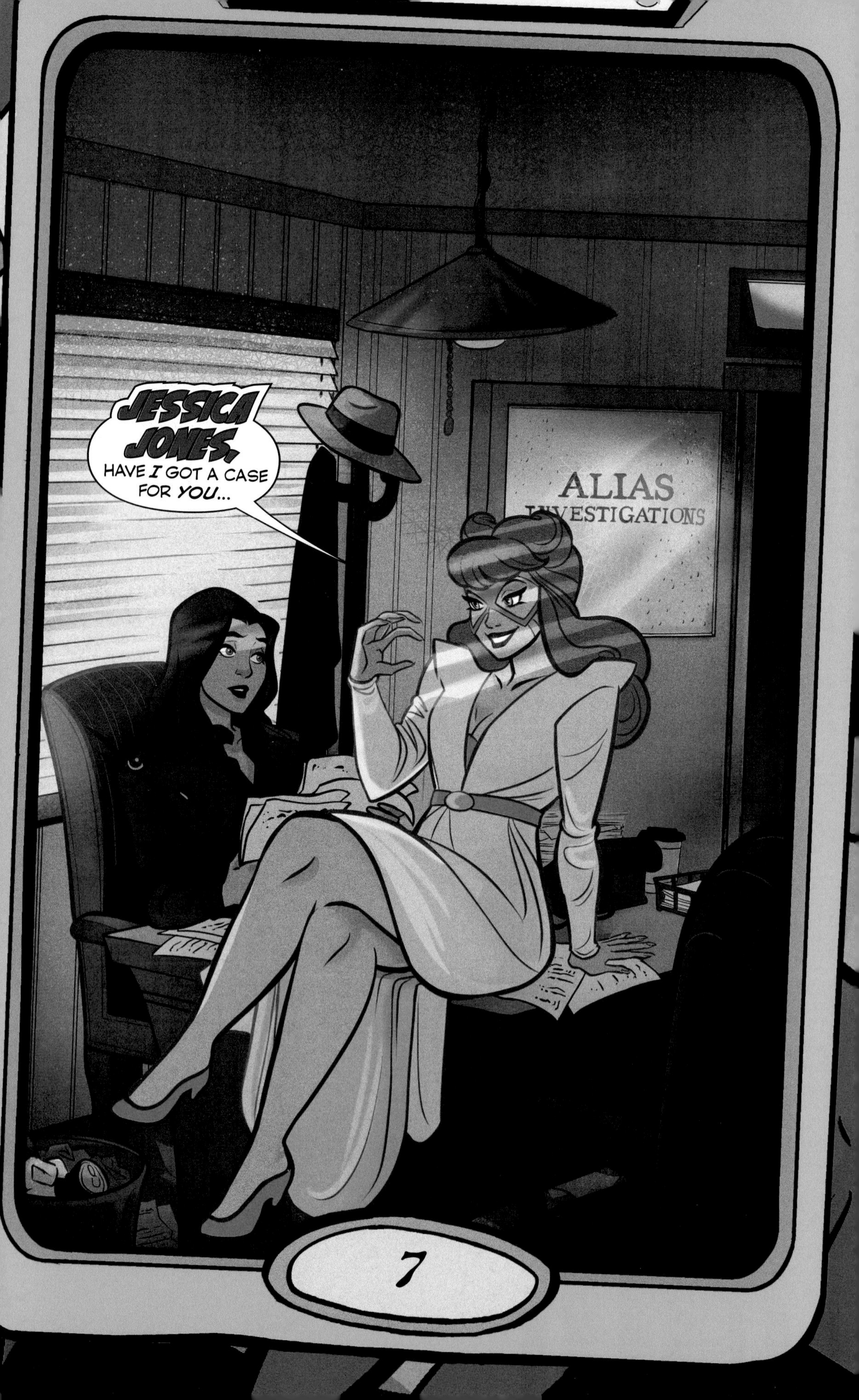
JESSICA JONES, HAVE I GOT A CASE FOR YOU...
ALIAS INVESTIGATIONS
7

Patsy Walker, A.K.A. HELLCAT!

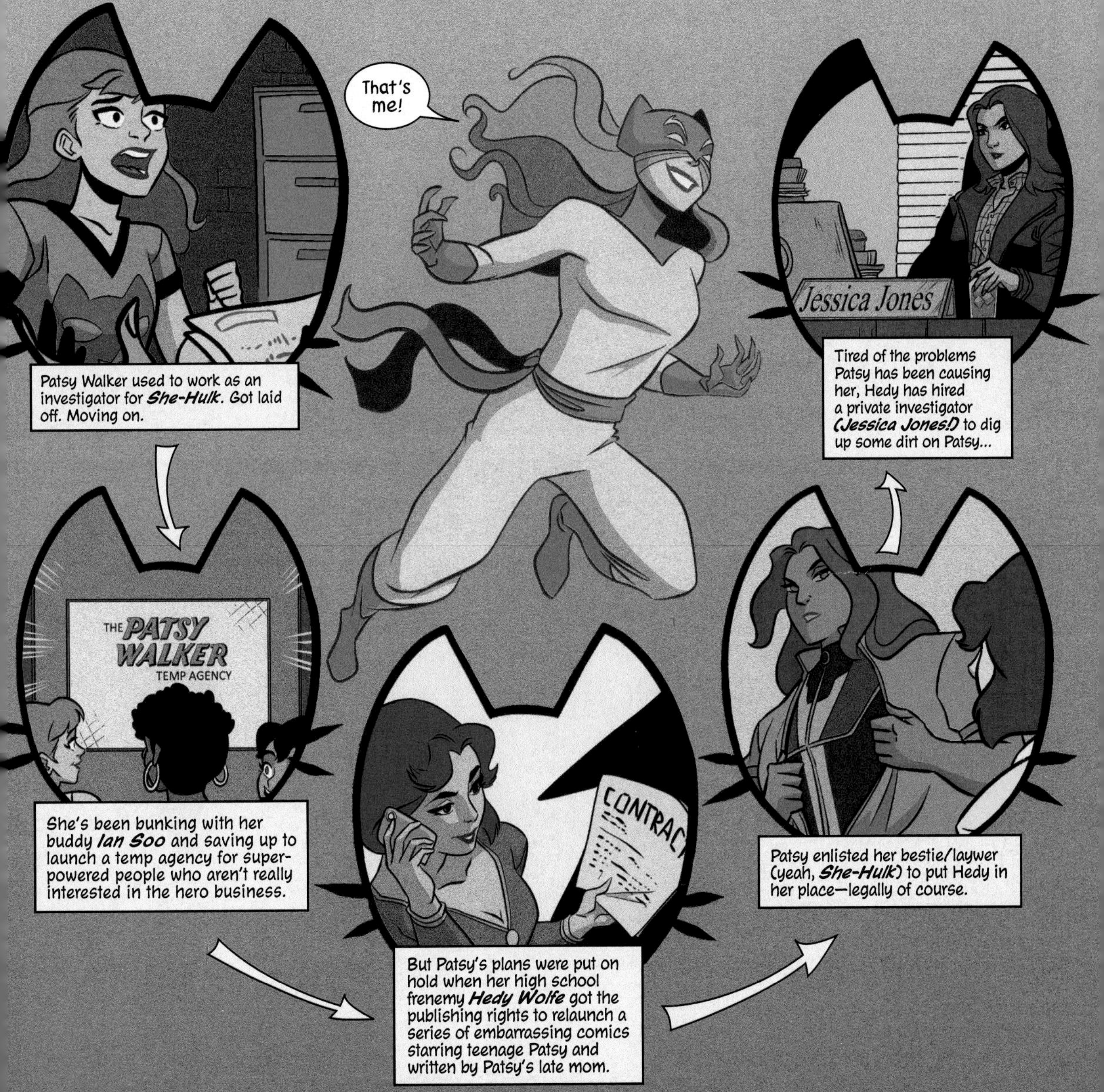
That's me!
Patsy Walker used to work as an investigator for She-Hulk. Got laid off. Moving on.
THE PATSY WALKER TEMP AGENCY
She's been bunking with her buddy Ian Soo and saving up to launch a temp agency for super-powered people who aren't really interested in the hero business.
CONTRACT
But Patsy's plans were put on hold when her high school frenemy Hedy Wolfe got the publishing rights to relaunch a series of embarrassing comics starring teenage Patsy and written by Patsy's late mom.
Patsy enlisted her bestie/laywer (yeah, She-Hulk) to put Hedy in her place—legally of course.
Tired of the problems Patsy has been causing her, Hedy has hired a private investigator (Jessica Jones!) to dig up some dirt on Patsy...
Jessica Jones

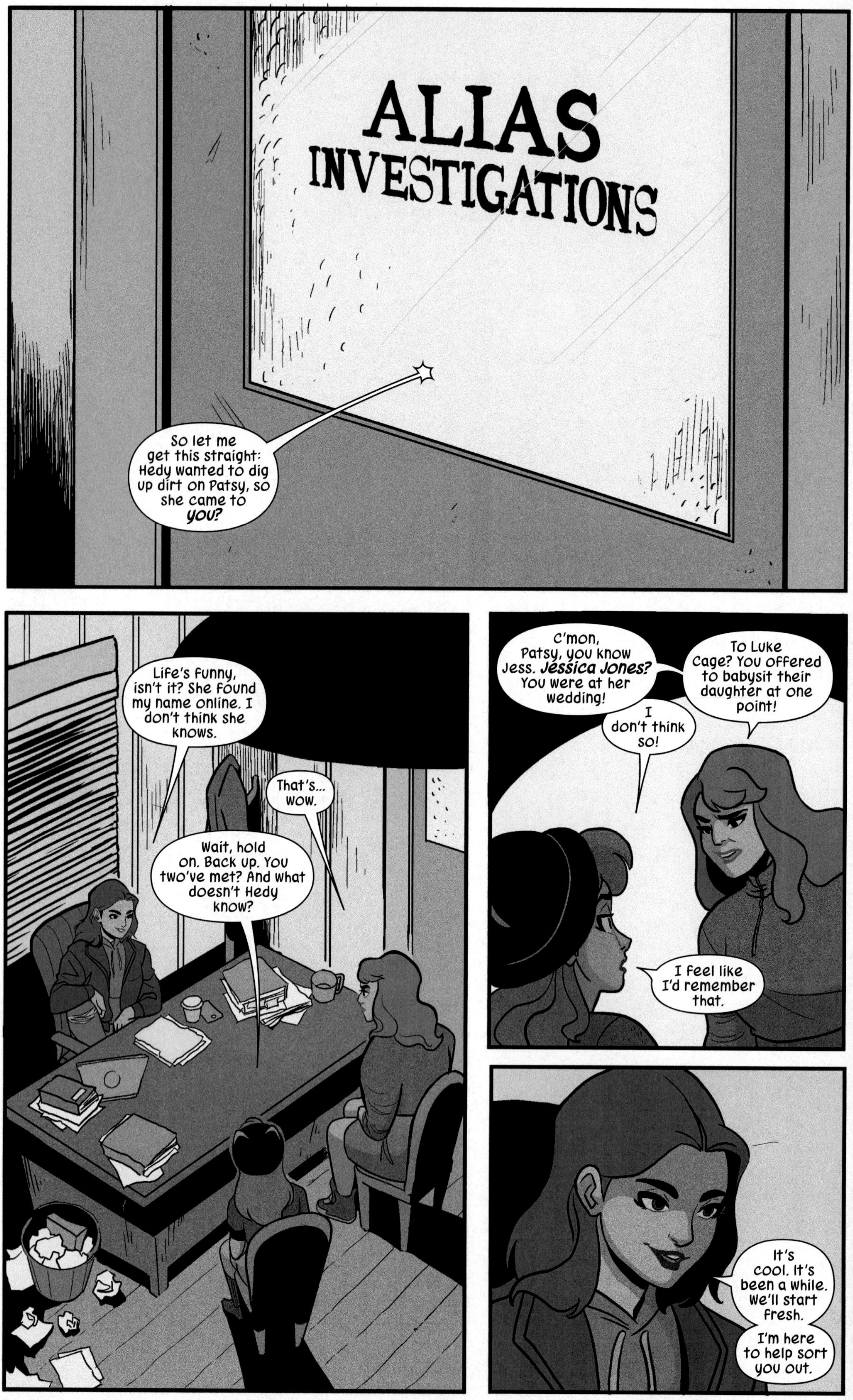
ALIAS INVESTIGATIONS
So let me get this straight: Hedy wanted to dig up dirt on Patsy, so she came to *YOU?*
Life's funny, isn't it? She found my name online. I don't think she knows.
That's... wow.
Wait, hold on. Back up. You two've met? And what doesn't Hedy know?
C'mon, Patsy, you know Jess. *Jessica Jones?* You were at her wedding!
To Luke Cage? You offered to babysit their daughter at one point!
I don't think so!
I feel like I'd remember that.
It's cool. It's been a while. We'll start fresh.
I'm here to help sort you out.

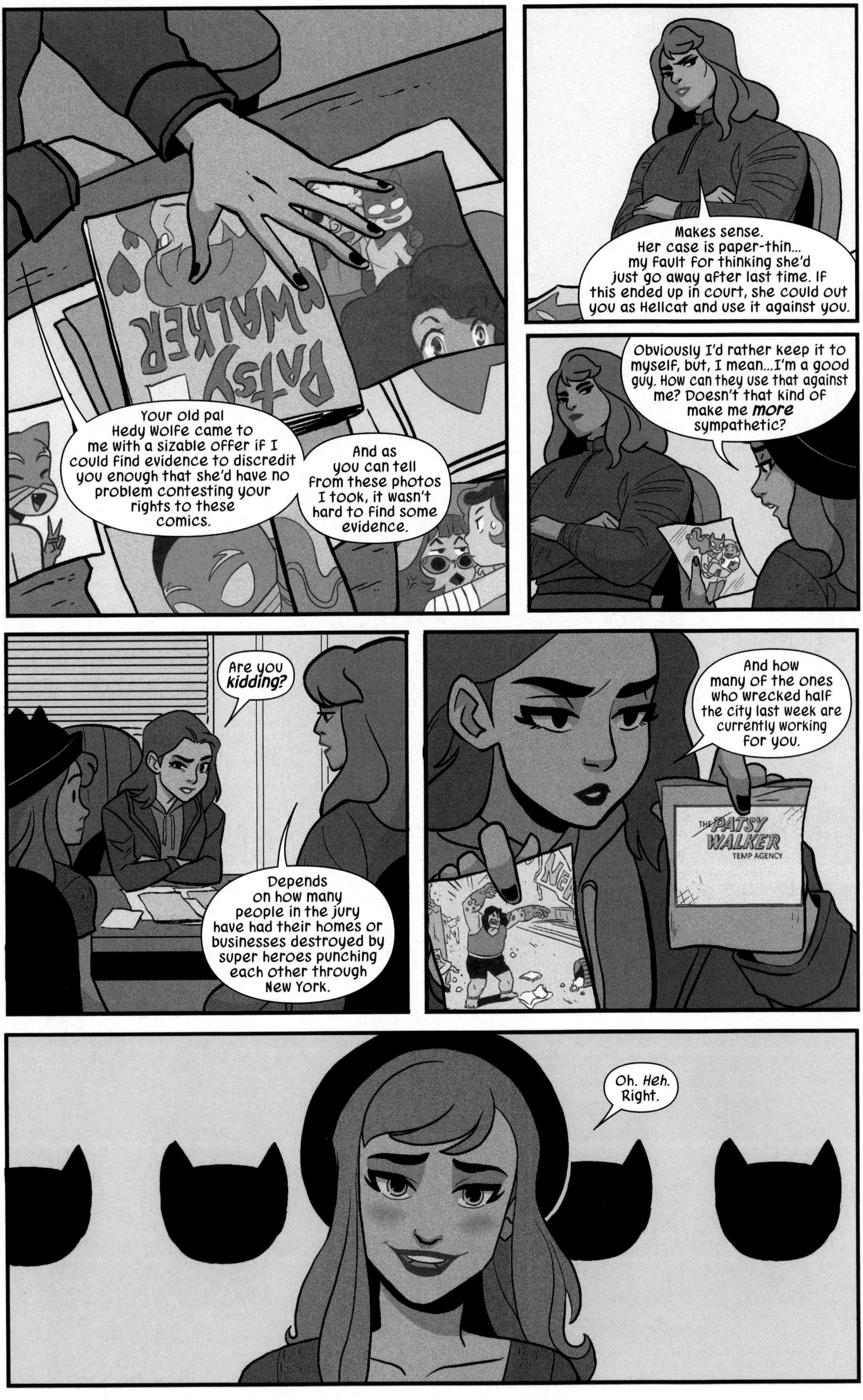
PATSY WALKER
Your old pal Hedy Wolfe came to me with a sizable offer if I could find evidence to discredit you enough that she'd have no problem contesting your rights to these comics.
And as you can tell from these photos I took, it wasn't hard to find some evidence.
Makes sense. Her case is paper-thin... my fault for thinking she'd just go away after last time. If this ended up in court, she could out you as Hellcat and use it against you.
Obviously I'd rather keep it to myself, but, I mean...I'm a good guy. How can they use that against me? Doesn't that kind of make me *more* sympathetic?
Are you *kidding?*
Depends on how many people in the jury have had their homes or businesses destroyed by super heroes punching each other through New York.
And how many of the ones who wrecked half the city last week are currently working for you.
THE PATSY WALKER TEMP AGENCY
Oh. Heh. Right.

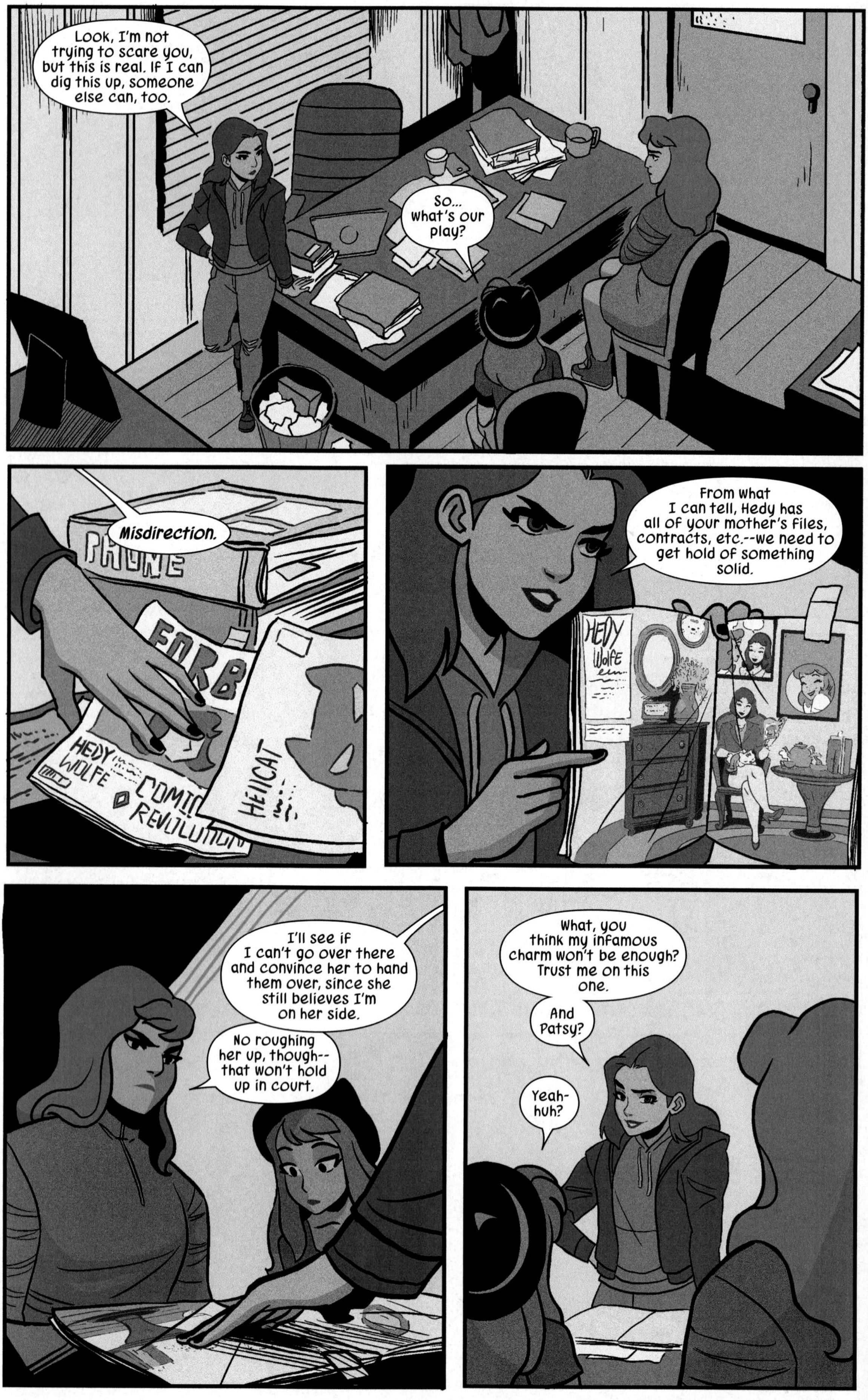
Look, I'm not trying to scare you, but this is real. If I can dig this up, someone else can, too.
So... what's our play?
Misdirection.
PHONE
FORB
HEDY WOLFE
COMIC REVOLUTION
HELLCAT
From what I can tell, Hedy has all of your mother's files, contracts, etc.--we need to get hold of something solid.
HEDY WOLFE
I'll see if I can't go over there and convince her to hand them over, since she still believes I'm on her side.
No roughing her up, though--that won't hold up in court.
What, you think my infamous charm won't be enough? Trust me on this one.
And Patsy?
Yeah-huh?

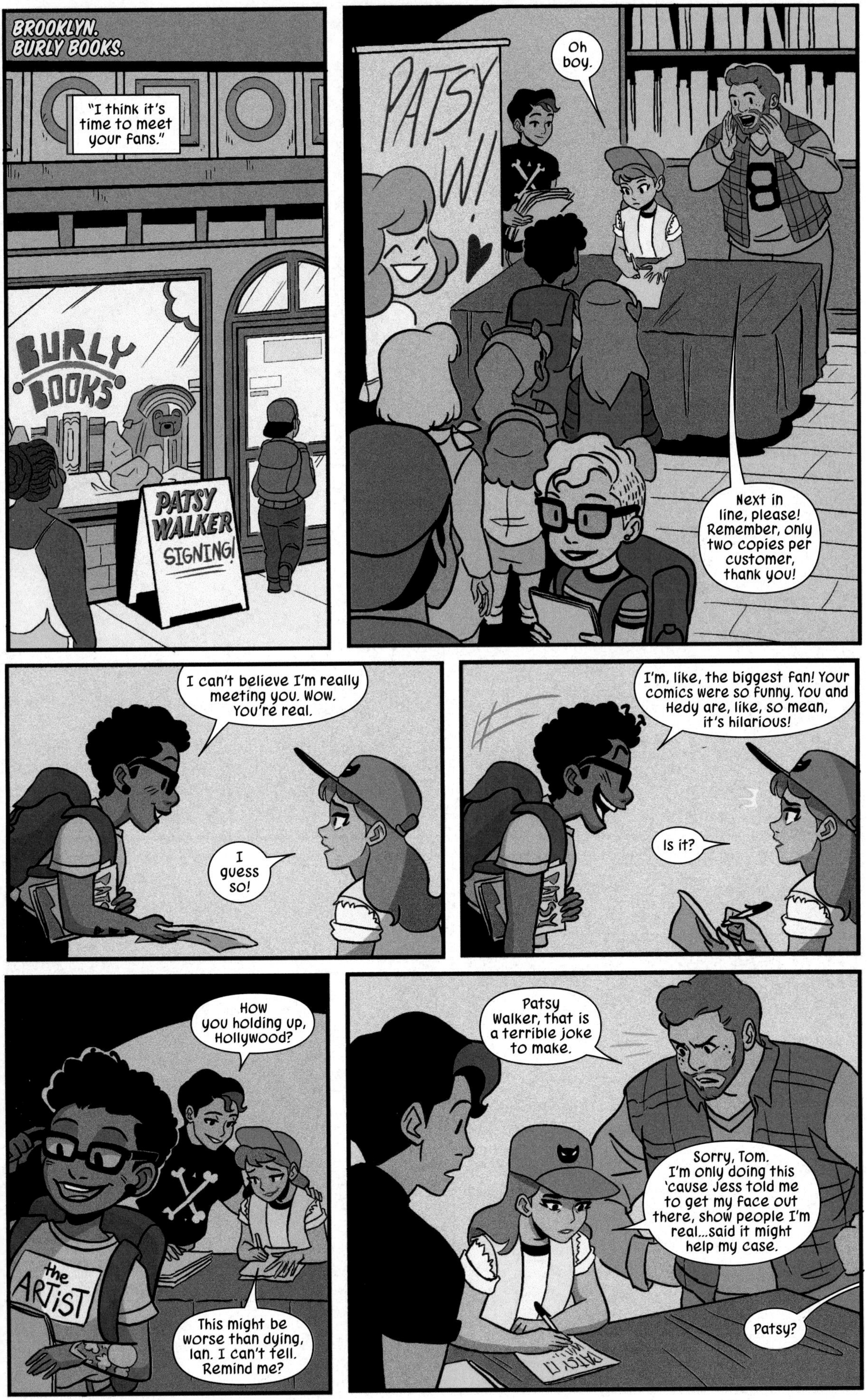
BROOKLYN.
BURLY BOOKS.
"I think it's time to meet your fans."
BURLY BOOKS
PATSY WALKER SIGNING!
PATSY W!
Oh boy.
Next in line, please! Remember, only two copies per customer, thank you!
I can't believe I'm really meeting you. Wow. You're real.
I guess so!
I'm, like, the biggest fan! Your comics were so funny. You and Hedy are, like, so mean, it's hilarious!
Is it?
How you holding up, Hollywood?
This might be worse than dying, Ian. I can't tell. Remind me?
the ARTIST
Patsy Walker, that is a terrible joke to make.
Sorry, Tom. I'm only doing this 'cause Jess told me to get my face out there, show people I'm real...said it might help my case.
Patsy?

Omigod, it IS her! I told you, didn't I?

Mmhmm.

You two! You put my photo on the Internet!*

PATSY WALKER

*P.W.A.H.! #2 -W.M.!

Well, duh! We were so excited, weren't we?

Mm.

Exactly. What she said.

You can't just do that without asking! You totally messed with my life!

WALKER STALKER

Patsy, don't.

Uhm...well, we didn't mean to...

We were just excited.

Sorry we bothered you.

Wait!

Do you want to take a...selfie?

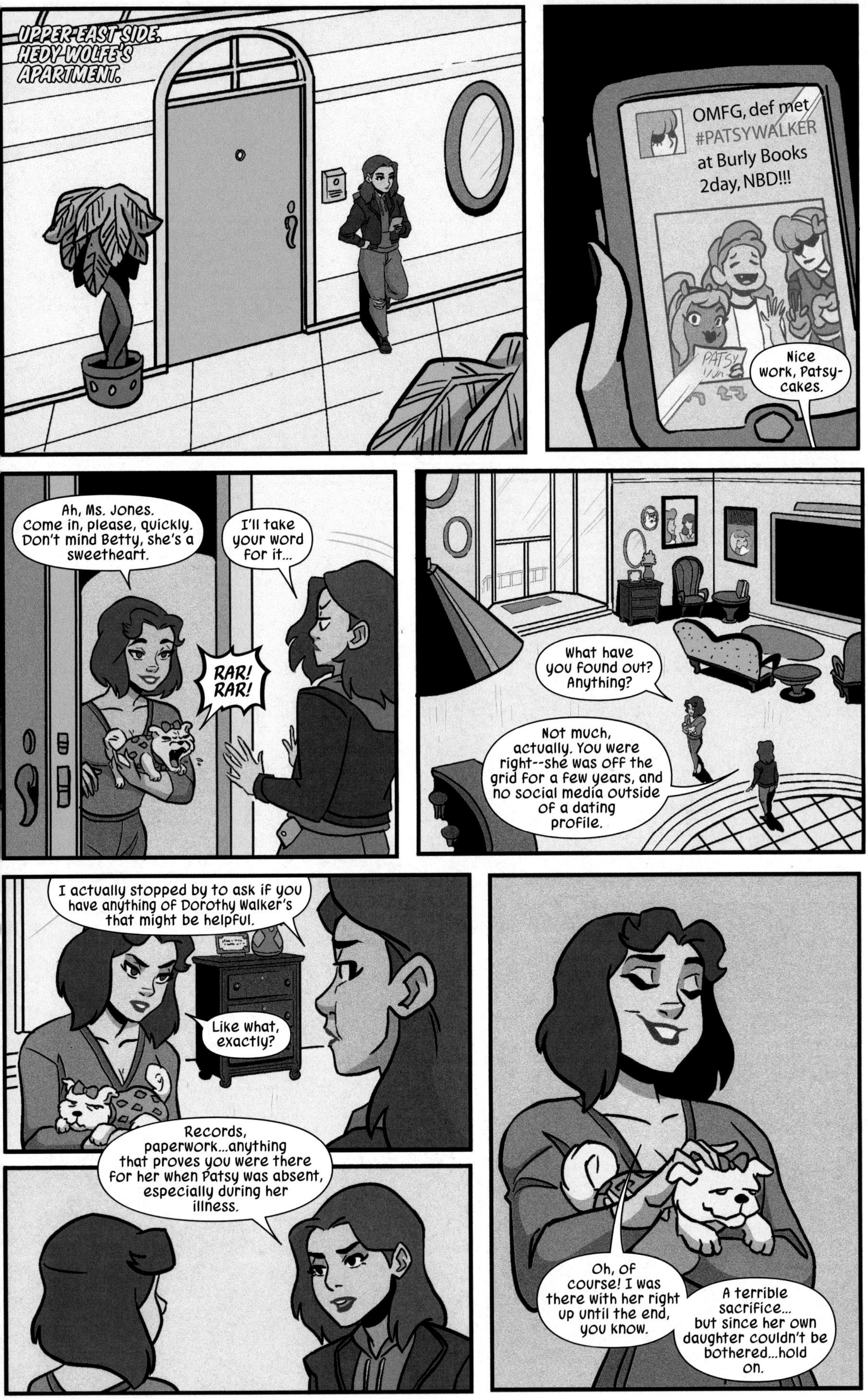
UPPER-EAST SIDE. HEDY WOLFE'S APARTMENT.
OMFG, def met #PATSYWALKER at Burly Books 2day, NBD!!!
PATSY
Nice work, Patsy-cakes.
Ah, Ms. Jones. Come in, please, quickly. Don't mind Betty, she's a sweetheart.
I'll take your word for it...
RAR! RAR!
What have you found out? Anything?
Not much, actually. You were right--she was off the grid for a few years, and no social media outside of a dating profile.
I actually stopped by to ask if you have anything of Dorothy Walker's that might be helpful.
Like what, exactly?
Records, paperwork...anything that proves you were there for her when Patsy was absent, especially during her illness.
Oh, of course! I was there with her right up until the end, you know.
A terrible sacrifice... but since her own daughter couldn't be bothered...hold on.

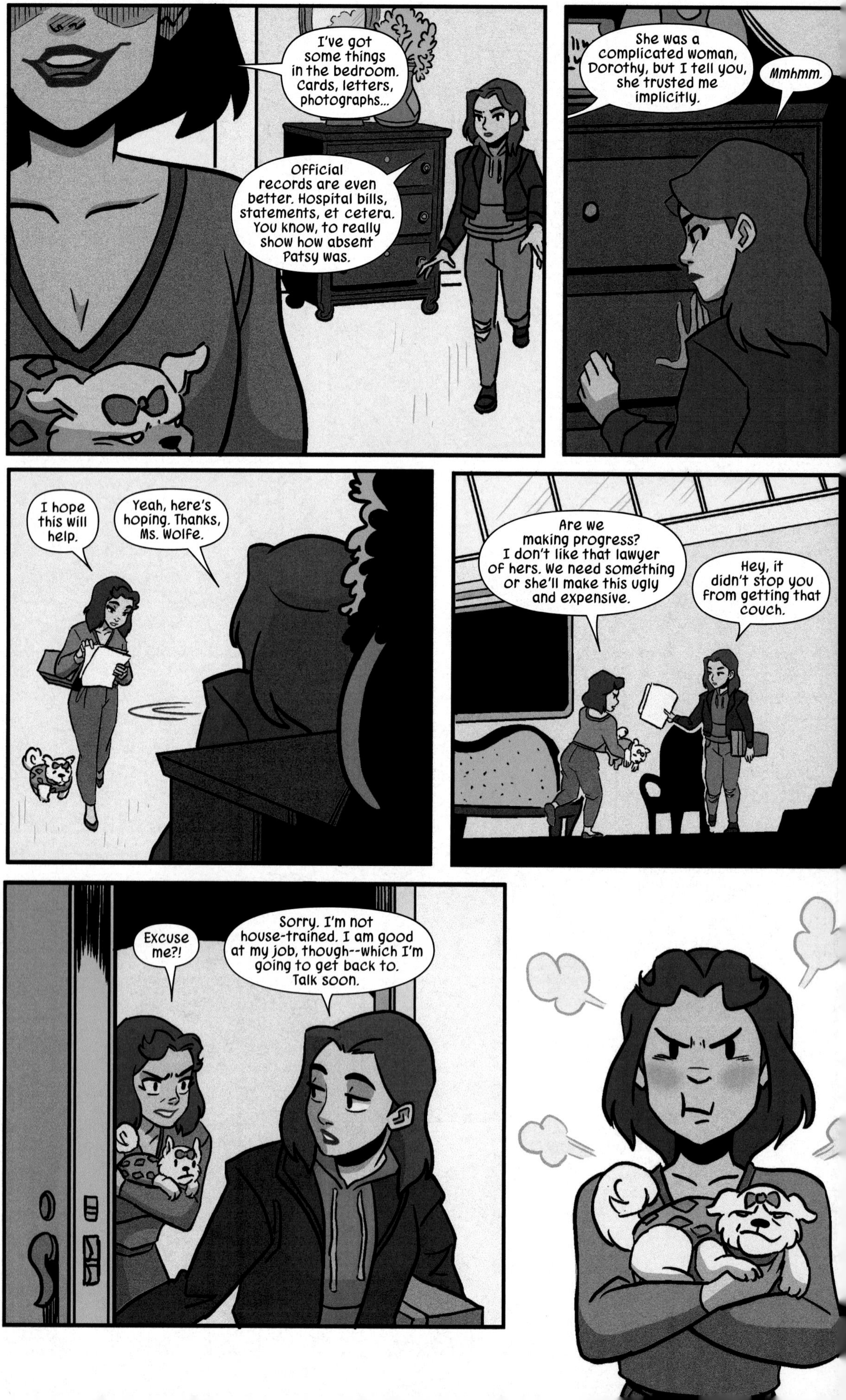
I've got some things in the bedroom. Cards, letters, photographs...
Official records are even better. Hospital bills, statements, et cetera. You know, to really show how absent Patsy was.
She was a complicated woman, Dorothy, but I tell you, she trusted me implicitly.
Mmhmm.
I hope this will help.
Yeah, here's hoping. Thanks, Ms. Wolfe.
Are we making progress? I don't like that lawyer of hers. We need something or she'll make this ugly and expensive.
Hey, it didn't stop you from getting that couch.
Excuse me?!
Sorry. I'm not house-trained. I am good at my job, though--which I'm going to get back to. Talk soon.

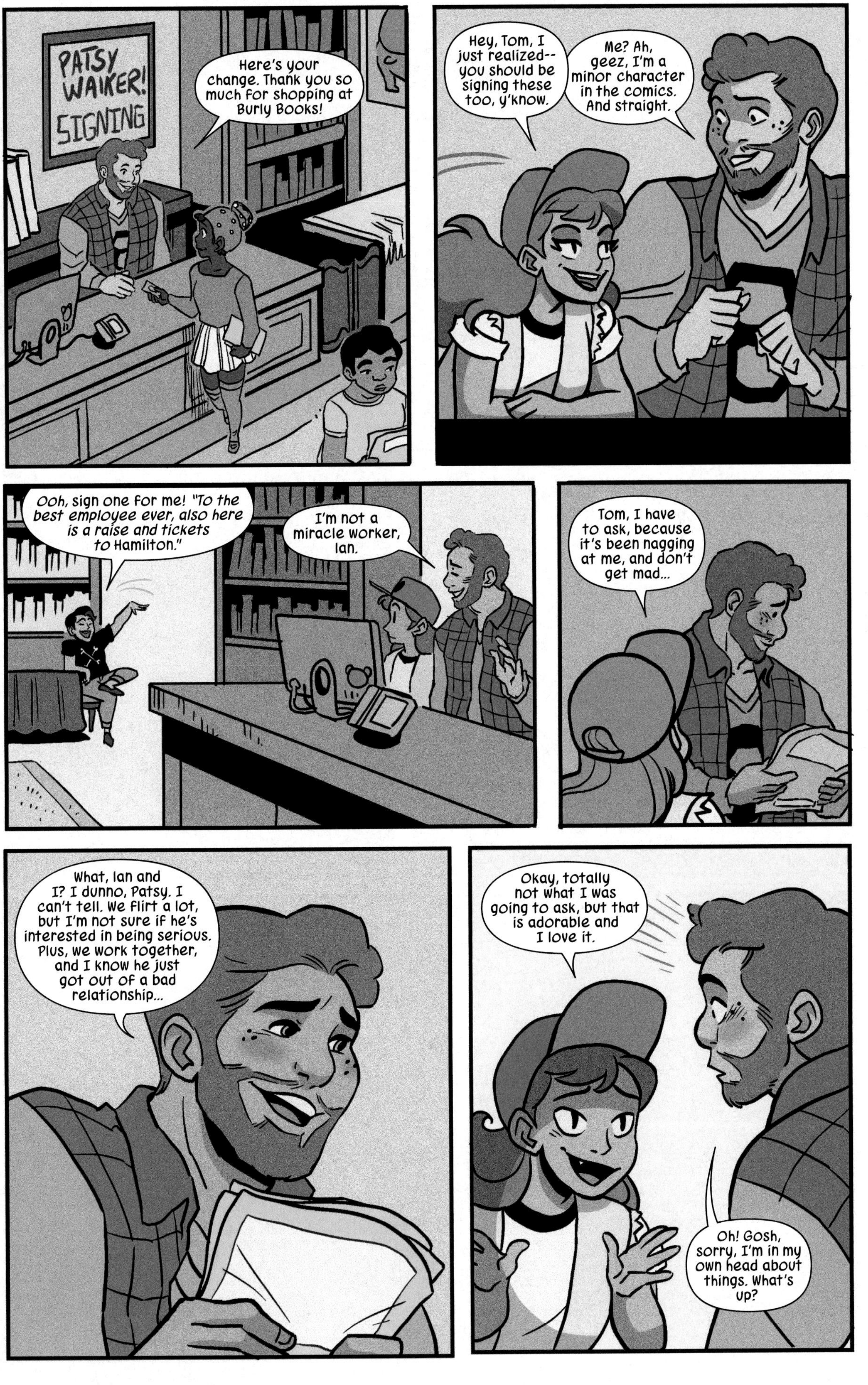
PATSY WALKER! SIGNING
Here's your change. Thank you so much for shopping at Burly Books!
Hey, Tom, I just realized-- you should be signing these too, y'know.
Me? Ah, geez, I'm a minor character in the comics. And straight.
Ooh, sign one for me! "To the best employee ever, also here is a raise and tickets to Hamilton."
I'm not a miracle worker, Ian.
Tom, I have to ask, because it's been nagging at me, and don't get mad...
What, Ian and I? I dunno, Patsy. I can't tell. We flirt a lot, but I'm not sure if he's interested in being serious. Plus, we work together, and I know he just got out of a bad relationship...
Okay, totally not what I was going to ask, but that is adorable and I love it.
Oh! Gosh, sorry, I'm in my own head about things. What's up?

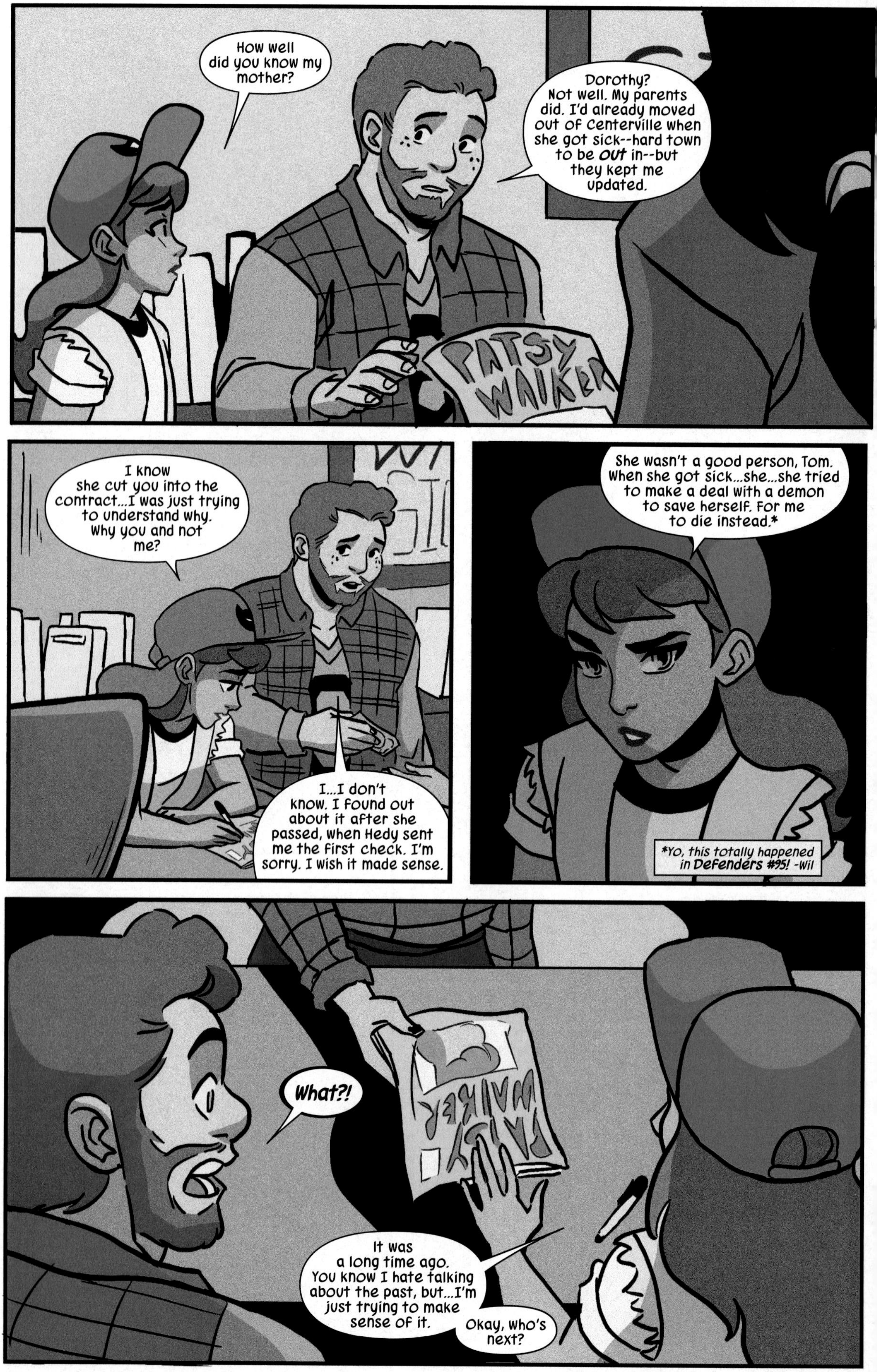
How well did you know my mother?
Dorothy? Not well. My parents did. I'd already moved out of Centerville when she got sick--hard town to be *out* in--but they kept me updated.
PATSY WALKER
I know she cut you into the contract...I was just trying to understand why. Why you and not me?
I...I don't know. I found out about it after she passed, when Hedy sent me the first check. I'm sorry. I wish it made sense.
She wasn't a good person, Tom. When she got sick...she...she tried to make a deal with a demon to save herself. For me to die instead.*
*Yo, this totally happened in Defenders #95! -Wil
What?!
It was a long time ago. You know I hate talking about the past, but...I'm just trying to make sense of it.
Okay, who's next?

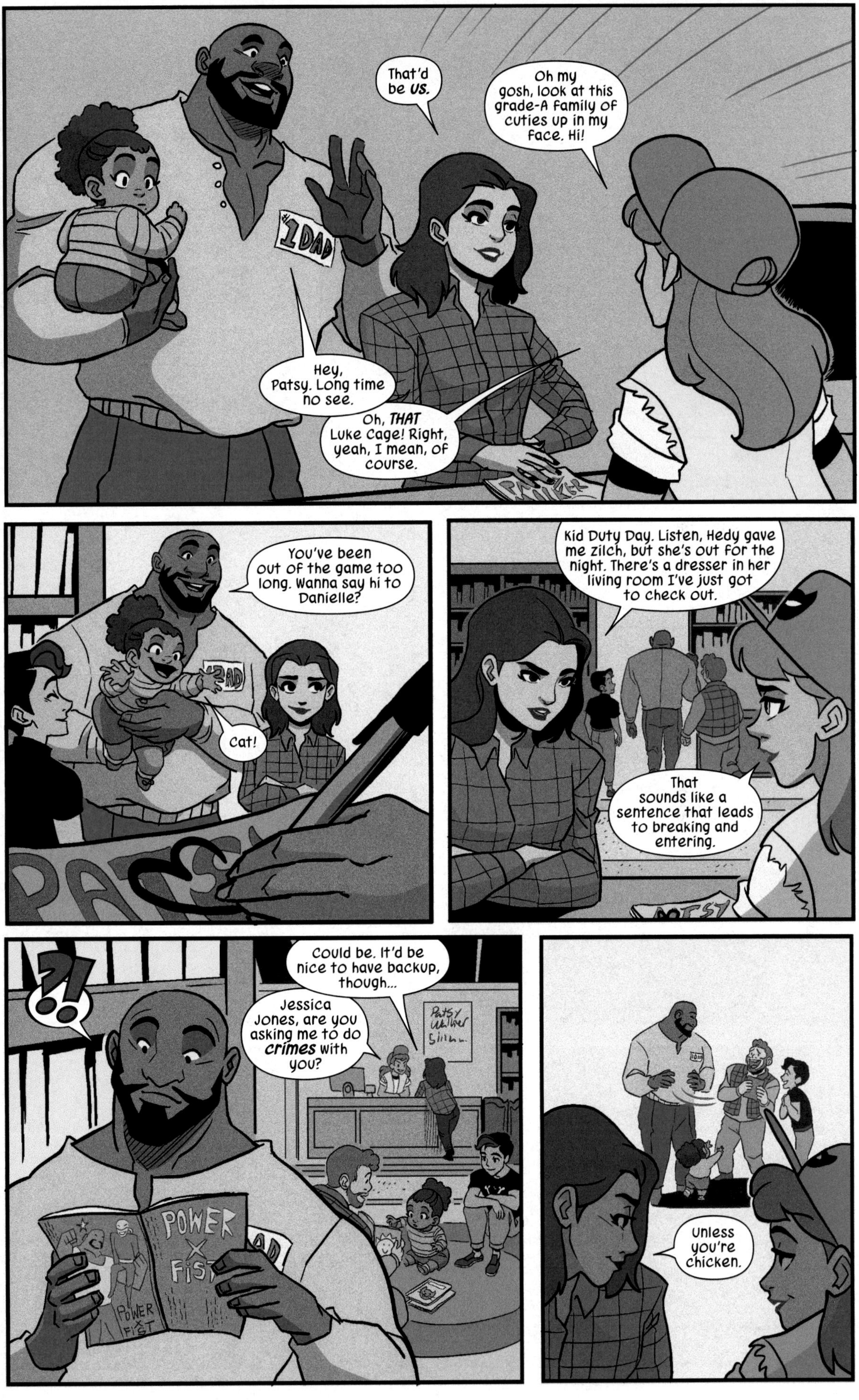

That'd be US.
Oh my gosh, look at this grade-A family of cuties up in my face. Hi!
#1 DAD
Hey, Patsy. Long time no see.
Oh, THAT Luke Cage! Right, yeah, I mean, of course.
You've been out of the game too long. Wanna say hi to Danielle?
Cat!
Kid Duty Day. Listen, Hedy gave me zilch, but she's out for the night. There's a dresser in her living room I've just got to check out.
That sounds like a sentence that leads to breaking and entering.
?!
Could be. It'd be nice to have backup, though...
Jessica Jones, are you asking me to do crimes with you?
POWER X FIST
Unless you're chicken.

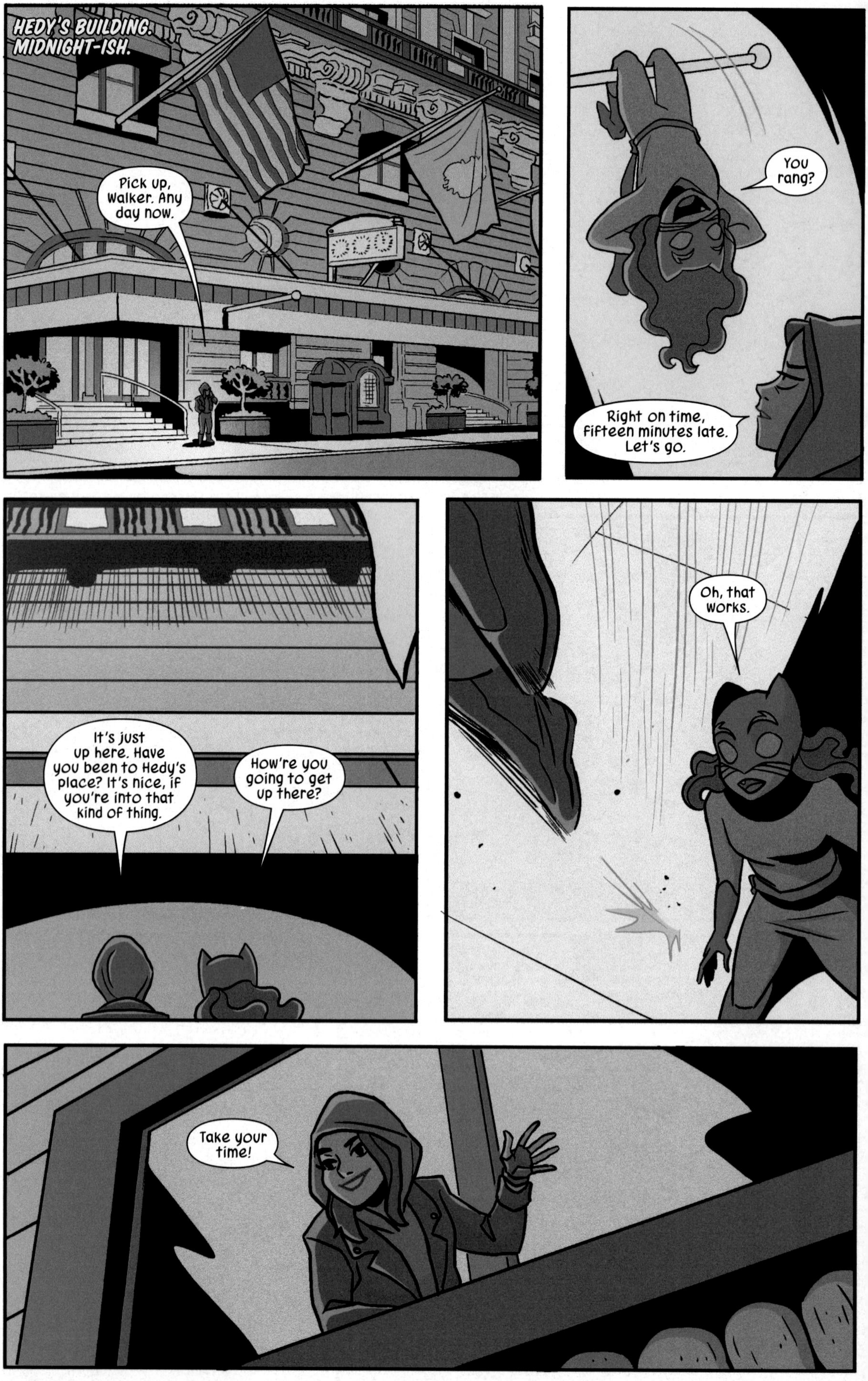
HEDY'S BUILDING. MIDNIGHT-ISH.
Pick up, Walker. Any day now.
You rang?
Right on time, fifteen minutes late. Let's go.
It's just up here. Have you been to Hedy's place? It's nice, if you're into that kind of thing.
How're you going to get up there?
Oh, that works.
Take your time!

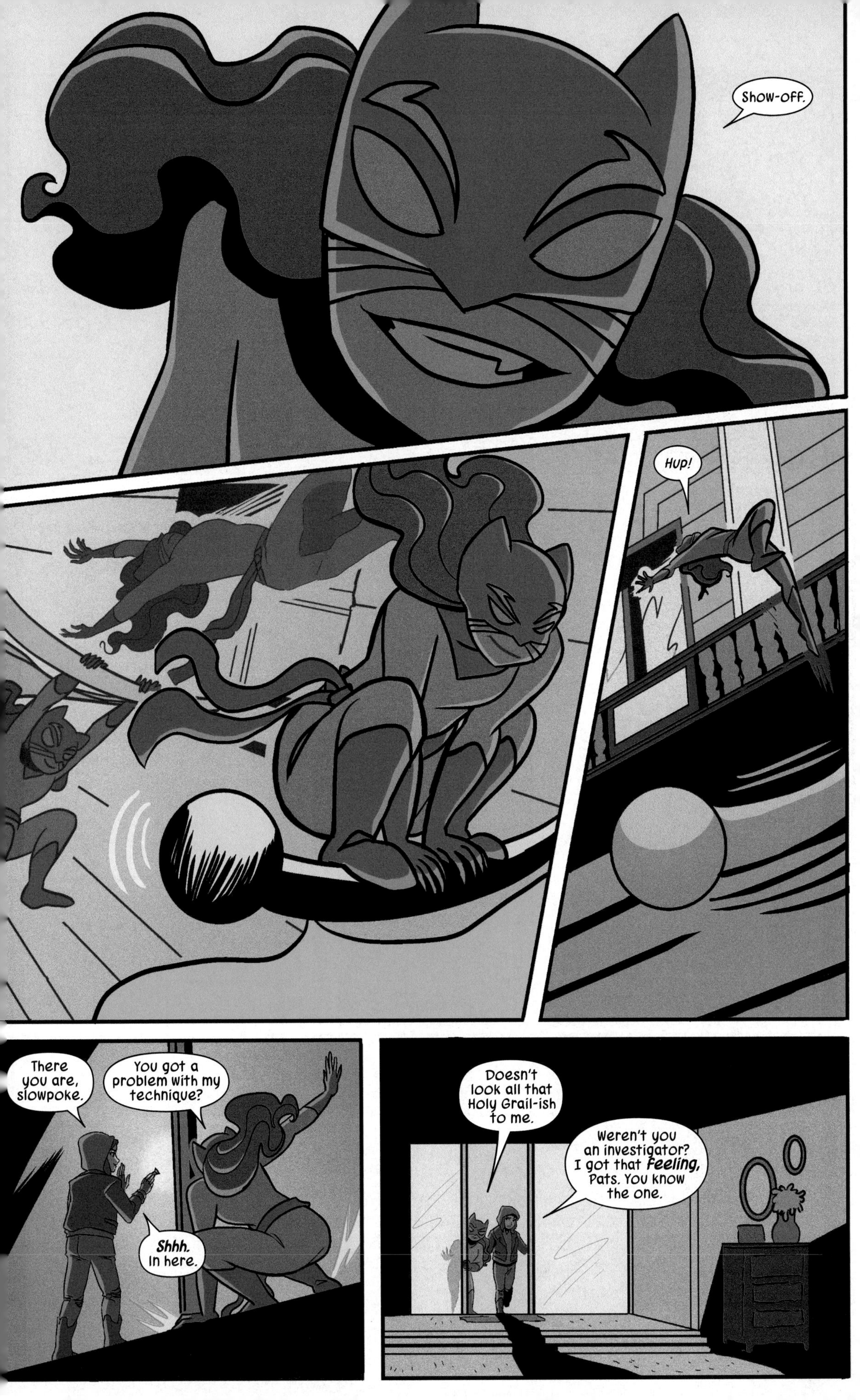
Show-off.
Hup!
There you are, slowpoke.
You got a problem with my technique?
Shhh. In here.
Doesn't look all that Holy Grail-ish to me.
Weren't you an investigator? I got that feeling, Pats. You know the one.

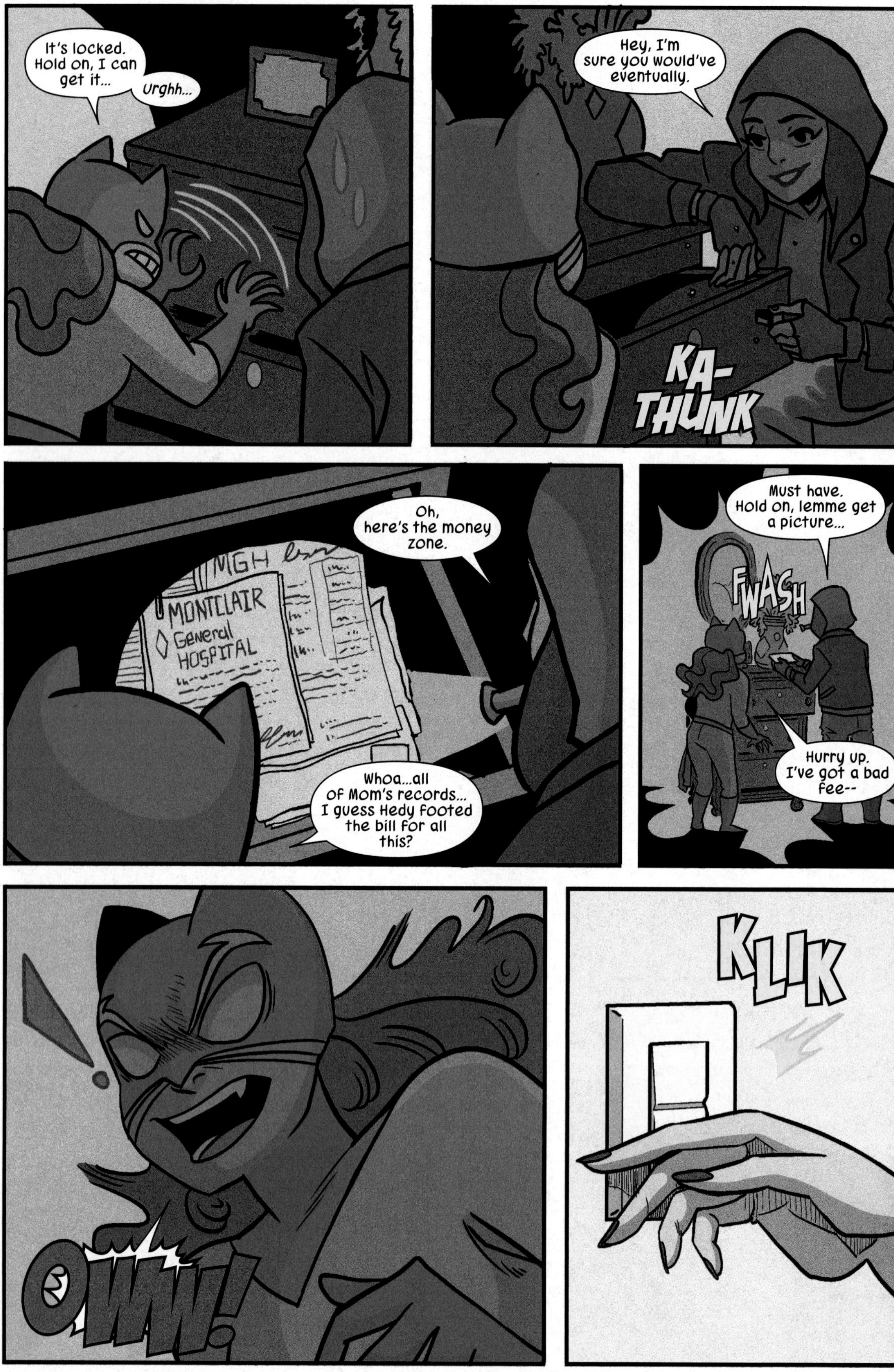
It's locked. Hold on, I can get it...
Urghh...
Hey, I'm sure you would've eventually.
KA-THUNK
Oh, here's the money zone.
MGH
MONTCLAIR General HOSPITAL
Whoa...all of Mom's records... I guess Hedy footed the bill for all this?
Must have. Hold on, lemme get a picture...
FWASH
Hurry up. I've got a bad fee--
OWW!
KLIK

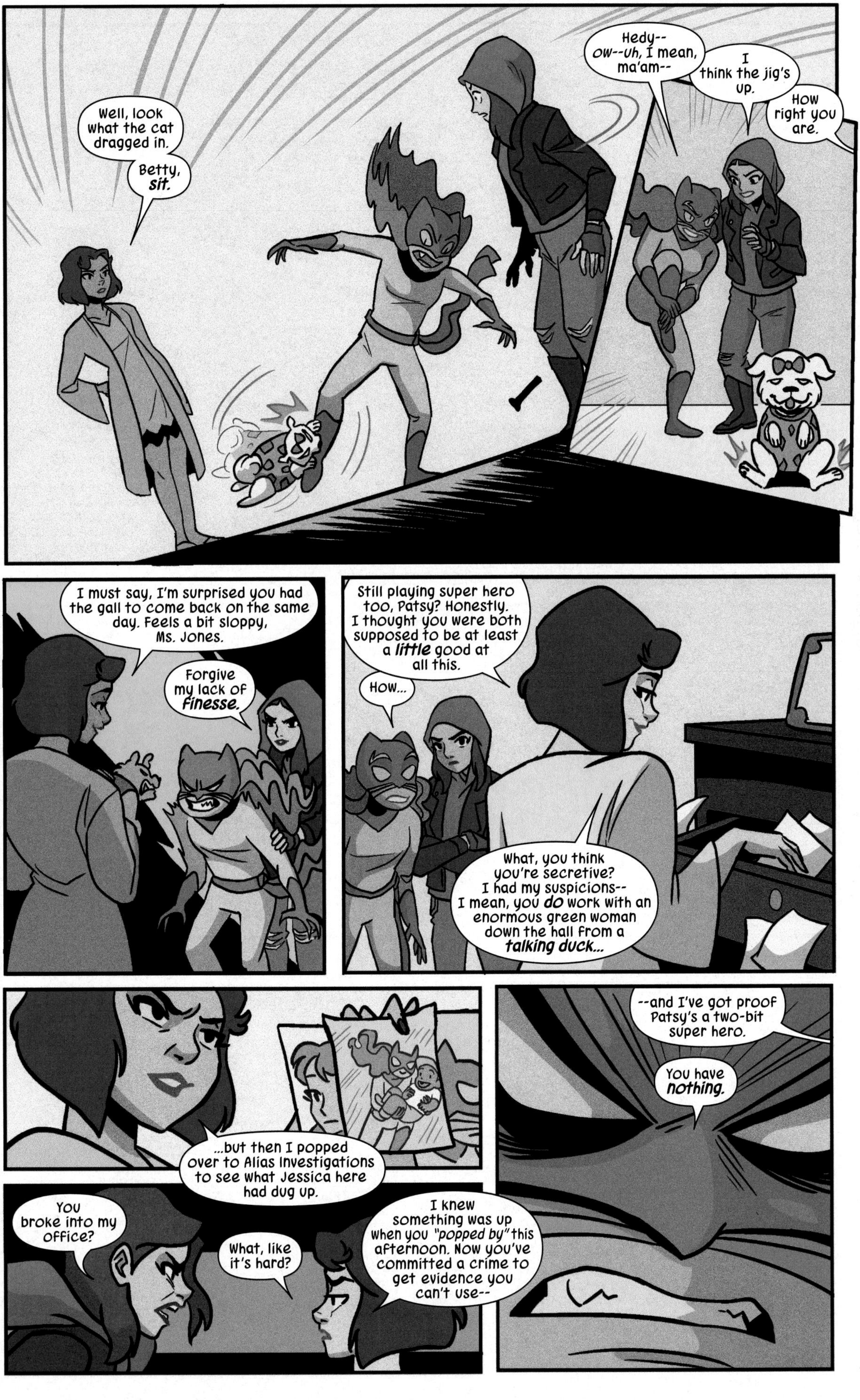
Well, look what the cat dragged in.
Betty, sit.
Hedy-- ow--uh, I mean, ma'am--
I think the jig's up.
How right you are.
I must say, I'm surprised you had the gall to come back on the same day. Feels a bit sloppy, Ms. Jones.
Forgive my lack of finesse.
Still playing super hero too, Patsy? Honestly. I thought you were both supposed to be at least a little good at all this.
How...
What, you think you're secretive? I had my suspicions-- I mean, you do work with an enormous green woman down the hall from a talking duck...
...but then I popped over to Alias Investigations to see what Jessica here had dug up.
You broke into my office?
What, like it's hard?
I knew something was up when you "popped by" this afternoon. Now you've committed a crime to get evidence you can't use--
--and I've got proof Patsy's a two-bit super hero.
You have nothing.

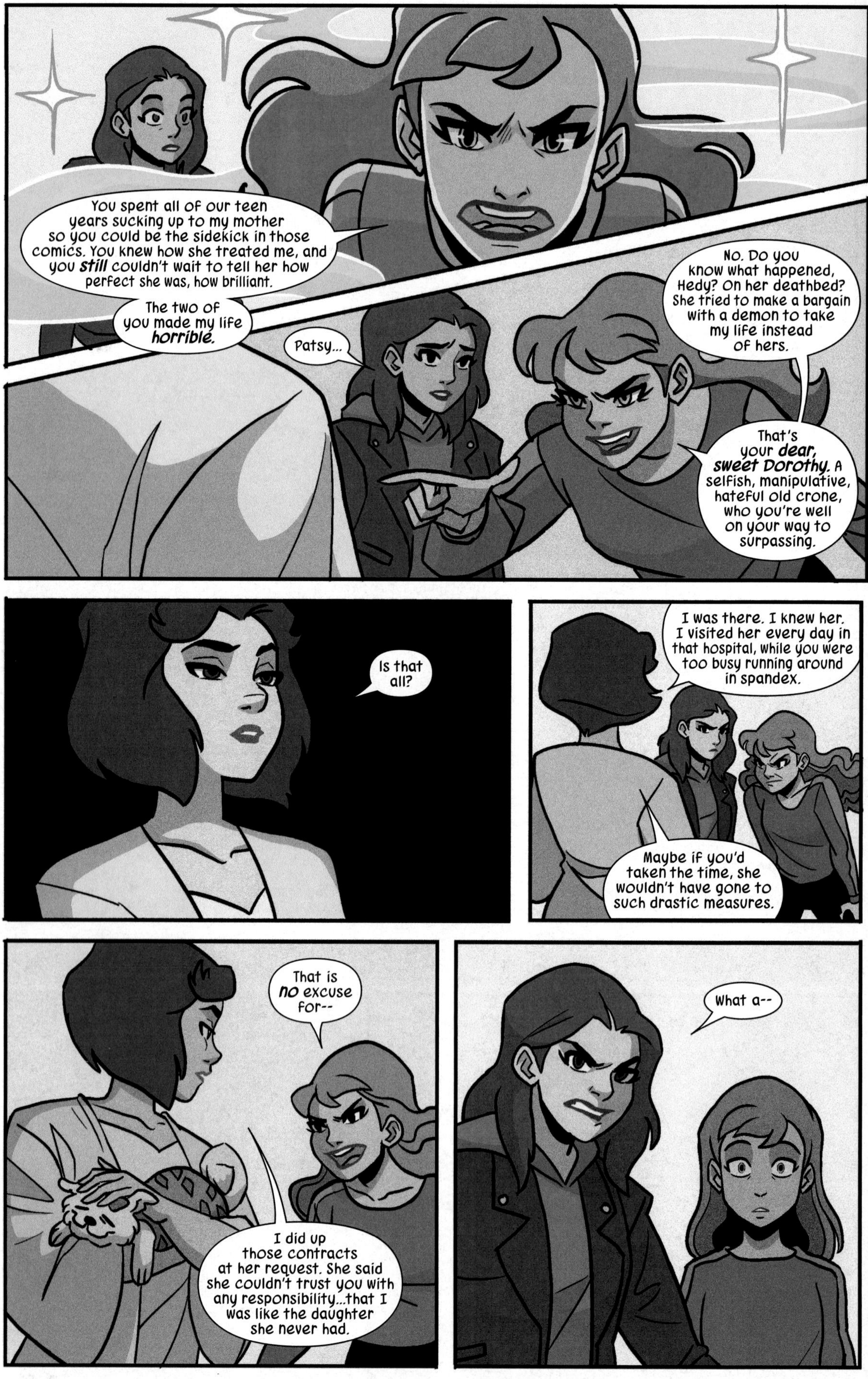
You spent all of our teen years sucking up to my mother so you could be the sidekick in those comics. You knew how she treated me, and you *still* couldn't wait to tell her how perfect she was, how brilliant.
The two of you made my life *horrible.*
Patsy...
No. Do you know what happened, Hedy? On her deathbed? She tried to make a bargain with a demon to take my life instead of hers.
That's your *dear, sweet Dorothy.* A selfish, manipulative, hateful old crone, who you're well on your way to surpassing.
Is that all?
I was there. I knew her. I visited her every day in that hospital, while you were too busy running around in spandex.
Maybe if you'd taken the time, she wouldn't have gone to such drastic measures.
That is *no* excuse for--
I did up those contracts at her request. She said she couldn't trust you with any responsibility...that I was like the daughter she never had.
What a--

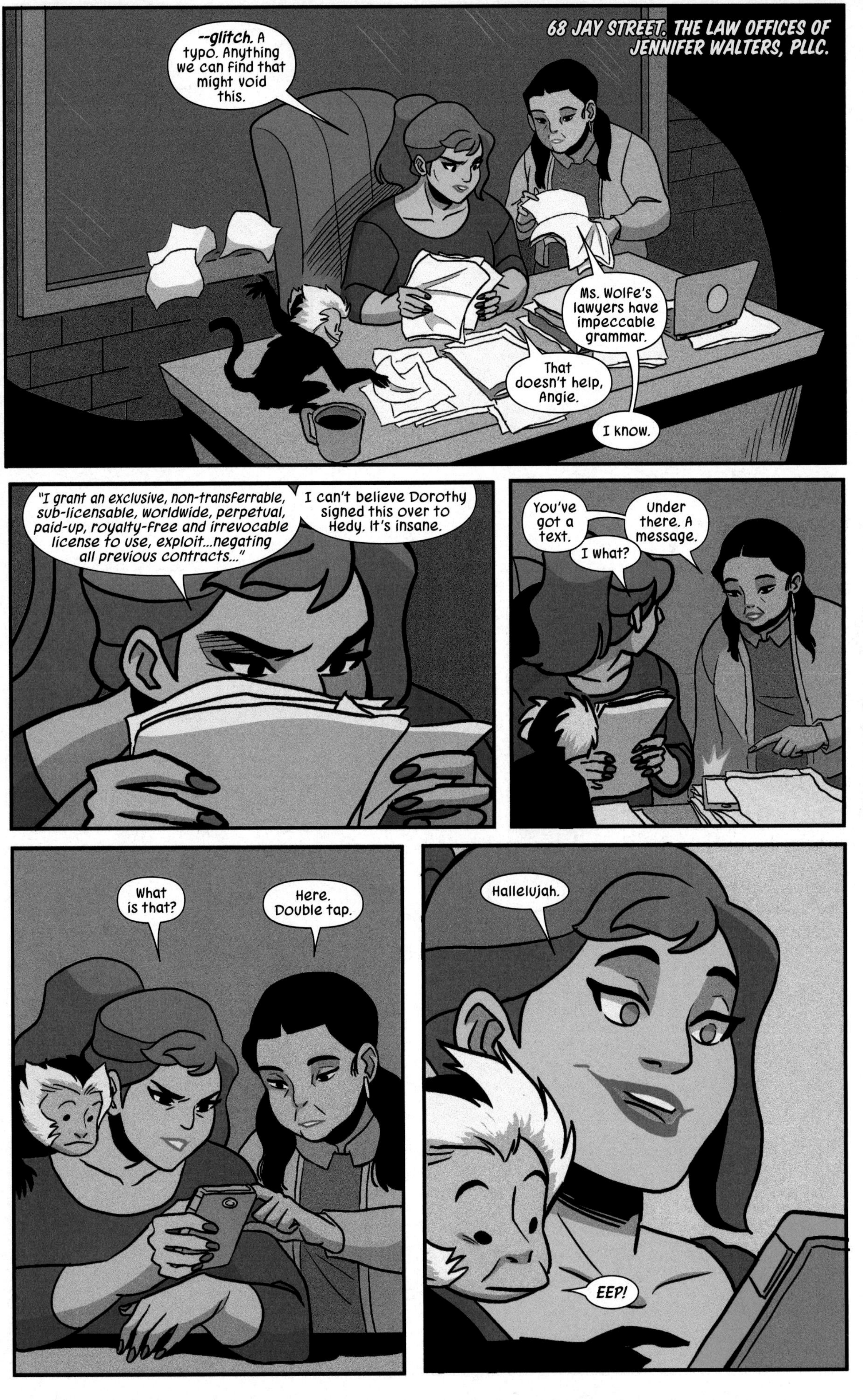
68 JAY STREET. THE LAW OFFICES OF JENNIFER WALTERS, PLLC.
--glitch. A typo. Anything we can find that might void this.
Ms. Wolfe's lawyers have impeccable grammar.
That doesn't help, Angie.
I know.
"I grant an exclusive, non-transferrable, sub-licensable, worldwide, perpetual, paid-up, royalty-free and irrevocable license to use, exploit...negating all previous contracts..."
I can't believe Dorothy signed this over to Hedy. It's insane.
You've got a text.
I what?
Under there. A message.
What is that?
Here. Double tap.
Hallelujah.
EEP!

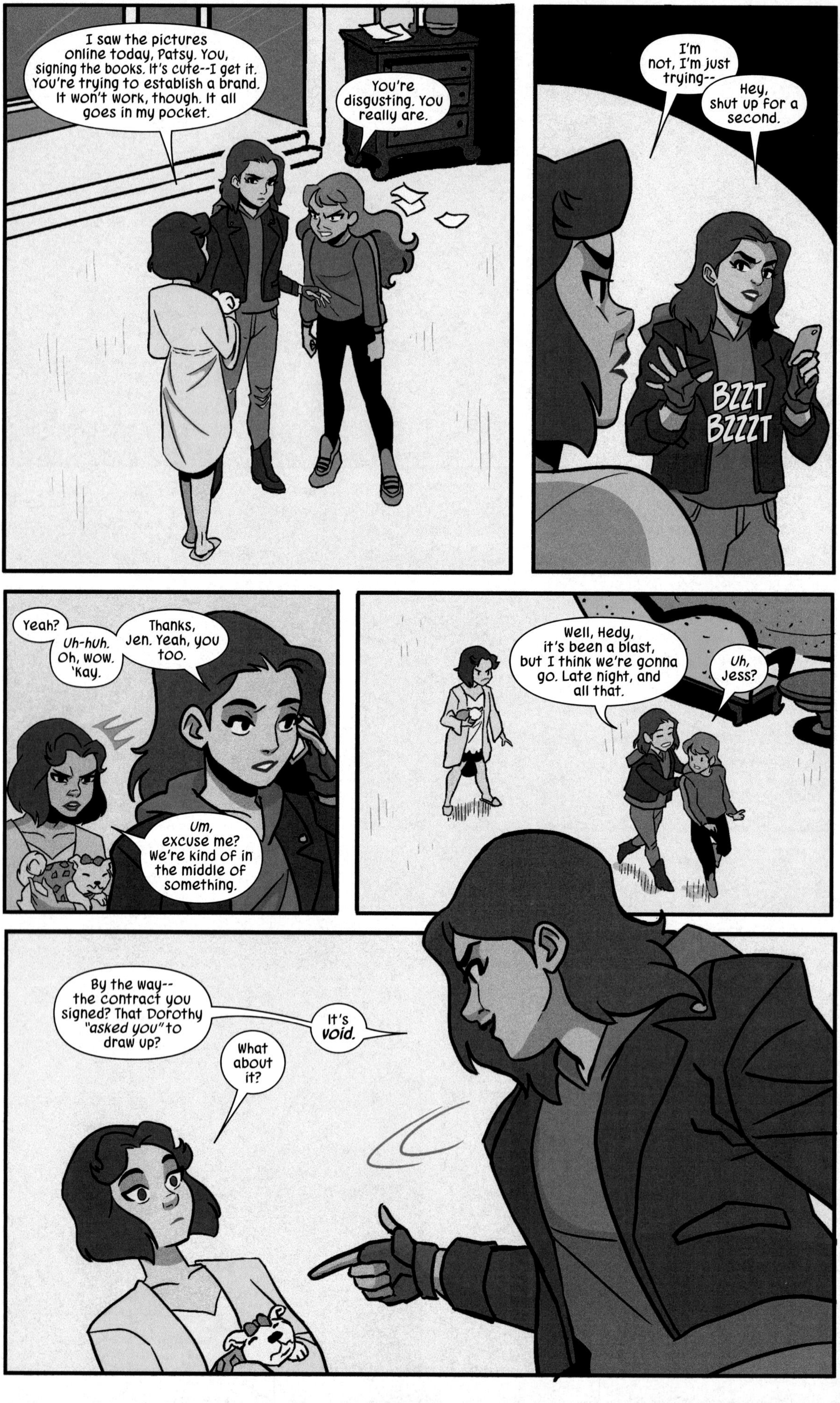
I saw the pictures online today, Patsy. You, signing the books. It's cute--I get it. You're trying to establish a brand. It won't work, though. It all goes in my pocket.
You're disgusting. You really are.
I'm not, I'm just trying--
Hey, shut up for a second.
BZZT BZZZT
Yeah?
Uh-huh. Oh, wow. 'Kay.
Thanks, Jen. Yeah, you too.
Um, excuse me? We're kind of in the middle of something.
Well, Hedy, it's been a blast, but I think we're gonna go. Late night, and all that.
Uh, Jess?
By the way-- the contract you signed? That Dorothy "asked you" to draw up?
What about it?
It's void.

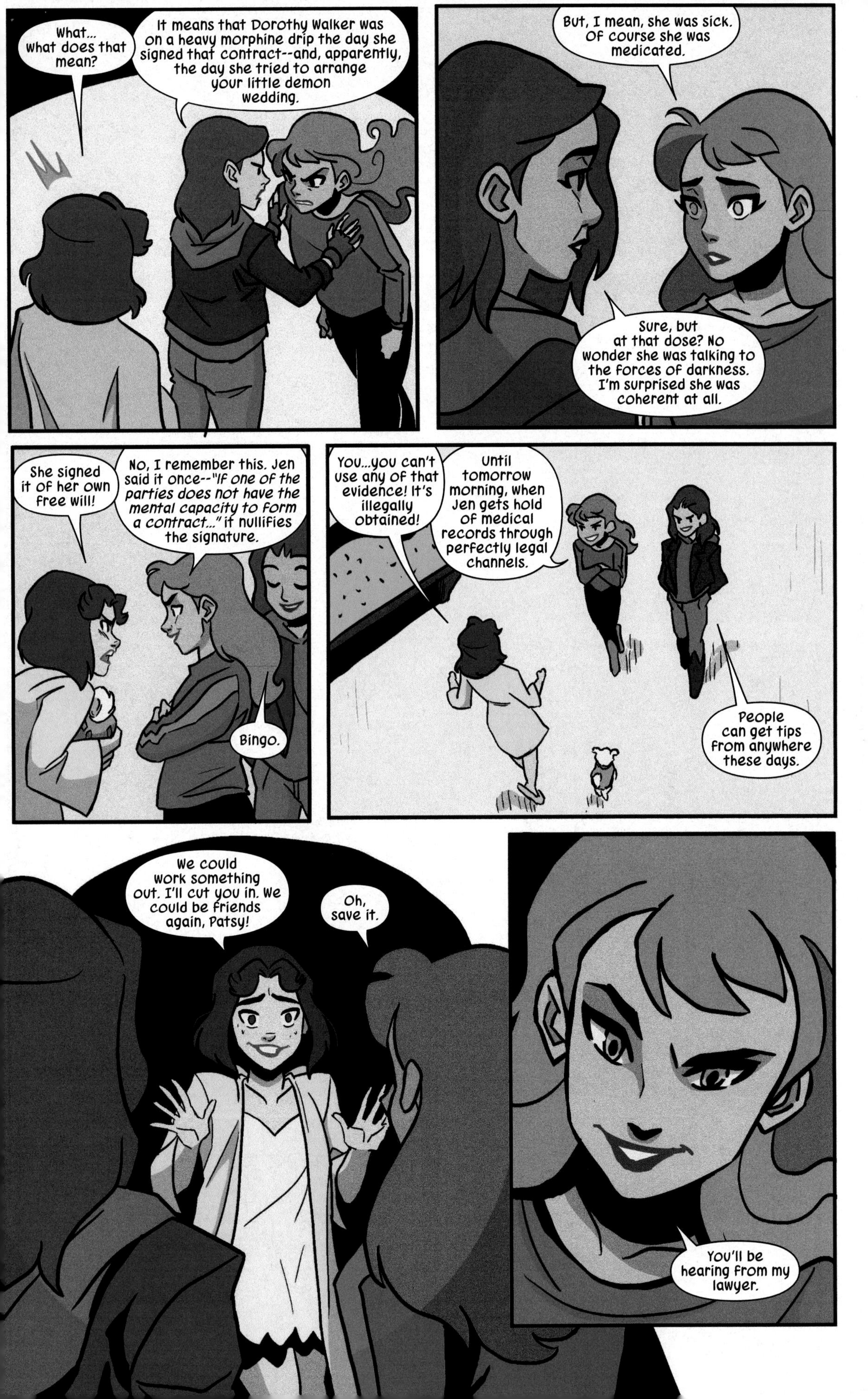
What... what does that mean?
It means that Dorothy Walker was on a heavy morphine drip the day she signed that contract--and, apparently, the day she tried to arrange your little demon wedding.
But, I mean, she was sick. Of course she was medicated.
Sure, but at that dose? No wonder she was talking to the forces of darkness. I'm surprised she was coherent at all.
She signed it of her own free will!
No, I remember this. Jen said it once--"If one of the parties does not have the mental capacity to form a contract..." it nullifies the signature.
Bingo.
You...you can't use any of that evidence! It's illegally obtained!
Until tomorrow morning, when Jen gets hold of medical records through perfectly legal channels.
People can get tips from anywhere these days.
We could work something out. I'll cut you in. We could be friends again, Patsy!
Oh, save it.
You'll be hearing from my lawyer.

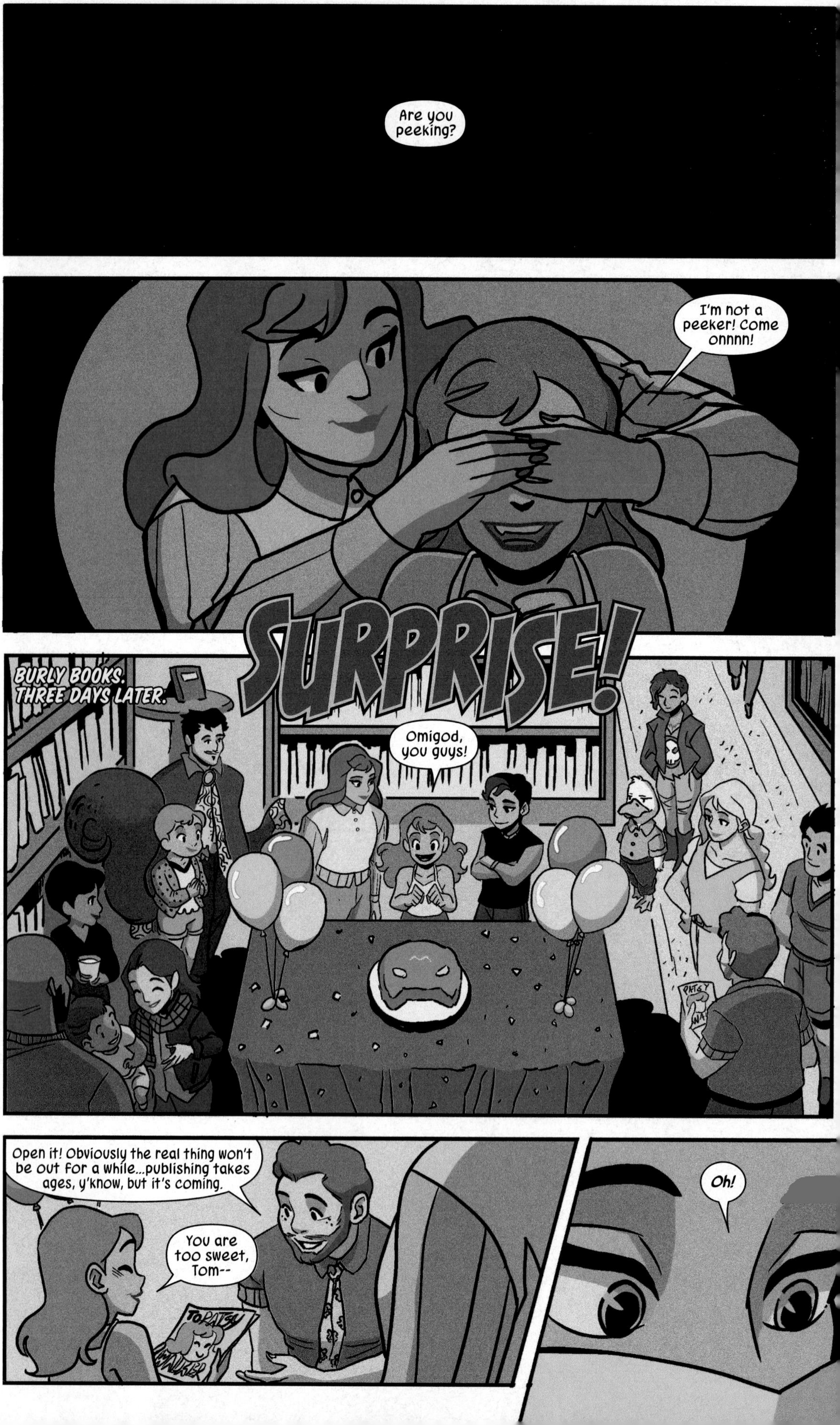

Are you peeking?
I'm not a peeker! Come onnnn!
SURPRISE!
BURLY BOOKS. THREE DAYS LATER.
Omigod, you guys!
Open it! Obviously the real thing won't be out for a while...publishing takes ages, y'know, but it's coming.
You are too sweet, Tom--
Oh!

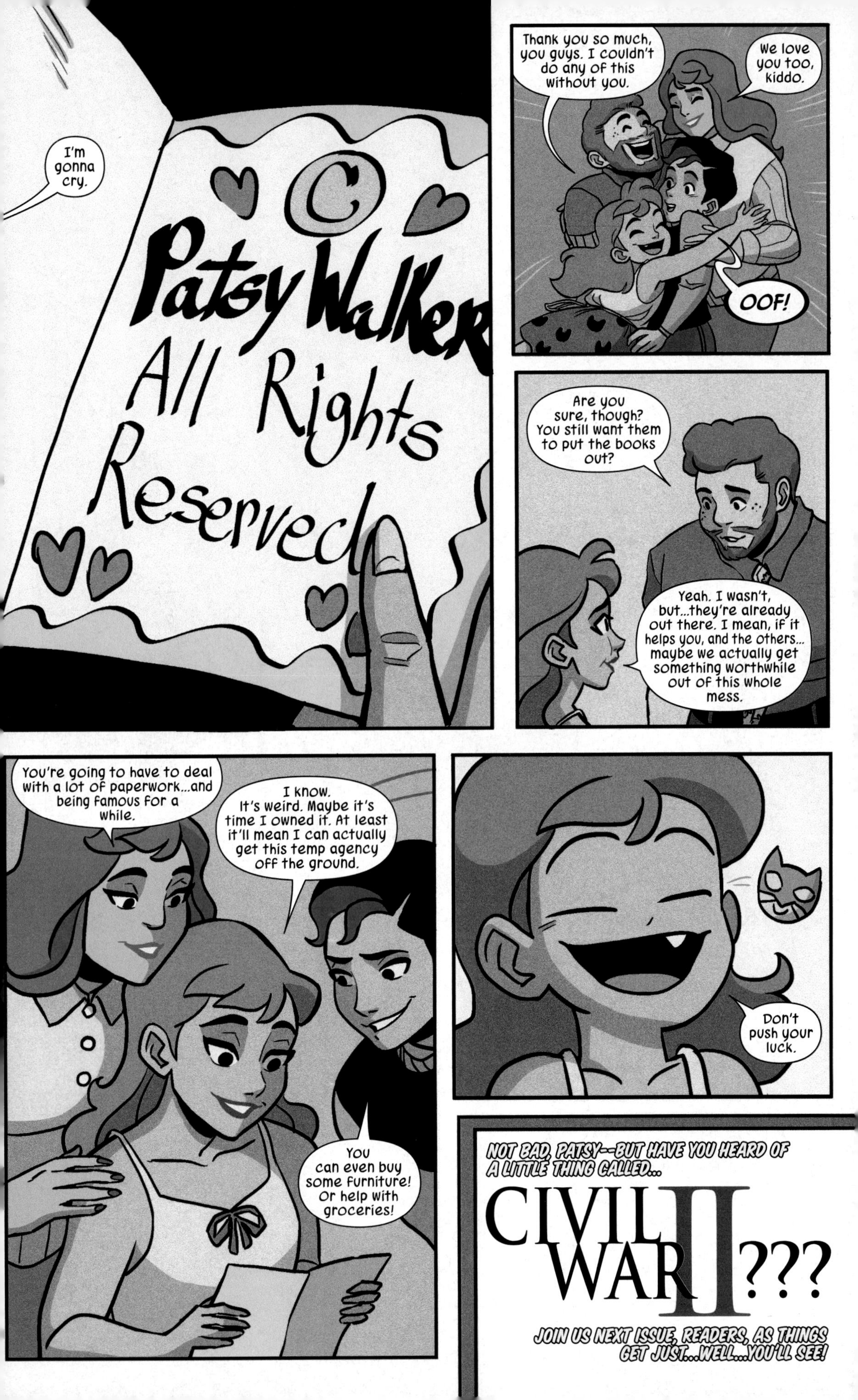
I'm gonna cry.
Patsy Walker All Rights Reserved
Thank you so much, you guys. I couldn't do any of this without you.
We love you too, kiddo.
OOF!
Are you sure, though? You still want them to put the books out?
Yeah. I wasn't, but...they're already out there. I mean, if it helps you, and the others... maybe we actually get something worthwhile out of this whole mess.
You're going to have to deal with a lot of paperwork...and being famous for a while.
I know. It's weird. Maybe it's time I owned it. At least it'll mean I can actually get this temp agency off the ground.
You can even buy some furniture! Or help with groceries!
Don't push your luck.
NOT BAD, PATSY--BUT HAVE YOU HEARD OF A LITTLE THING CALLED...
CIVIL WAR II???
JOIN US NEXT ISSUE, READERS, AS THINGS GET JUST...WELL...YOU'LL SEE!

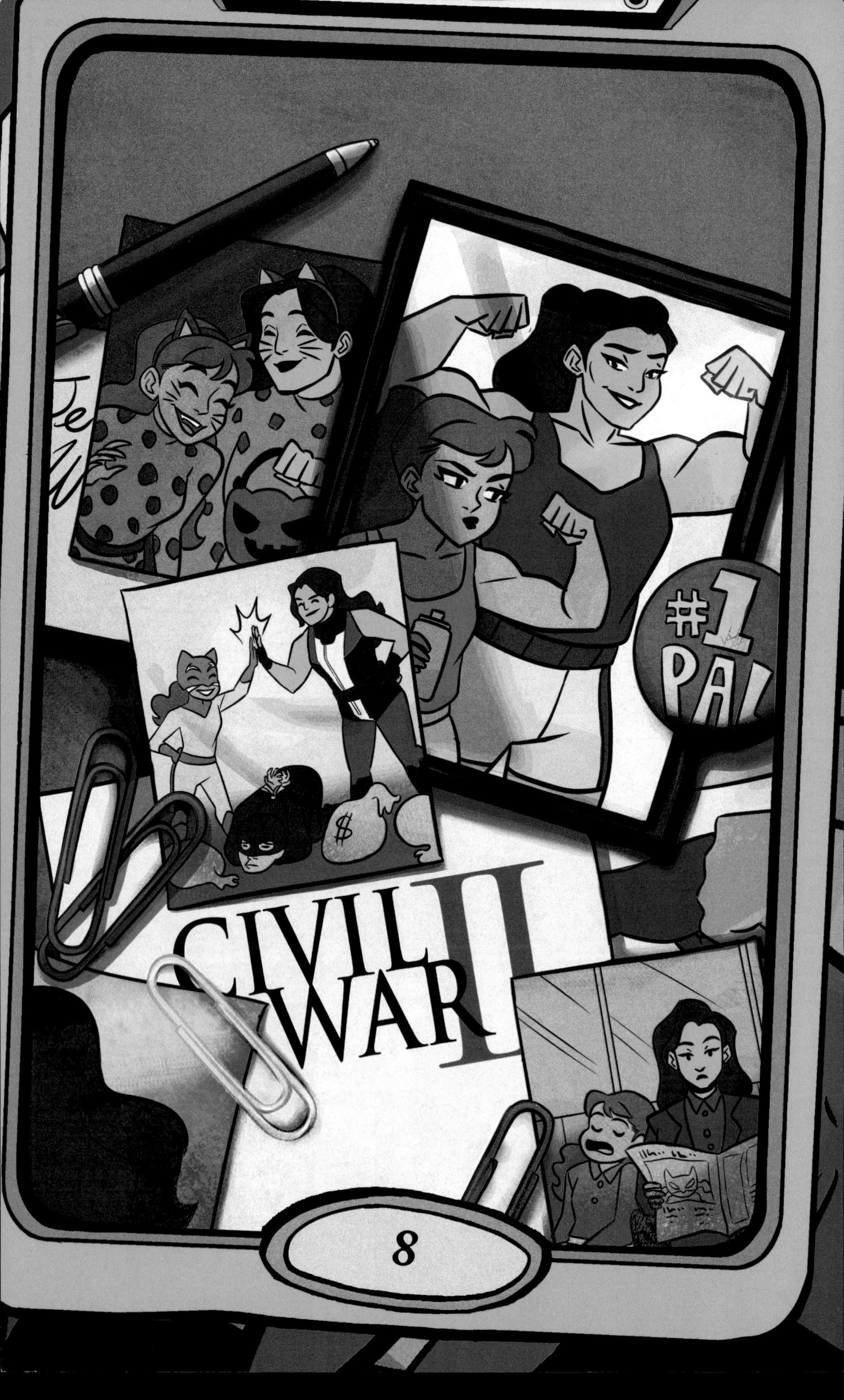
#1
PAL
CIVIL WAR II

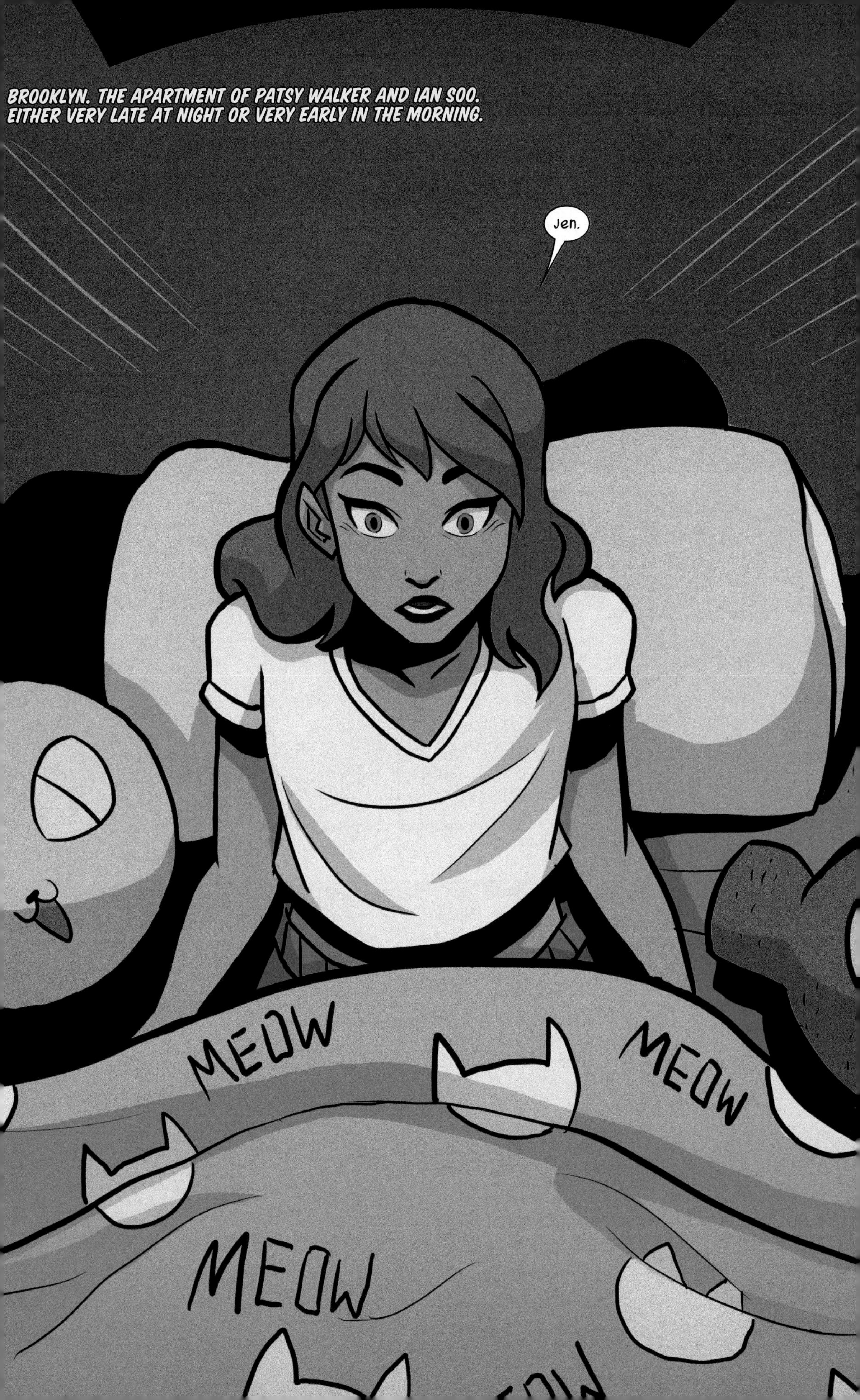
BROOKLYN. THE APARTMENT OF PATSY WALKER AND IAN SOO.
EITHER VERY LATE AT NIGHT OR VERY EARLY IN THE MORNING.
Jen.
MEOW
MEOW
MEOW

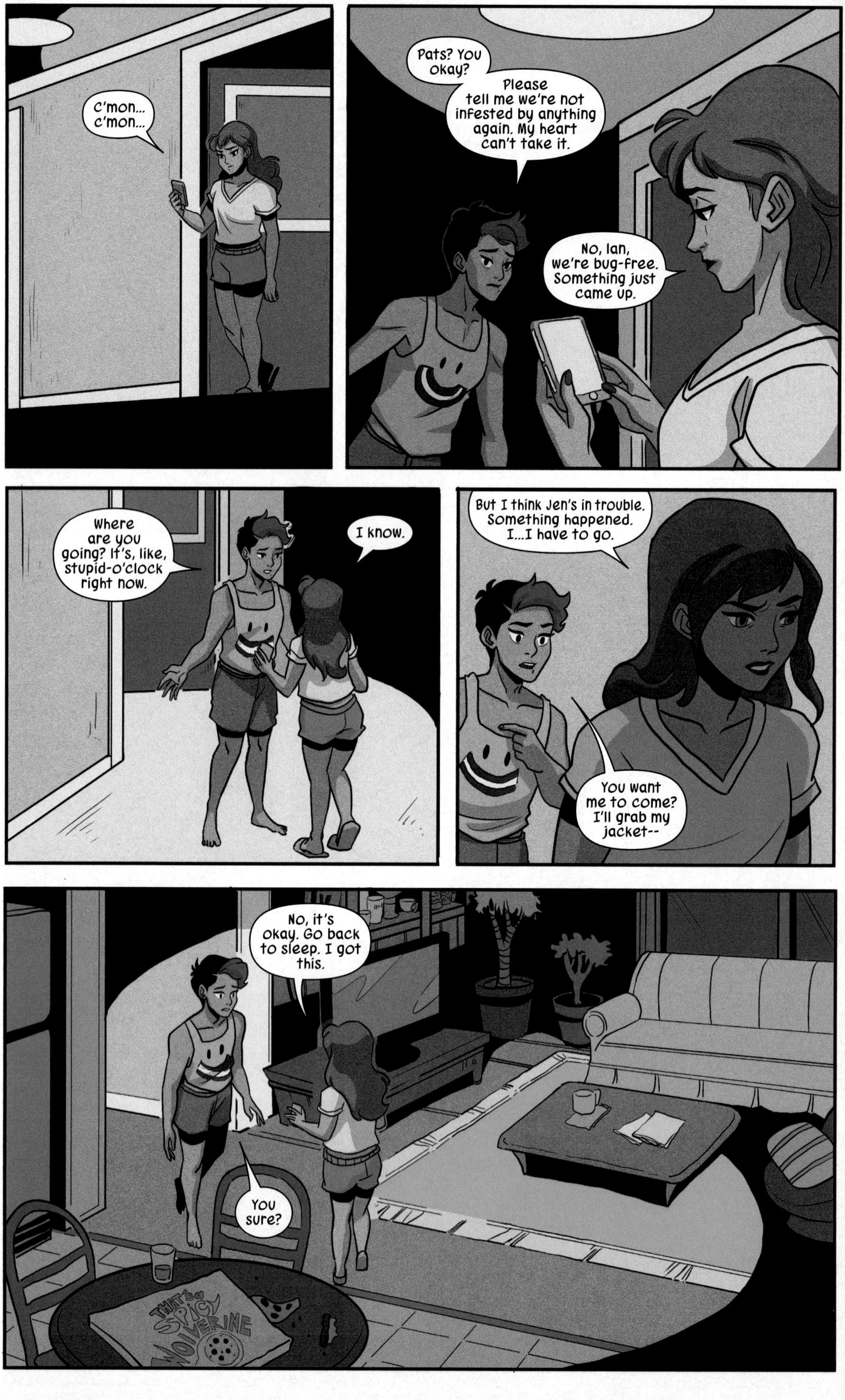
C'mon... c'mon...
Pats? You okay?
Please tell me we're not infested by anything again. My heart can't take it.
No, Ian, we're bug-free. Something just came up.
Where are you going? It's, like, stupid-o'clock right now.
I know.
But I think Jen's in trouble. Something happened. I...I have to go.
You want me to come? I'll grab my jacket--
No, it's okay. Go back to sleep. I got this.
You sure?
THAT'S a SPICY WOLVERINE

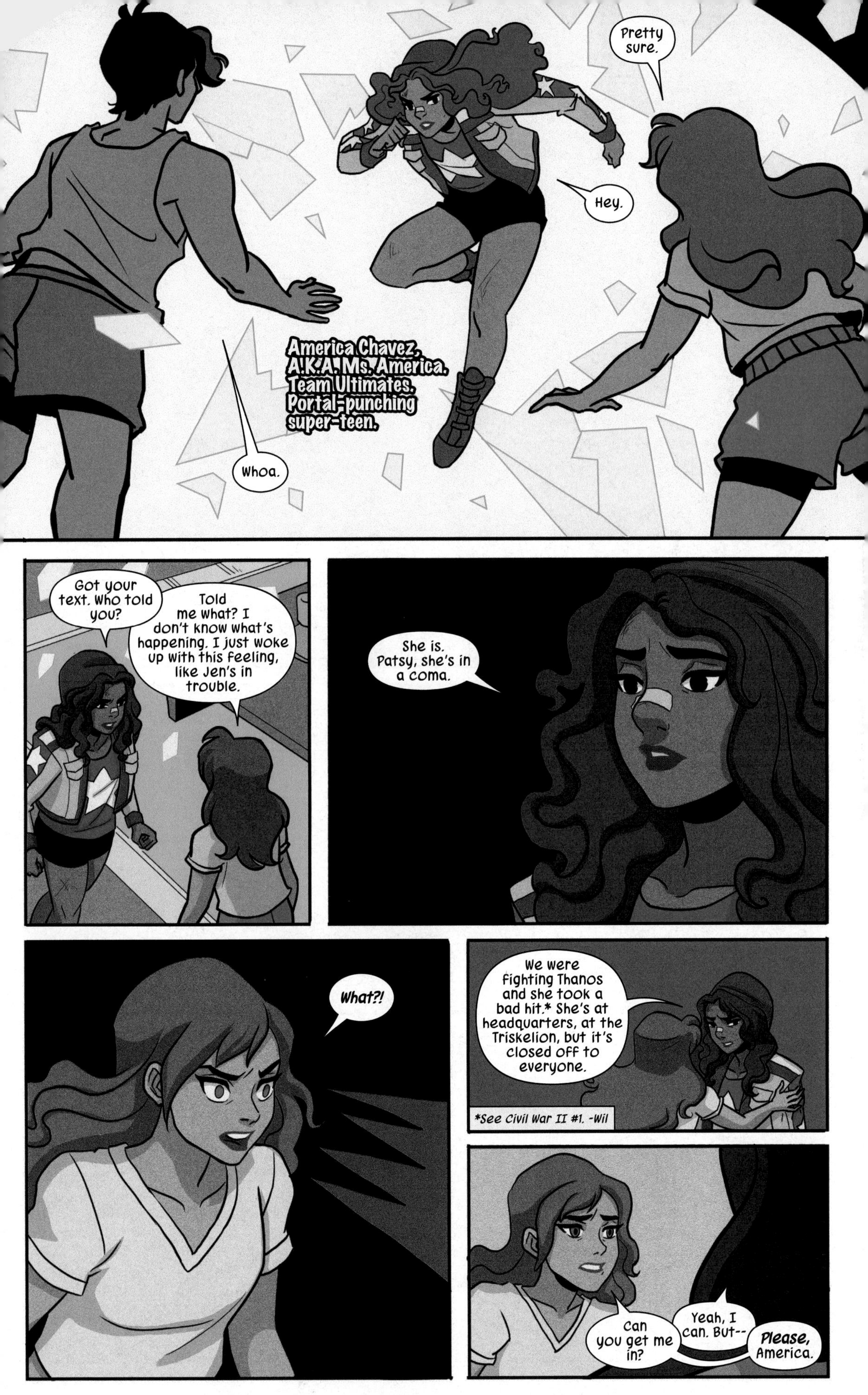
Pretty sure.
Hey.
America Chavez, A.K.A. Ms. America. Team Ultimates. Portal-punching super-teen.
Whoa.
Got your text. Who told you?
Told me what? I don't know what's happening. I just woke up with this feeling, like Jen's in trouble.
She is. Patsy, she's in a coma.
What?!
We were fighting Thanos and she took a bad hit.* She's at headquarters, at the Triskelion, but it's closed off to everyone.
*See Civil War II #1. -Wil
Can you get me in?
Yeah, I can. But--
Please, America.

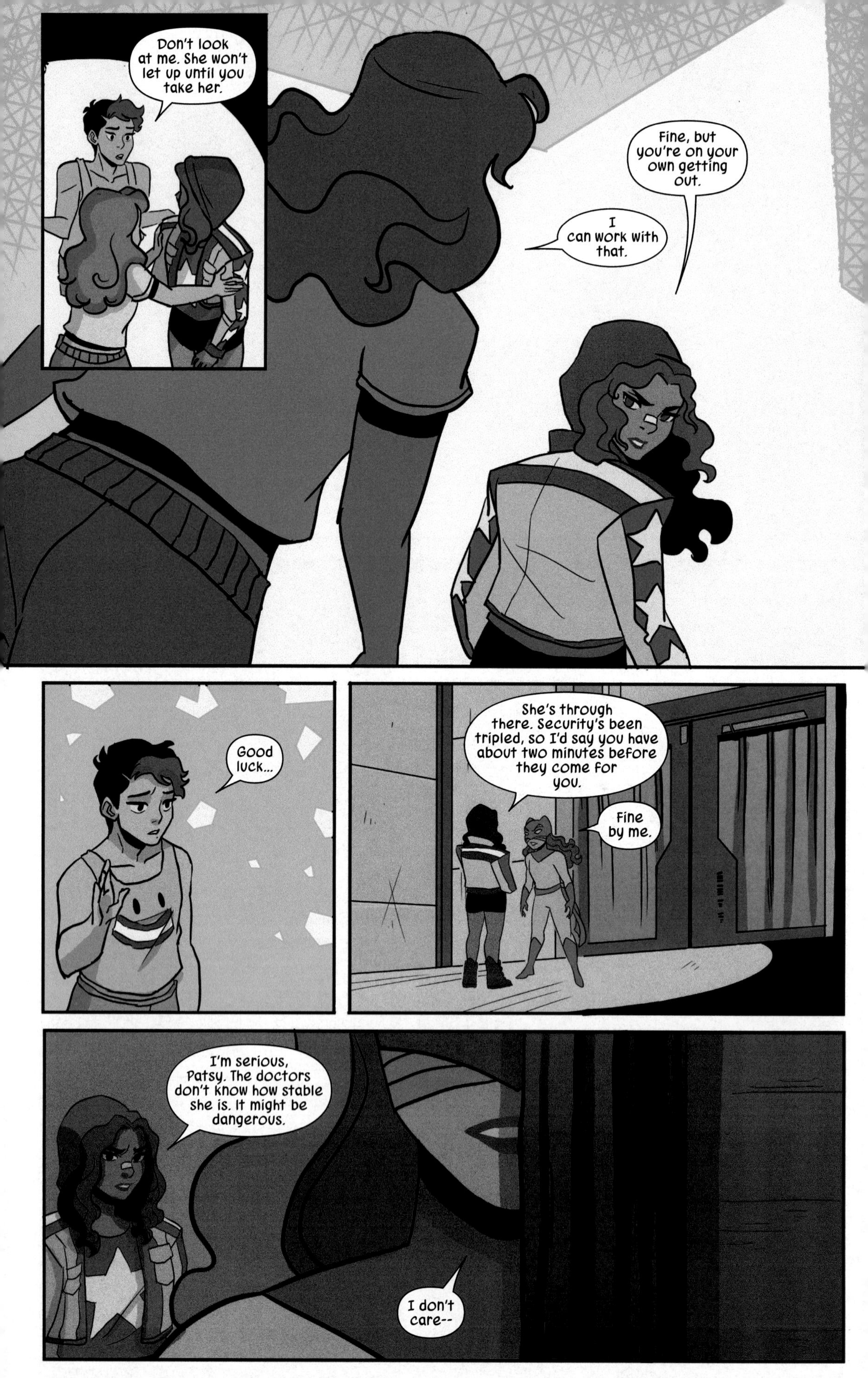
Don't look at me. She won't let up until you take her.
Fine, but you're on your own getting out.
I can work with that.
Good luck...
She's through there. Security's been tripled, so I'd say you have about two minutes before they come for you.
Fine by me.
I'm serious, Patsy. The doctors don't know how stable she is. It might be dangerous.
I don't care--

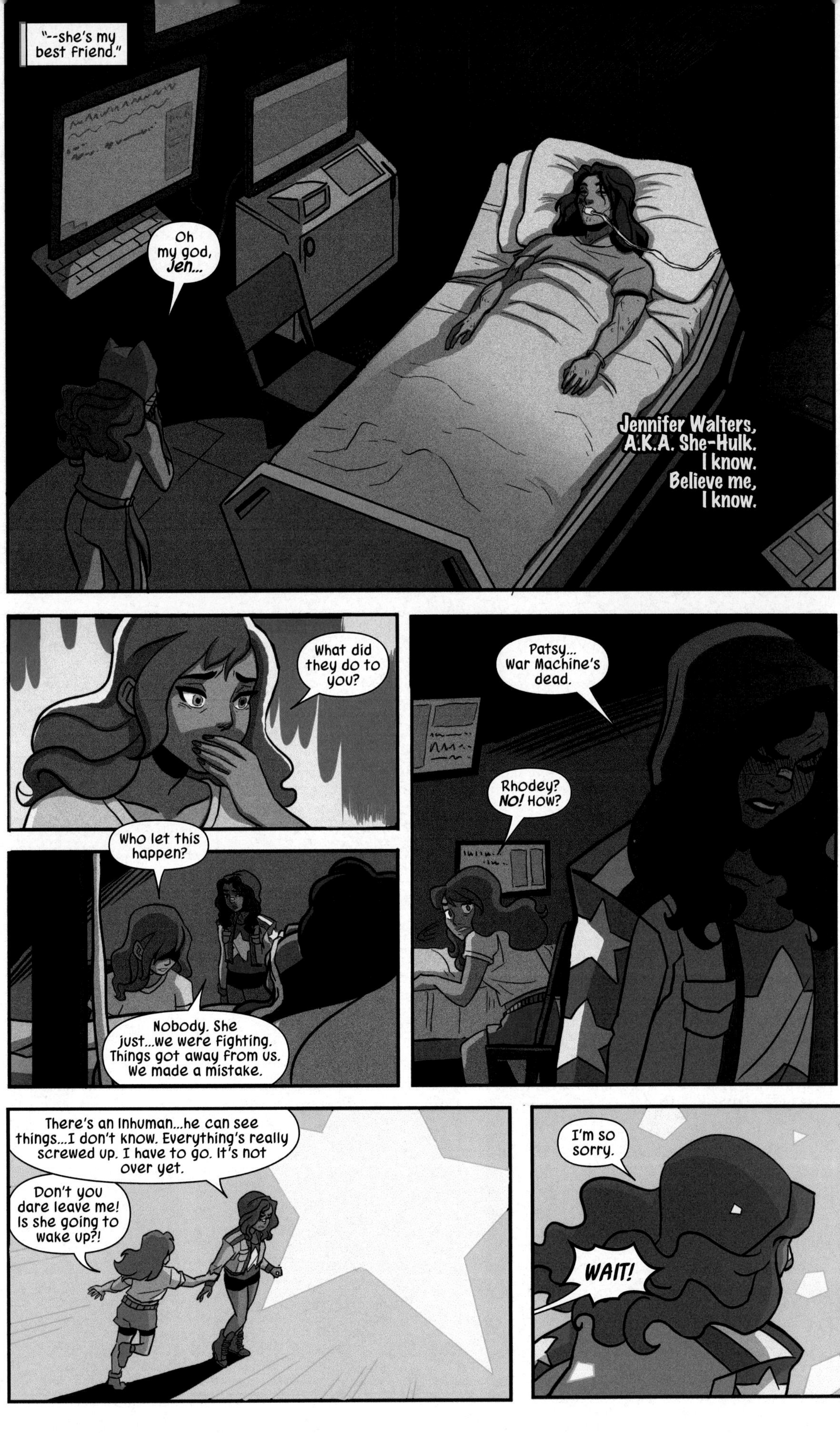
"--she's my best friend."
Oh my god, Jen...
Jennifer Walters, A.K.A. She-Hulk. I know. Believe me, I know.
What did they do to you?
Who let this happen?
Nobody. She just...we were fighting. Things got away from us. We made a mistake.
Patsy... War Machine's dead.
Rhodey? NO! How?
There's an Inhuman...he can see things...I don't know. Everything's really screwed up. I have to go. It's not over yet.
Don't you dare leave me! Is she going to wake up?!
I'm so sorry.
WAIT!

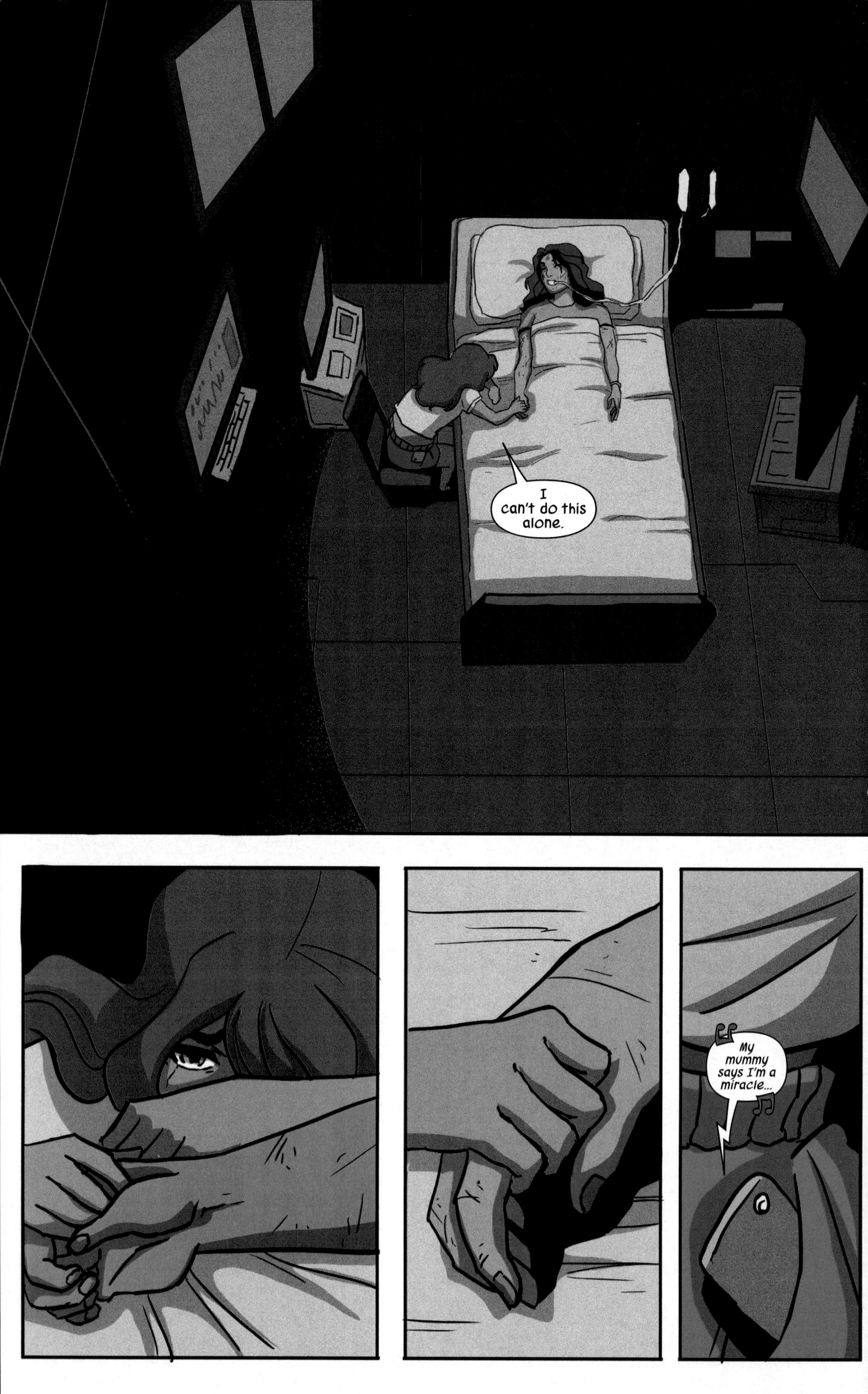
I can't do this alone.
My mummy says I'm a miracle...

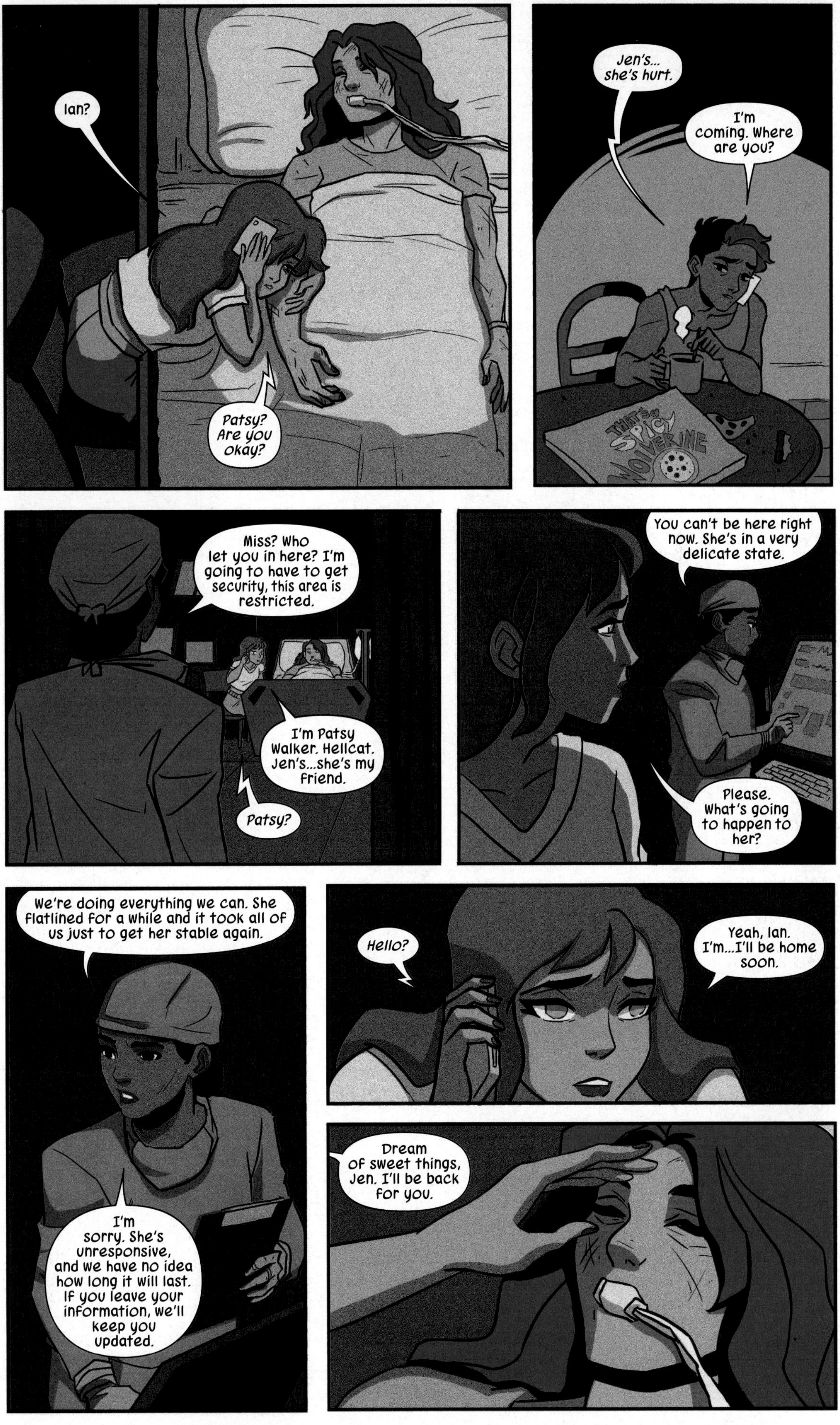
Ian?
Patsy? Are you Okay?
Jen's... she's hurt.
I'm coming. Where are you?
THAT'S a SPICY WOLVERINE
Miss? Who let you in here? I'm going to have to get security, this area is restricted.
I'm Patsy Walker. Hellcat. Jen's...she's my friend.
Patsy?
You can't be here right now. She's in a very delicate state.
Please. What's going to happen to her?
We're doing everything we can. She flatlined for a while and it took all of us just to get her stable again.
I'm sorry. She's unresponsive, and we have no idea how long it will last. If you leave your information, we'll keep you updated.
Hello?
Yeah, Ian. I'm...I'll be home soon.
Dream of sweet things, Jen. I'll be back for you.

"So, the facts are these."

James Rhodes is dead. Jen is in a coma. They're not sure...they don't know when she'll wake up. Or *if*.

Which is why I called you all here.

I don't know what to do.

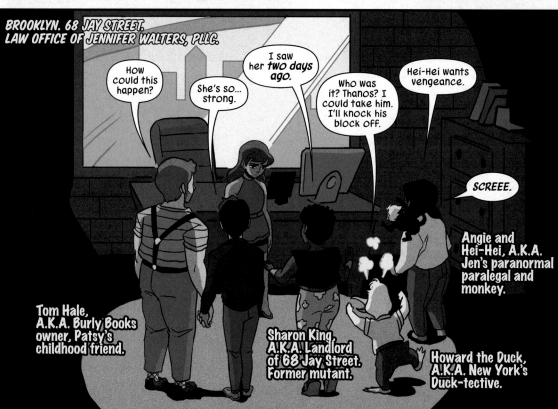

BROOKLYN. 68 JAY STREET.
LAW OFFICE OF JENNIFER WALTERS, PLLC.

How could this happen?

She's so... strong.

I saw her *two days ago*.

Who was it? Thanos? I could take him. I'll knock his block off.

Hei-Hei wants vengeance.

SCREEE.

Tom Hale, A.K.A. Burly Books owner, Patsy's childhood friend.

Sharon King, A.K.A. Landlord of 68 Jay Street. Former mutant.

Angie and Hei-Hei, A.K.A. Jen's paranormal paralegal and monkey.

Howard the Duck, A.K.A. New York's Duck-tective.

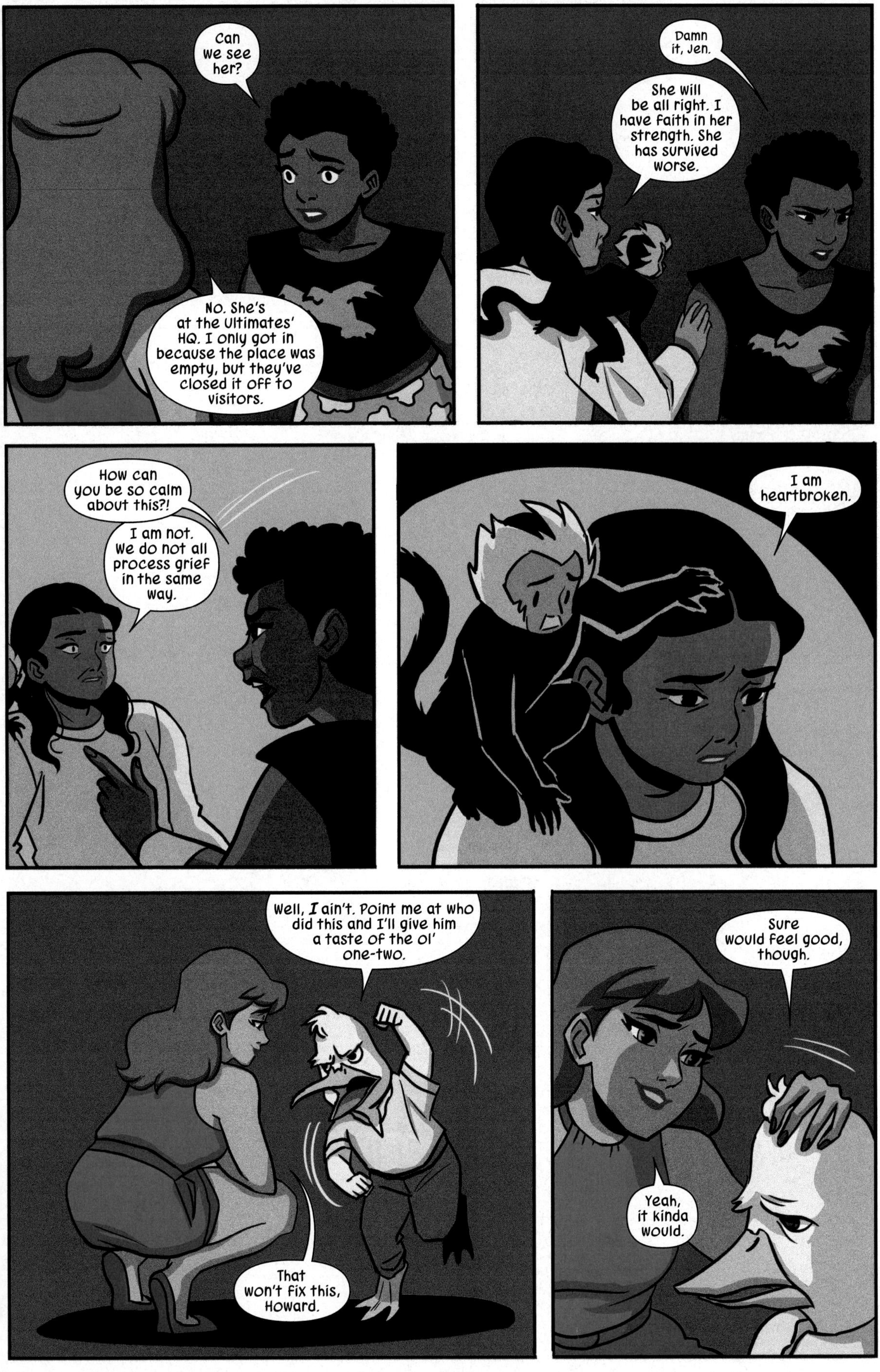
Can we see her?
No. She's at the Ultimates' HQ. I only got in because the place was empty, but they've closed it off to visitors.
Damn it, Jen.
She will be all right. I have faith in her strength. She has survived worse.
How can you be so calm about this?!
I am not. We do not all process grief in the same way.
I am heartbroken.
Well, *I* ain't. Point me at who did this and I'll give him a taste of the ol' one-two.
That won't fix this, Howard.
Sure would feel good, though.
Yeah, it kinda would.

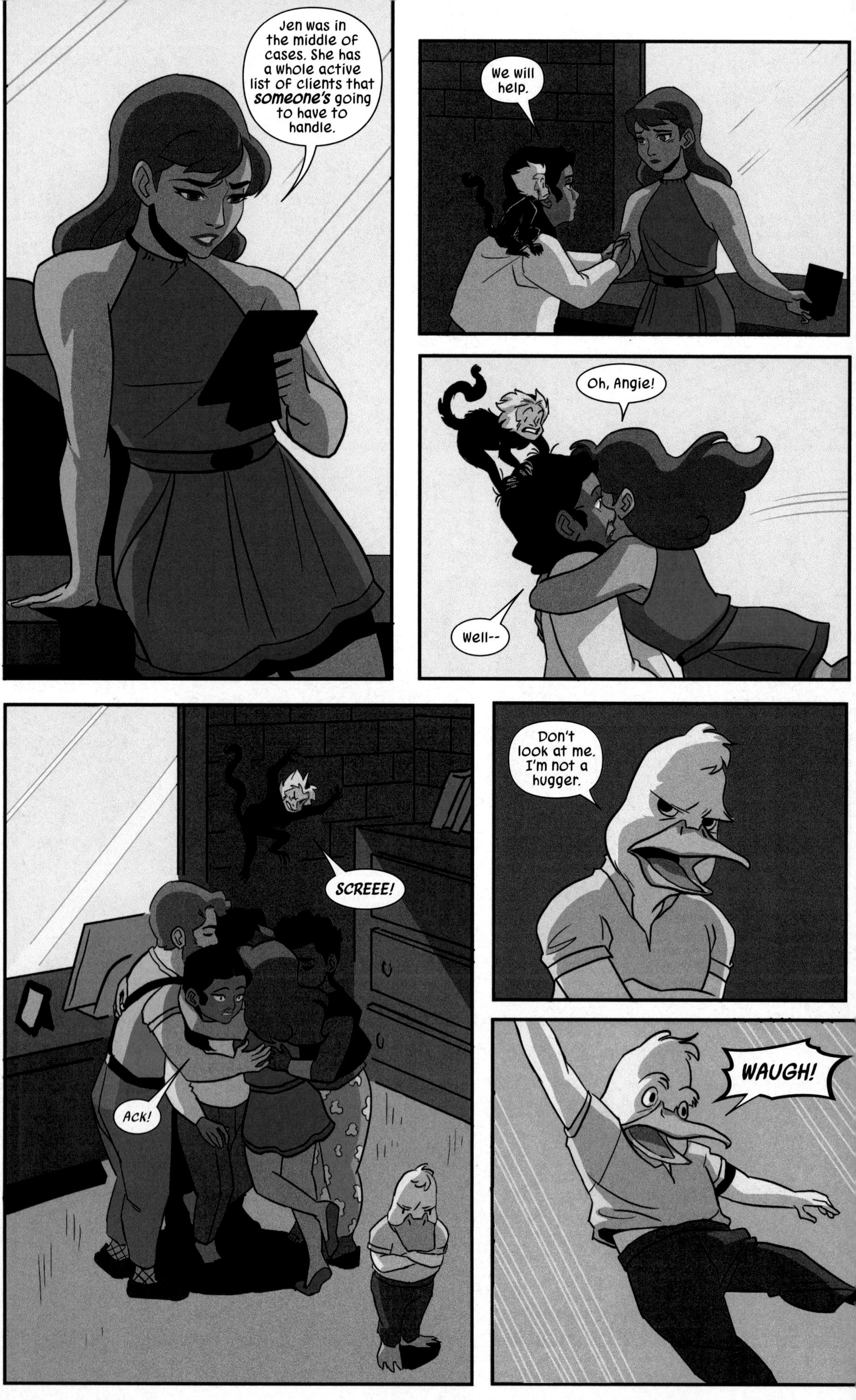
Jen was in the middle of cases. She has a whole active list of clients that *someone's* going to have to handle.
We will help.
Oh, Angie!
Well--
SCREEE!
Ack!
Don't look at me. I'm not a hugger.
WAUGH!

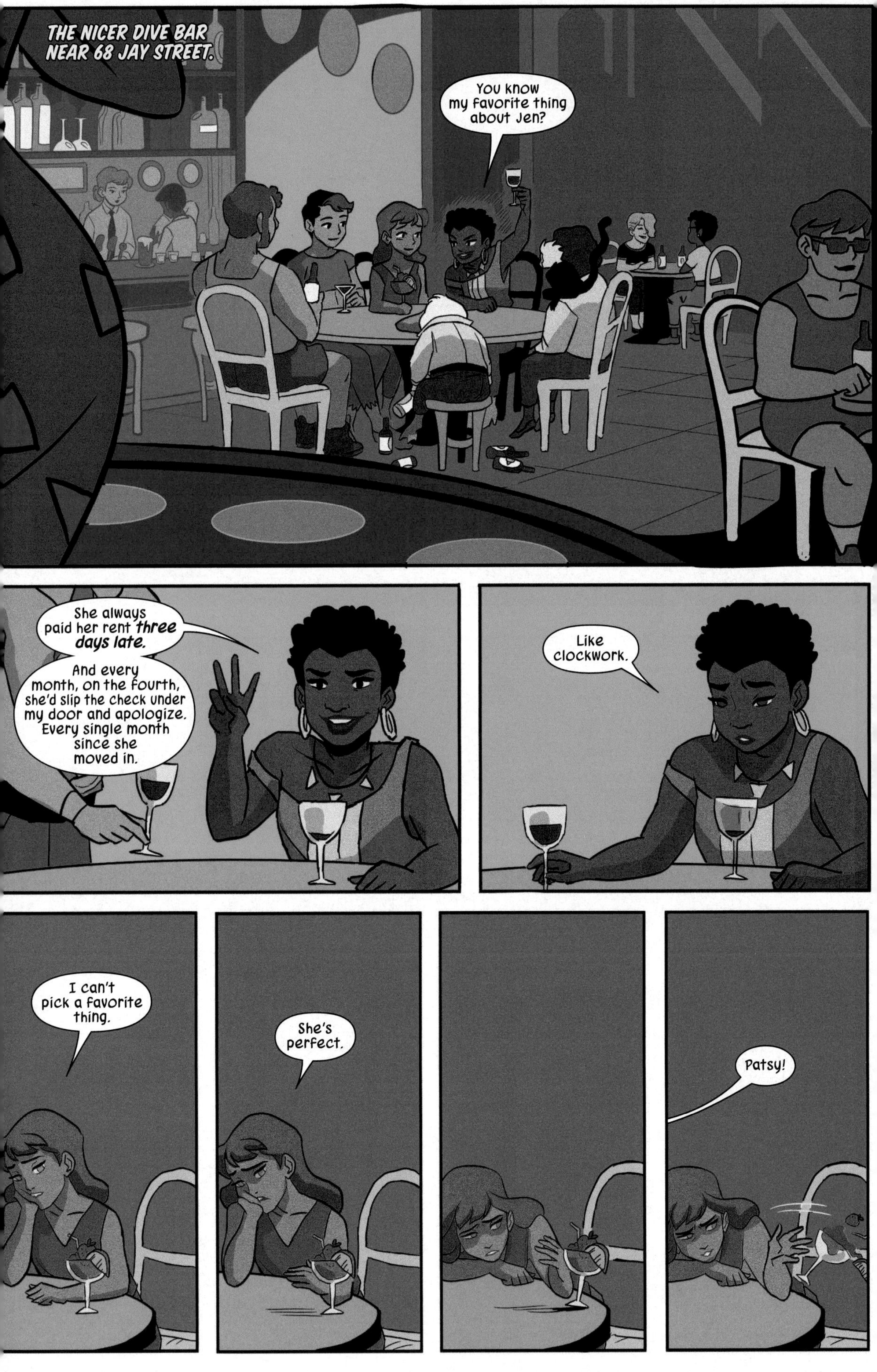
THE NICER DIVE BAR NEAR 68 JAY STREET.
You know my favorite thing about Jen?
She always paid her rent three days late.
And every month, on the fourth, she'd slip the check under my door and apologize. Every single month since she moved in.
Like clockwork.
I can't pick a favorite thing.
She's perfect.
Patsy!

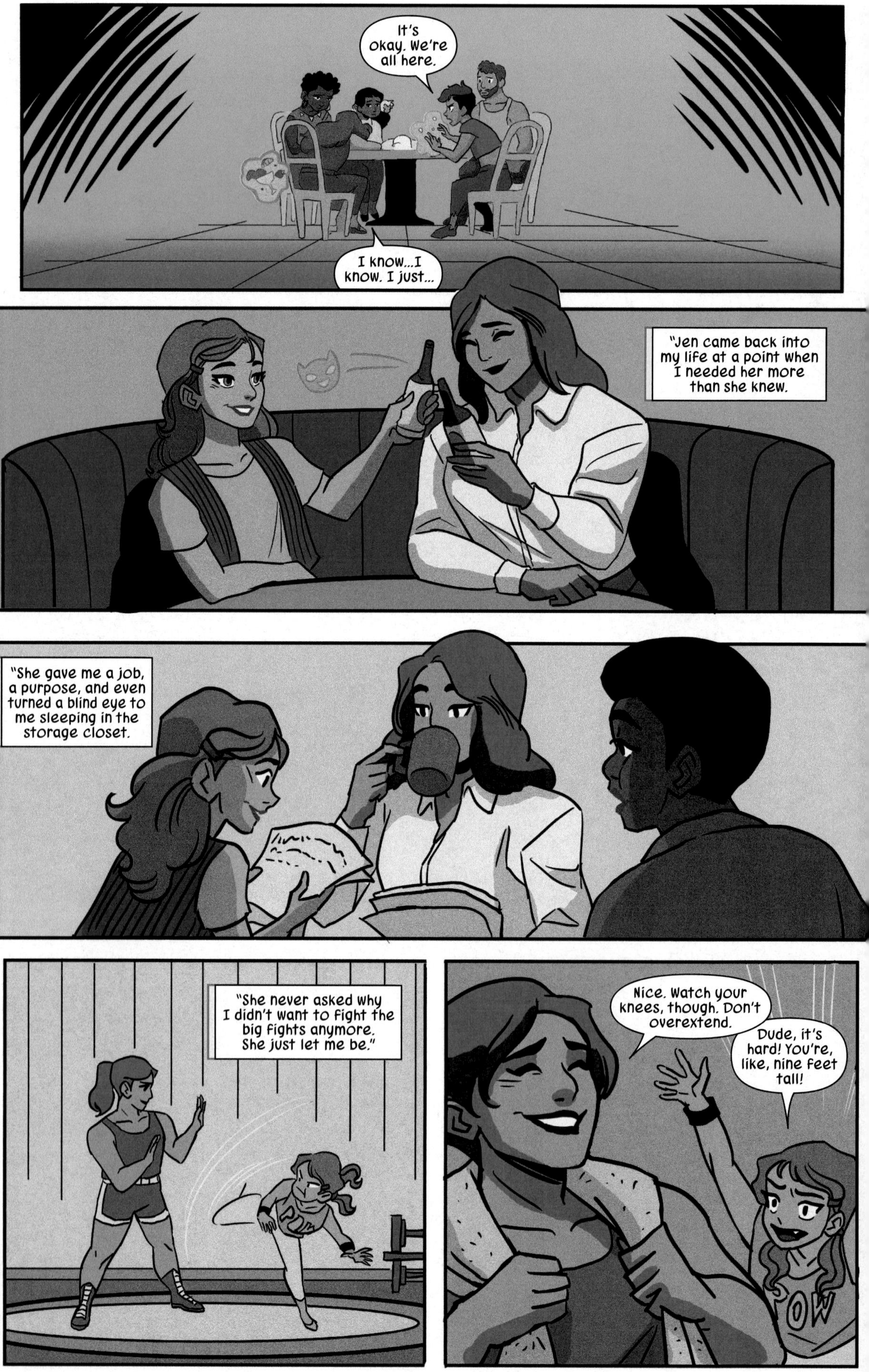
It's okay. We're all here.
I know...I know. I just...
"Jen came back into my life at a point when I needed her more than she knew.
"She gave me a job, a purpose, and even turned a blind eye to me sleeping in the storage closet.
"She never asked why I didn't want to fight the big fights anymore. She just let me be."
Nice. Watch your knees, though. Don't overextend.
Dude, it's hard! You're, like, nine feet tall!
POW

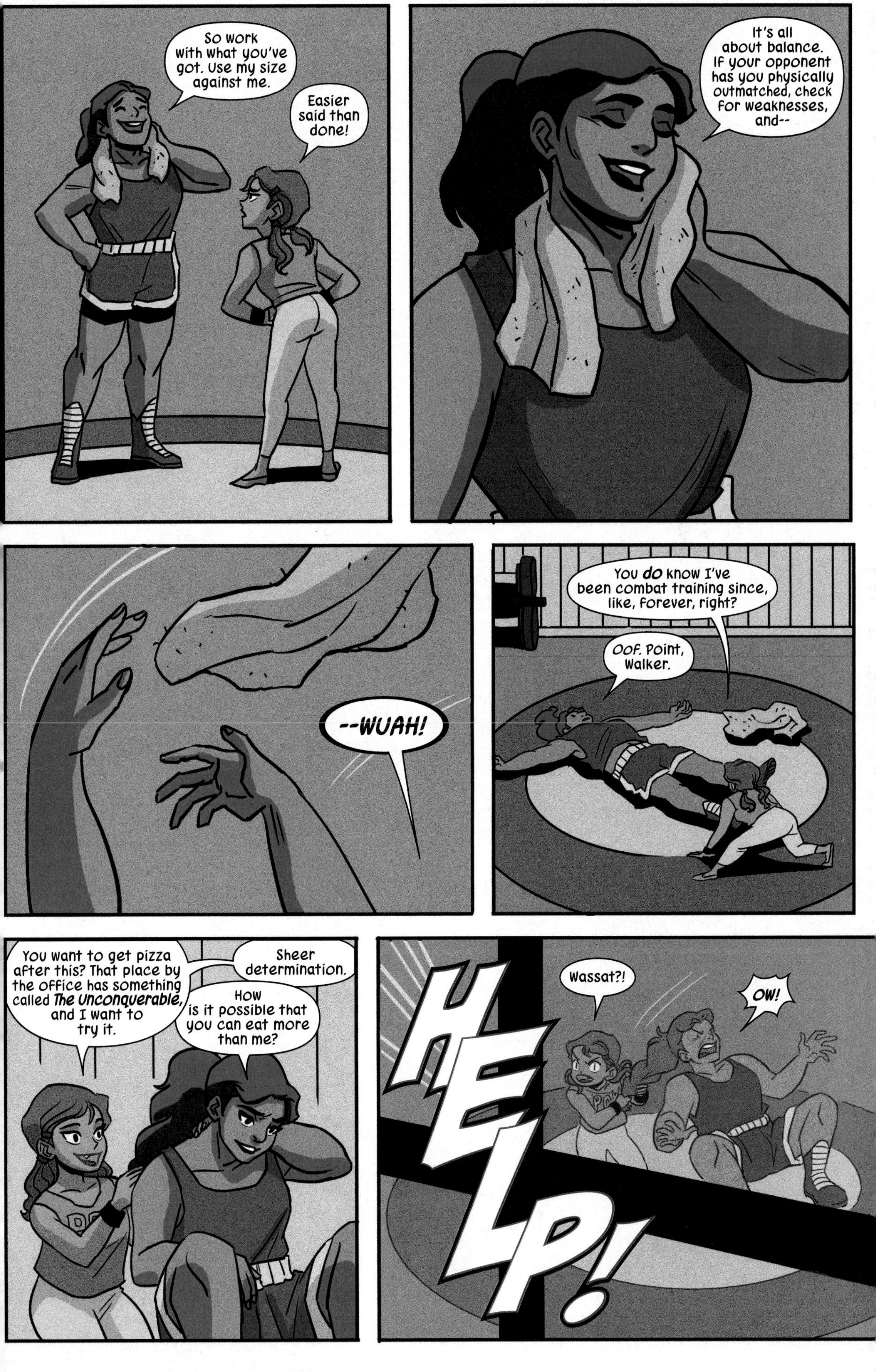
So work with what you've got. Use my size against me.
Easier said than done!
It's all about balance. If your opponent has you physically outmatched, check for weaknesses, and--
--WUAH!
You do know I've been combat training since, like, forever, right?
Oof. Point, Walker.
You want to get pizza after this? That place by the office has something called The Unconquerable, and I want to try it.
How is it possible that you can eat more than me?
Sheer determination.
HELP!
Wassat?!
OW!

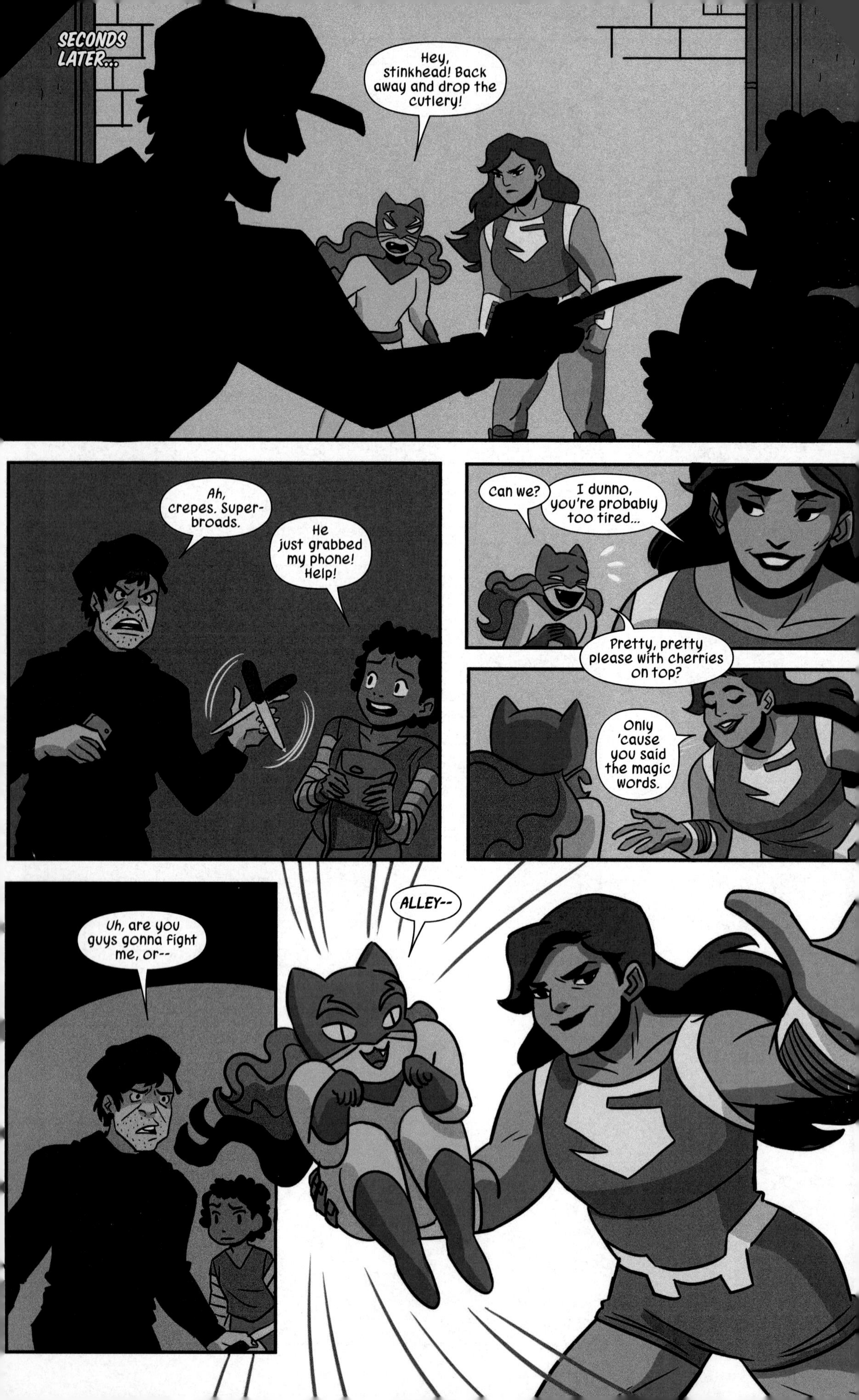
SECONDS LATER...
Hey, stinkhead! Back away and drop the cutlery!
Ah, crepes. Super-broads.
He just grabbed my phone! Help!
Can we?
I dunno, you're probably too tired...
Pretty, pretty please with cherries on top?
Only 'cause you said the magic words.
Uh, are you guys gonna fight me, or--
ALLEY--

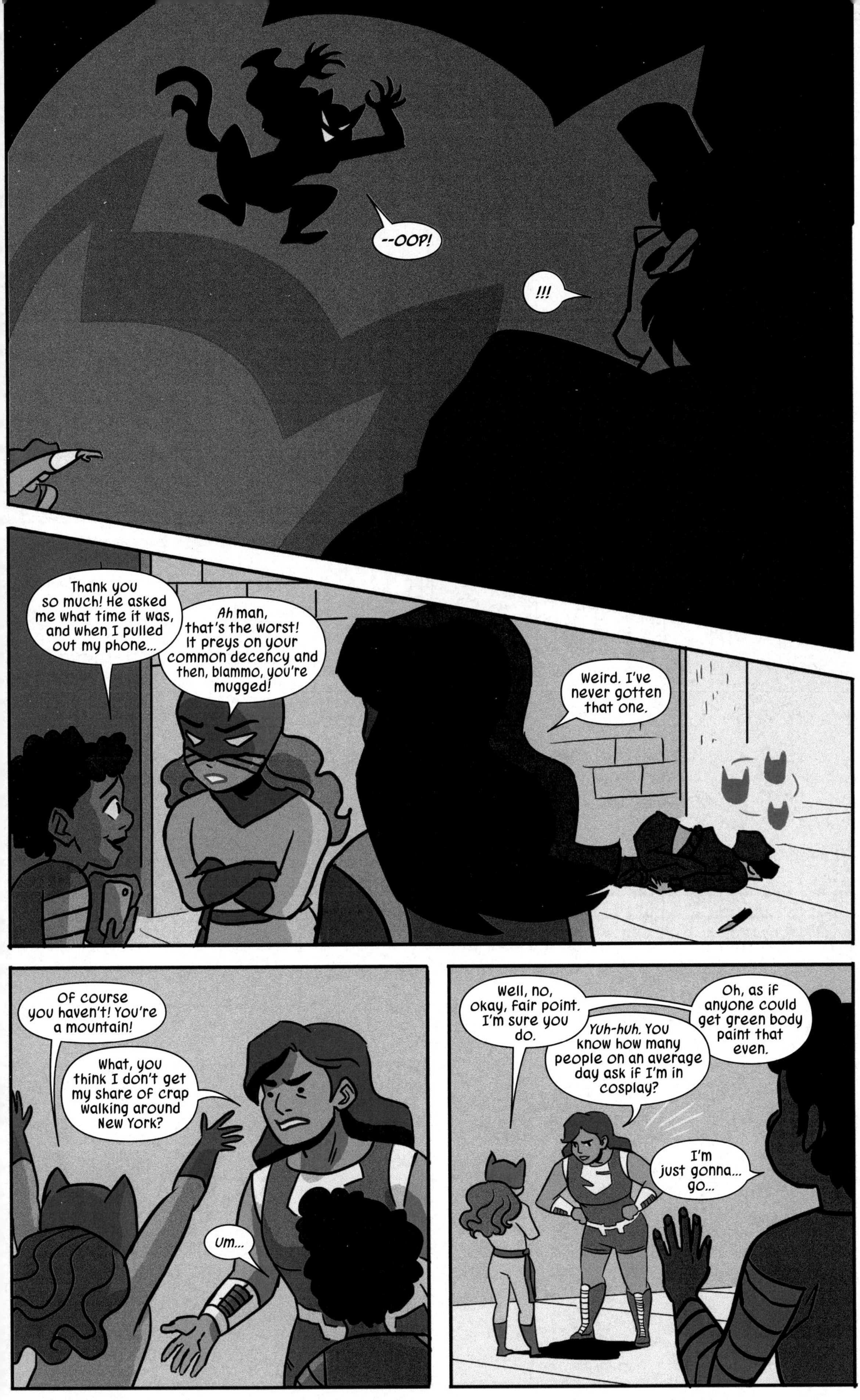
--OOP!
!!!
Thank you so much! He asked me what time it was, and when I pulled out my phone...
Ah man, that's the worst! It preys on your common decency and then, blammo, you're mugged!
Weird. I've never gotten that one.
Of course you haven't! You're a mountain!
What, you think I don't get my share of crap walking around New York?
Um...
Well, no, okay, fair point. I'm sure you do.
Yuh-huh. You know how many people on an average day ask if I'm in cosplay?
Oh, as if anyone could get green body paint that even.
I'm just gonna... go...

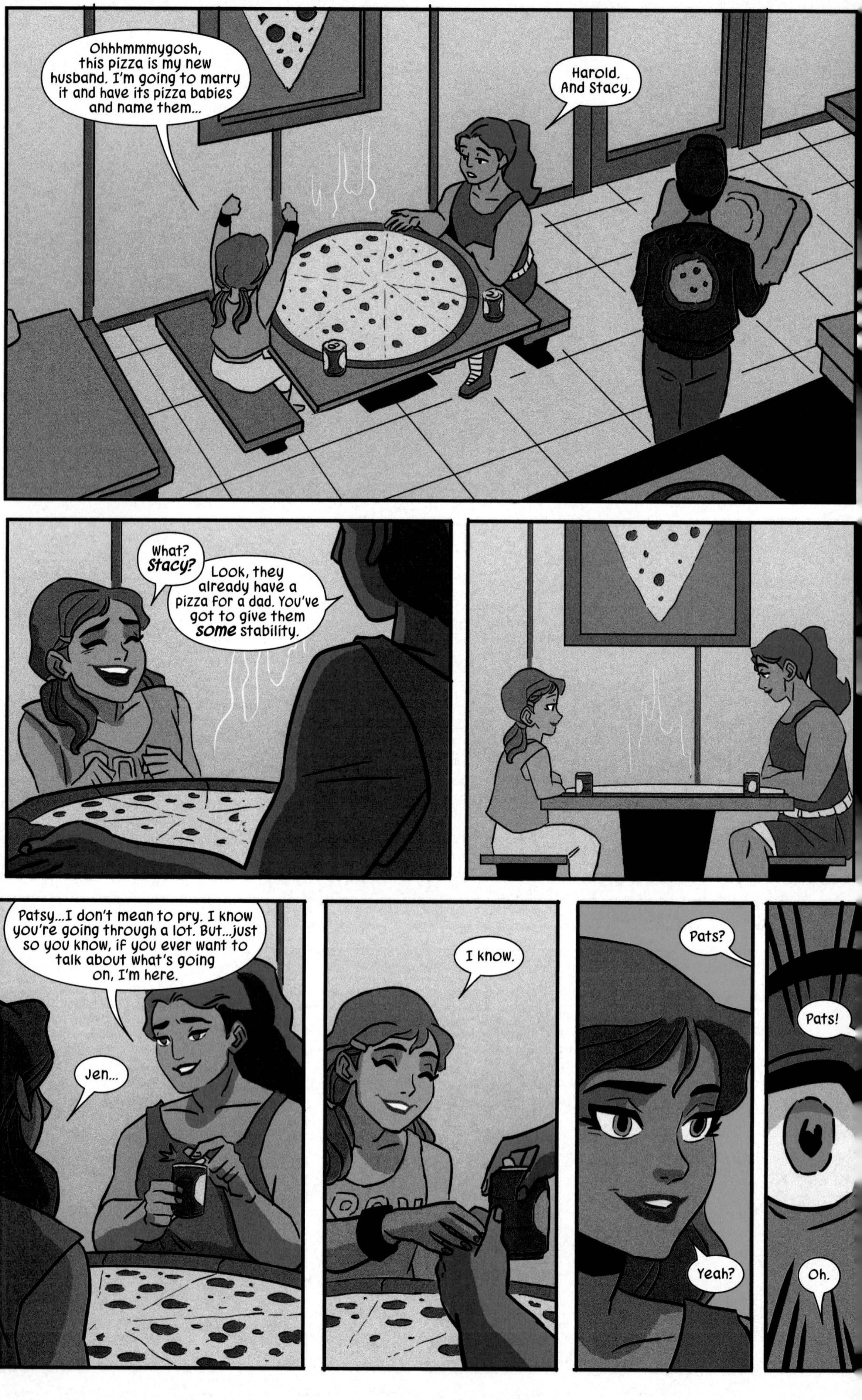
Ohhhmmmygosh, this pizza is my new husband. I'm going to marry it and have its pizza babies and name them...
Harold. And Stacy.
What? Stacy?
Look, they already have a pizza for a dad. You've got to give them SOME stability.
Patsy...I don't mean to pry. I know you're going through a lot. But...just so you know, if you ever want to talk about what's going on, I'm here.
Jen...
I know.
Pats?
Yeah?
Pats!
Oh.

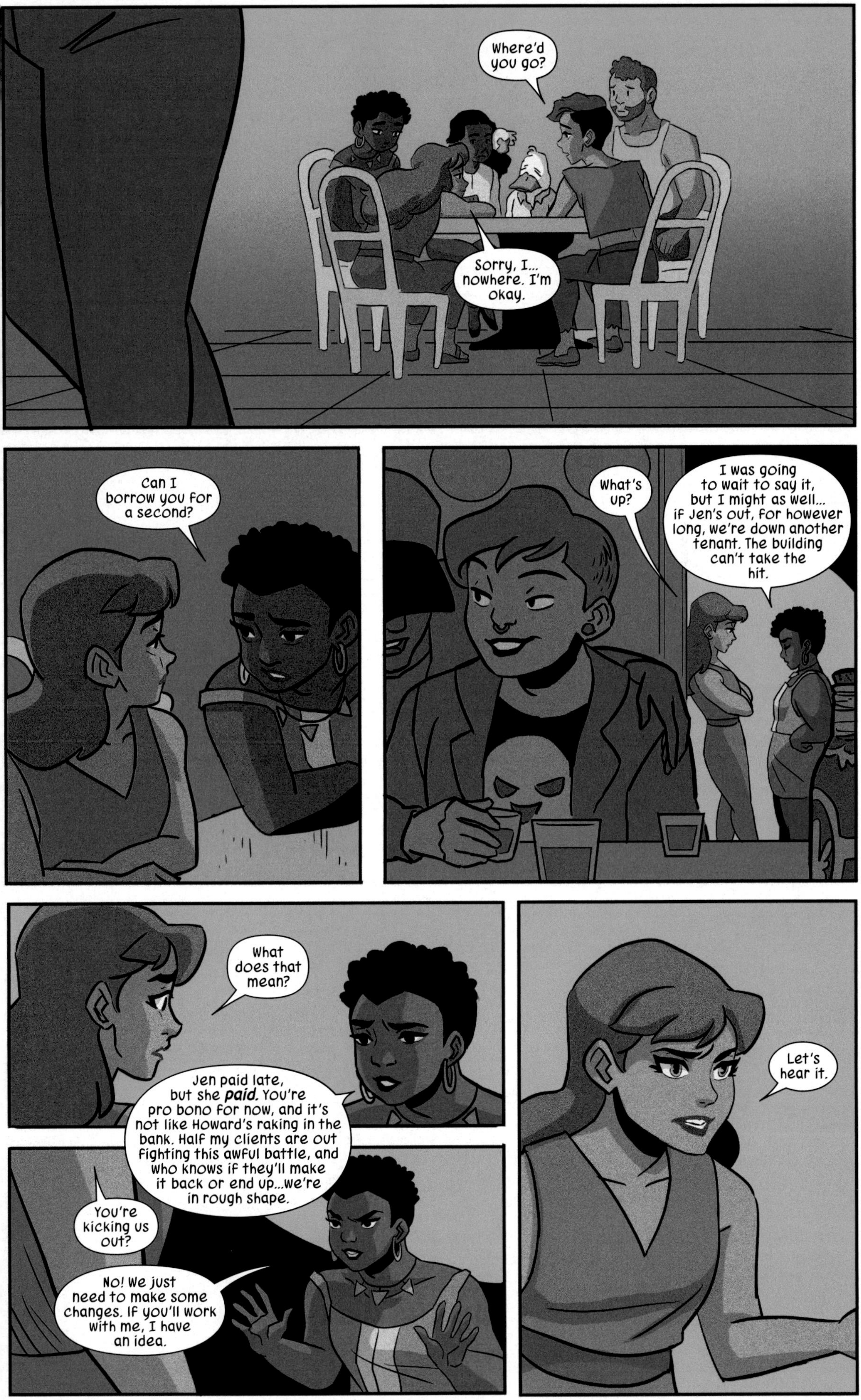
Where'd you go?
Sorry, I... nowhere. I'm okay.
Can I borrow you for a second?
What's up?
I was going to wait to say it, but I might as well... if Jen's out, for however long, we're down another tenant. The building can't take the hit.
What does that mean?
Jen paid late, but she **paid.** You're pro bono for now, and it's not like Howard's raking in the bank. Half my clients are out fighting this awful battle, and who knows if they'll make it back or end up...we're in rough shape.
You're kicking us out?
No! We just need to make some changes. If you'll work with me, I have an idea.
Let's hear it.

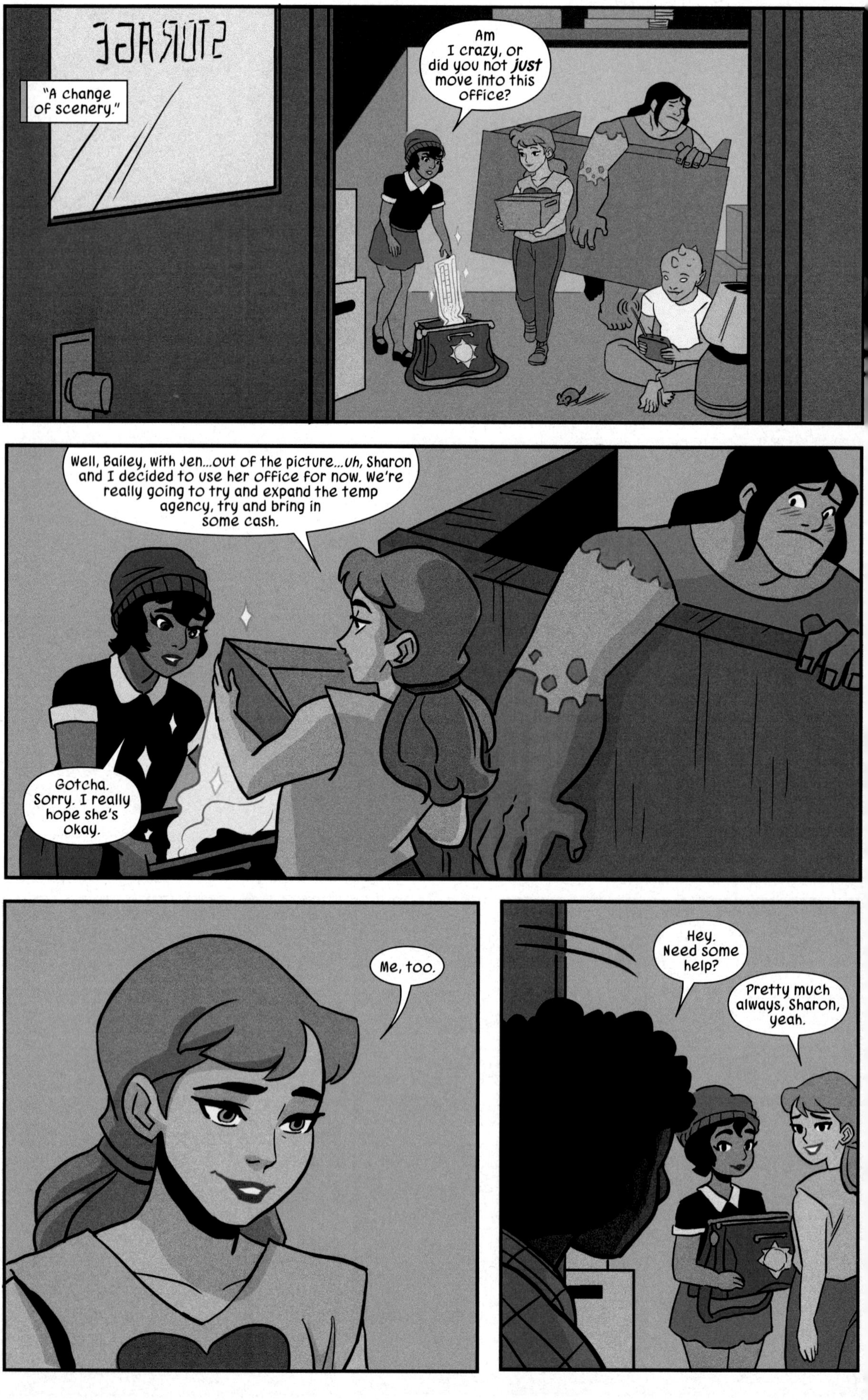
"A change of scenery."
Am I crazy, or did you not *just* move into this office?
Well, Bailey, with Jen...out of the picture...*uh*, Sharon and I decided to use her office for now. We're really going to try and expand the temp agency, try and bring in some cash.
Gotcha. Sorry. I really hope she's okay.
Me, too.
Hey. Need some help?
Pretty much always, Sharon, yeah.

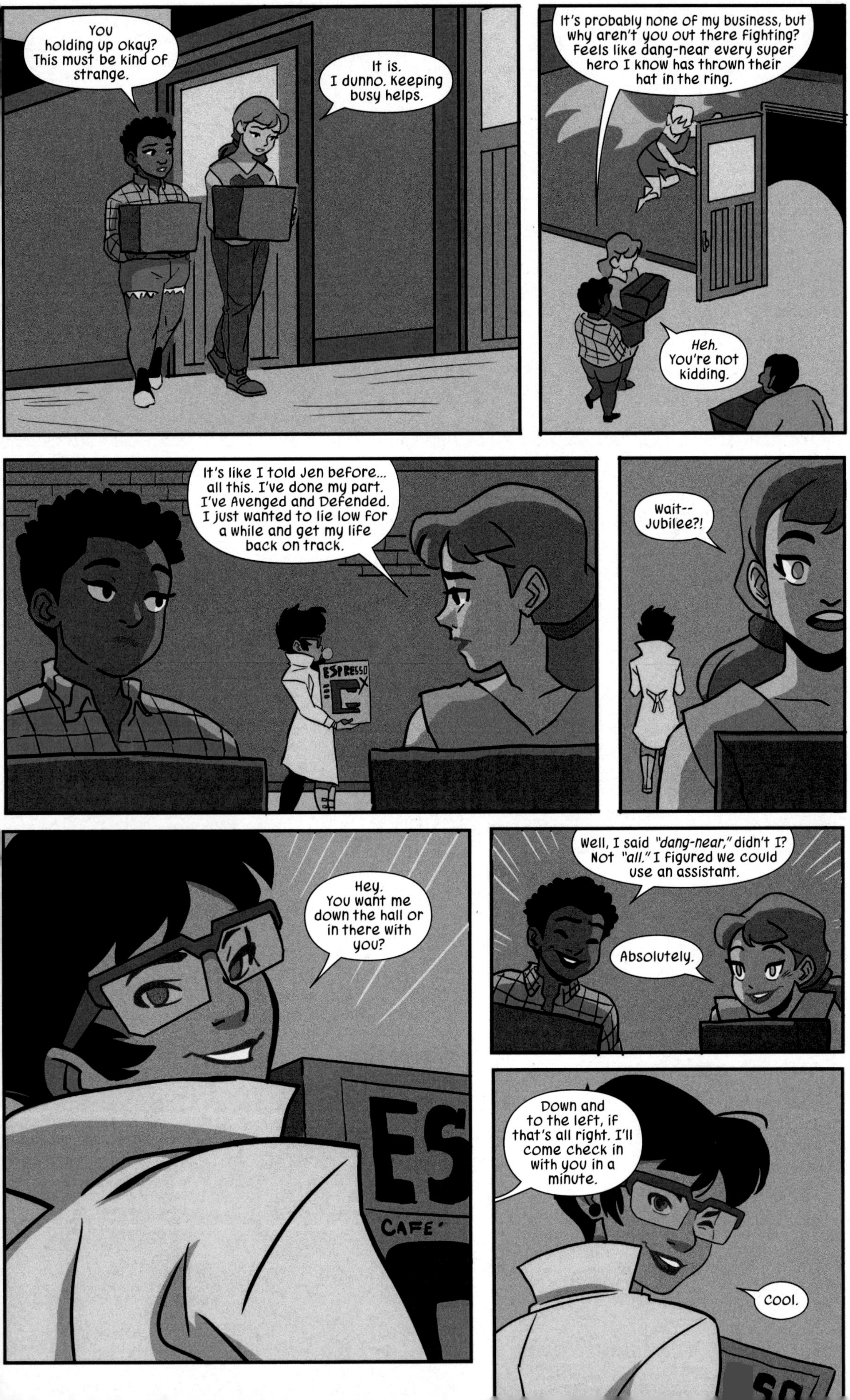
You holding up okay? This must be kind of strange.
It is. I dunno. Keeping busy helps.
It's probably none of my business, but why aren't you out there fighting? Feels like dang-near every super hero I know has thrown their hat in the ring.
Heh. You're not kidding.
It's like I told Jen before... all this. I've done my part. I've Avenged and Defended. I just wanted to lie low for a while and get my life back on track.
ESPRESSO
Wait-- Jubilee?!
Hey. You want me down the hall or in there with you?
ES
CAFE'
Well, I said "dang-near," didn't I? Not "all." I figured we could use an assistant.
Absolutely.
Down and to the left, if that's all right. I'll come check in with you in a minute.
Cool.

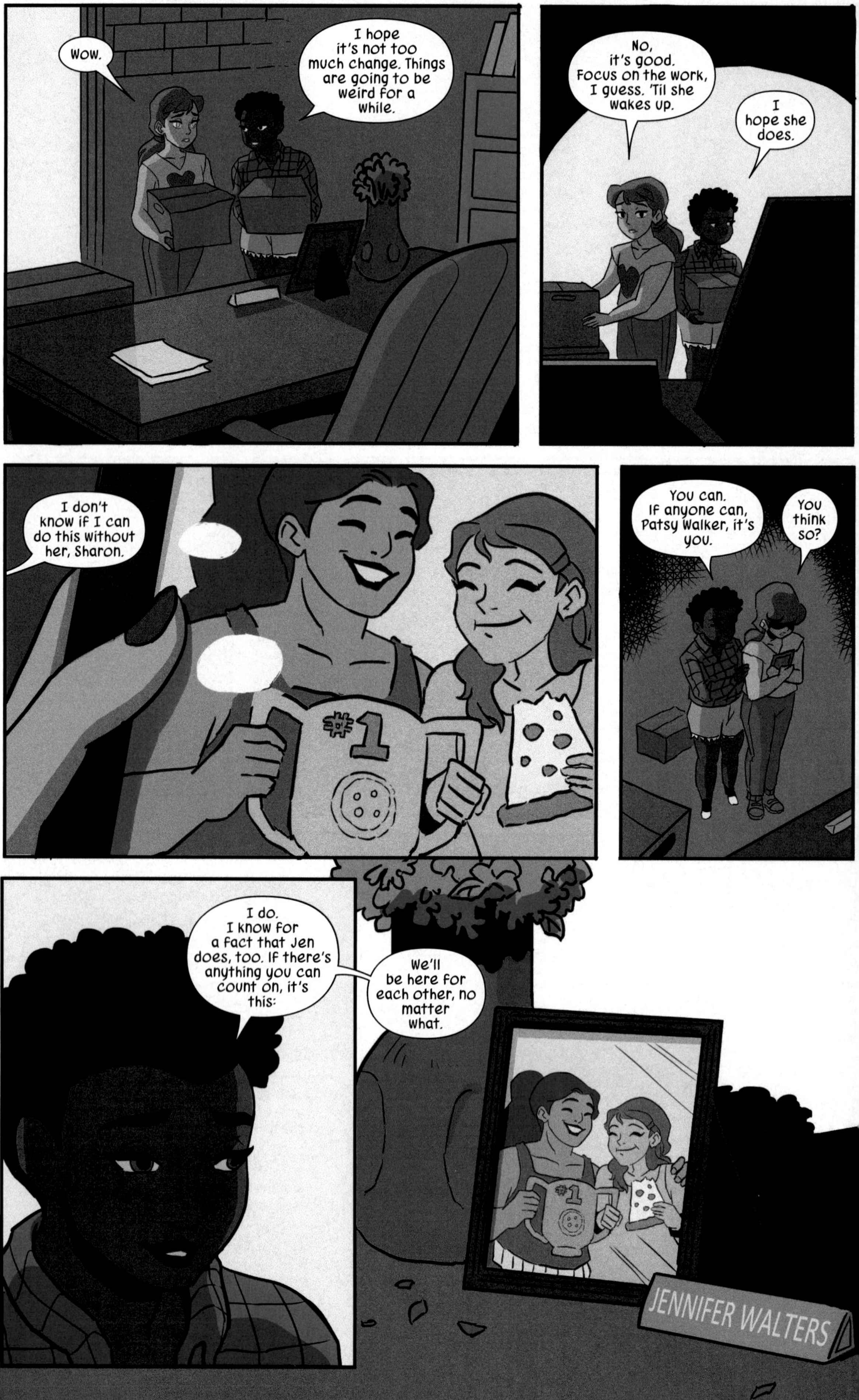
WOW.
I hope it's not too much change. Things are going to be weird for a while.
No, it's good. Focus on the work, I guess. 'Til she wakes up.
I hope she does.
I don't know if I can do this without her, Sharon.
#1
You can. If anyone can, Patsy Walker, it's you.
You think so?
I do. I know for a fact that Jen does, too. If there's anything you can count on, it's this:
We'll be here for each other, no matter what.
JENNIFER WALTERS

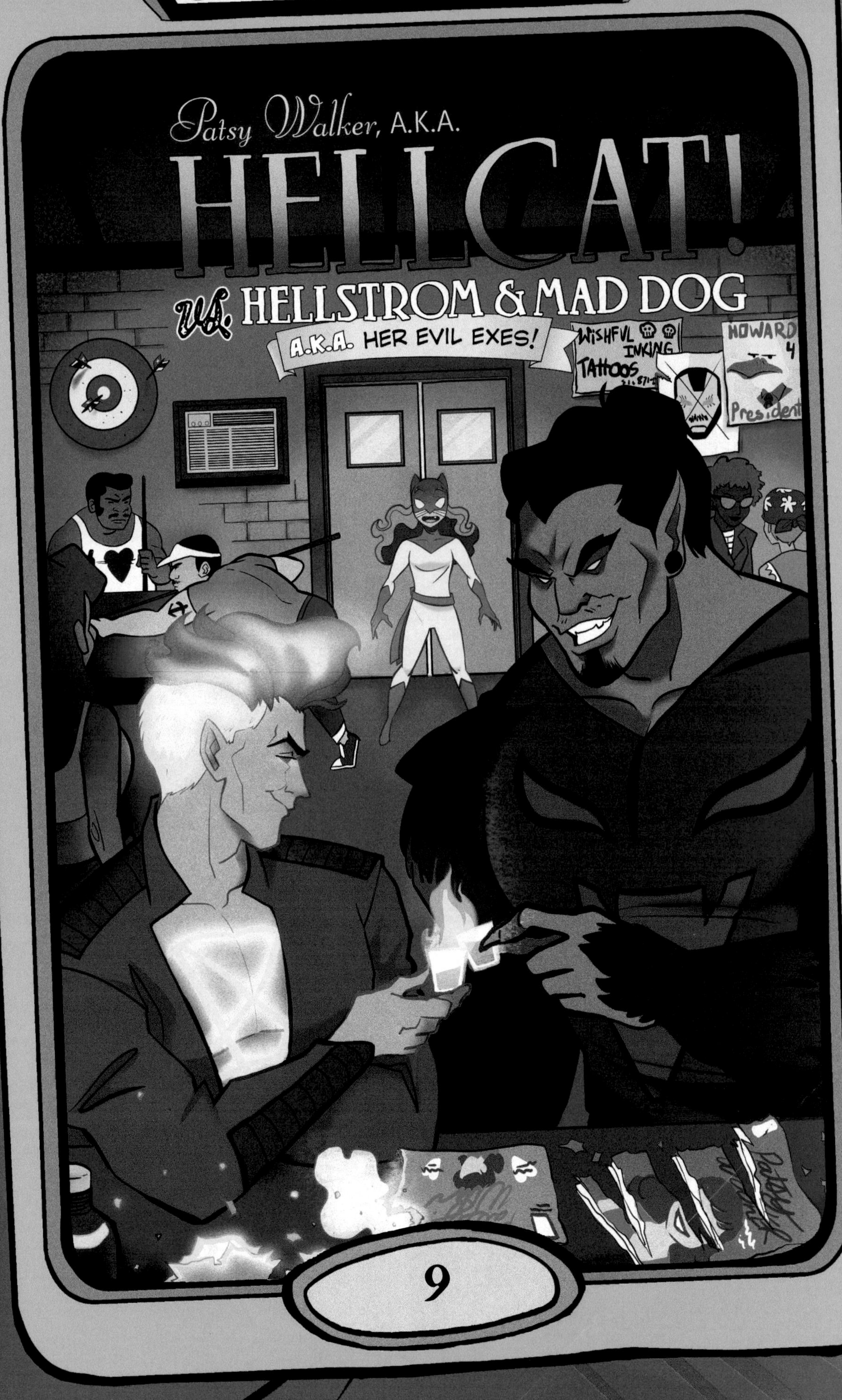
Patsy Walker, A.K.A.
HELLCAT!
vs. HELLSTROM & MAD DOG
A.K.A. HER EVIL EXES!
WISHFUL INKING TATTOOS
HOWARD 4 President
9

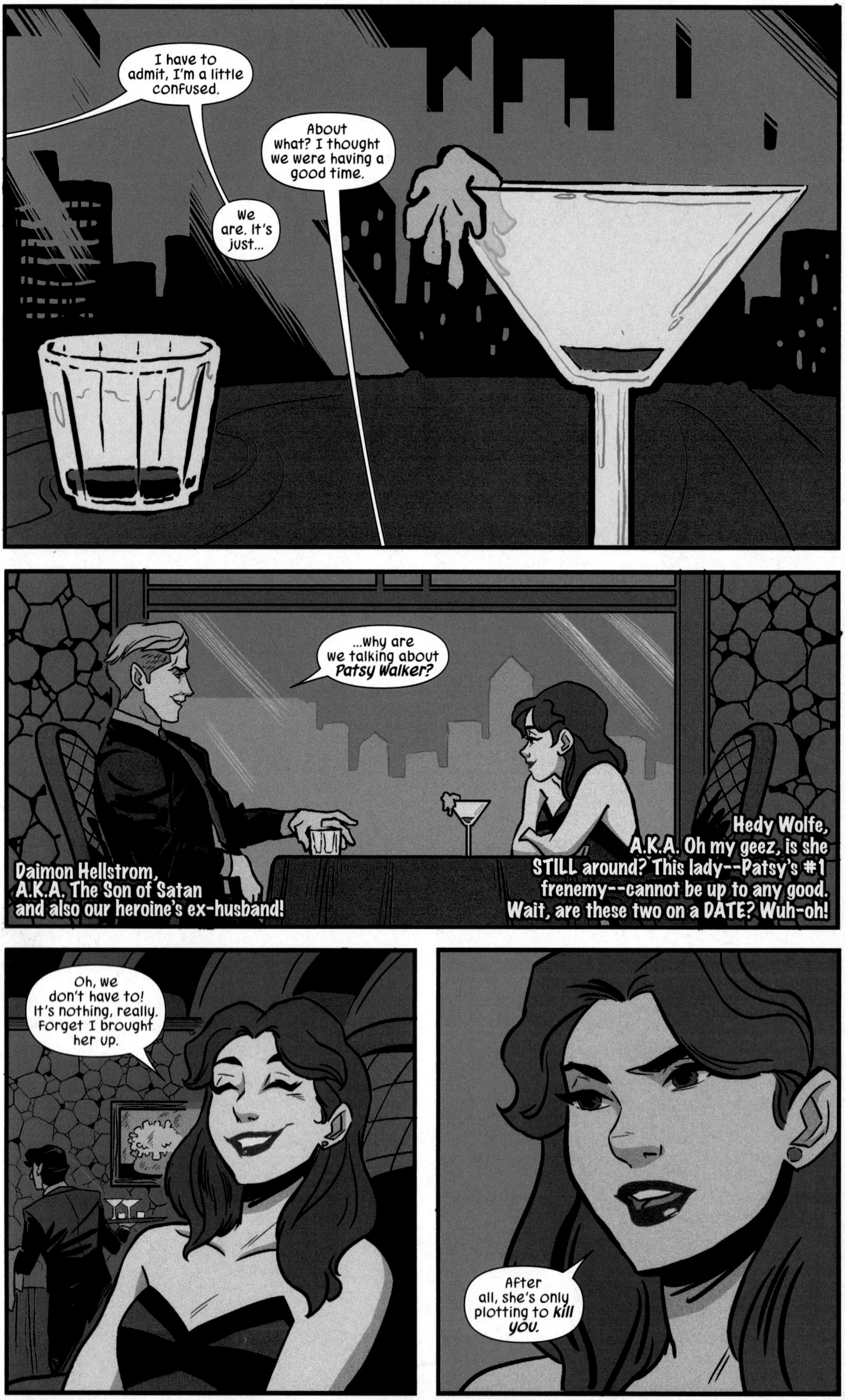

I have to admit, I'm a little confused.
About what? I thought we were having a good time.
We are. It's just...
...why are we talking about Patsy Walker?
Daimon Hellstrom, A.K.A. The Son of Satan and also our heroine's ex-husband!
Hedy Wolfe, A.K.A. Oh my geez, is she STILL around? This lady--Patsy's #1 frenemy--cannot be up to any good. Wait, are these two on a DATE? Wuh-oh!
Oh, we don't have to! It's nothing, really. Forget I brought her up.
After all, she's only plotting to kill you.

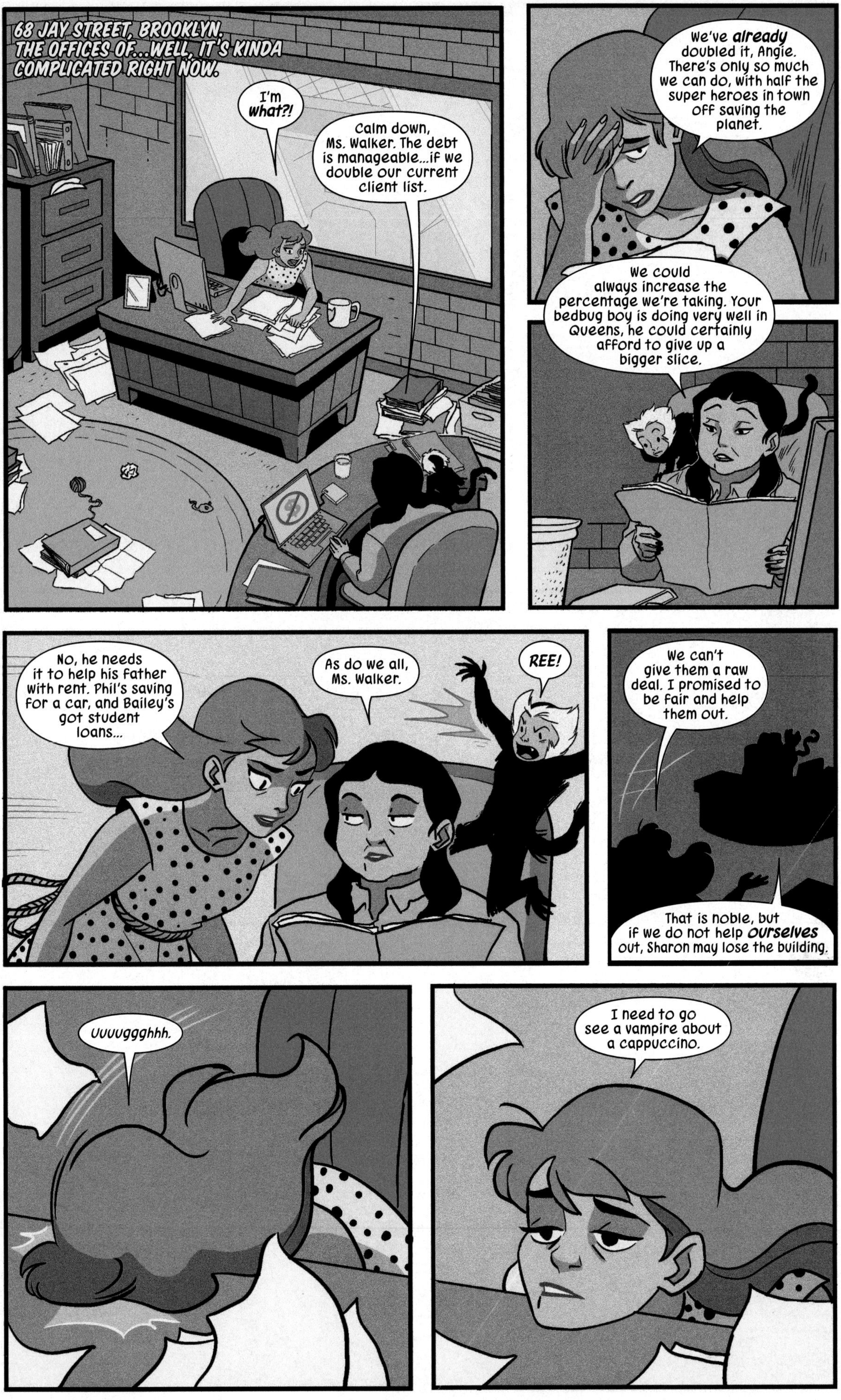
68 JAY STREET, BROOKLYN. THE OFFICES OF...WELL, IT'S KINDA COMPLICATED RIGHT NOW.
I'm what?!
Calm down, Ms. Walker. The debt is manageable...if we double our current client list.
We've already doubled it, Angie. There's only so much we can do, with half the super heroes in town off saving the planet.
We could always increase the percentage we're taking. Your bedbug boy is doing very well in Queens, he could certainly afford to give up a bigger slice.
No, he needs it to help his father with rent. Phil's saving for a car, and Bailey's got student loans...
As do we all, Ms. Walker.
REE!
We can't give them a raw deal. I promised to be fair and help them out.
That is noble, but if we do not help ourselves out, Sharon may lose the building.
Uuuugghhh.
I need to go see a vampire about a cappuccino.

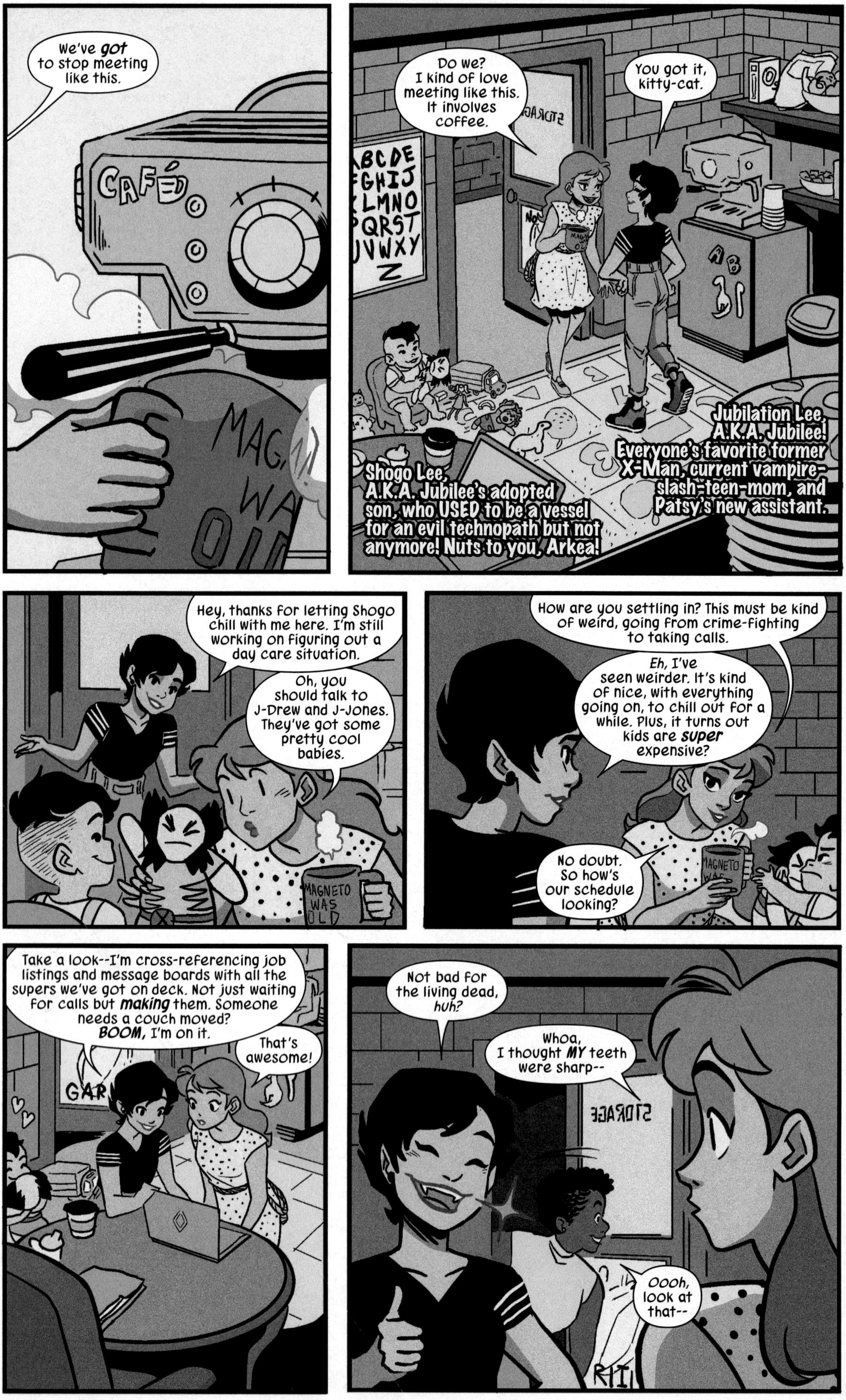

We've got to stop meeting like this.
CAFÉ
MAGNETO WAS OLD
Do we? I kind of love meeting like this. It involves coffee.
You got it, kitty-cat.
STORAGE
ABCDE FGHIJ KLMNO PQRST UVWXY Z
Shogo Lee, A.K.A. Jubilee's adopted son, who USED to be a vessel for an evil technopath but not anymore! Nuts to you, Arkea!
Jubilation Lee, A.K.A. Jubilee! Everyone's favorite former X-Man, current vampire-slash-teen-mom, and Patsy's new assistant.
Hey, thanks for letting Shogo chill with me here. I'm still working on figuring out a day care situation.
Oh, you should talk to J-Drew and J-Jones. They've got some pretty cool babies.
MAGNETO WAS OLD
How are you settling in? This must be kind of weird, going from crime-fighting to taking calls.
Eh, I've seen weirder. It's kind of nice, with everything going on, to chill out for a while. Plus, it turns out kids are super expensive?
No doubt. So how's our schedule looking?
Take a look--I'm cross-referencing job listings and message boards with all the supers we've got on deck. Not just waiting for calls but making them. Someone needs a couch moved? BOOM, I'm on it.
That's awesome!
Not bad for the living dead, huh?
Whoa, I thought MY teeth were sharp--
STORAGE
Oooh, look at that--

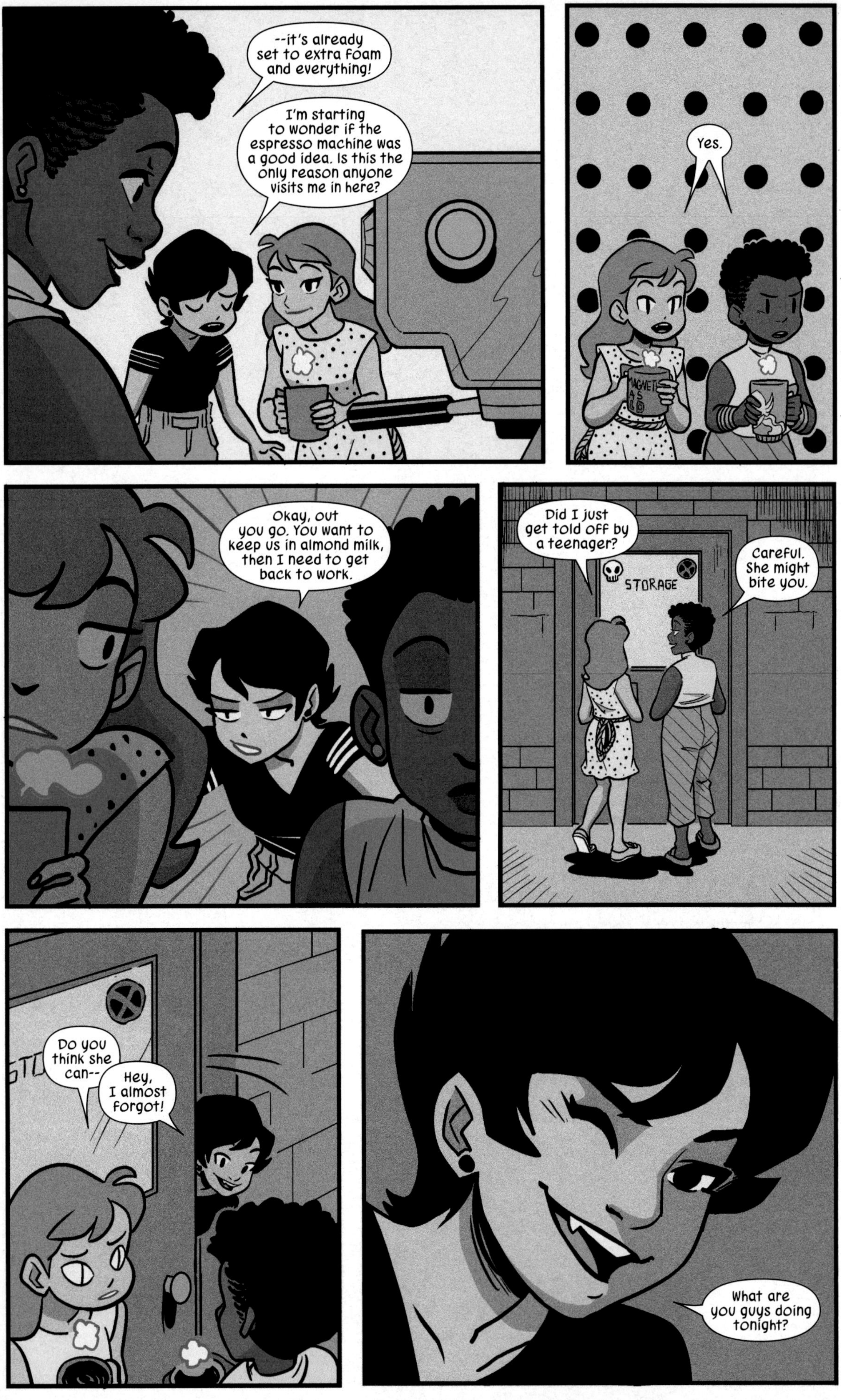
--it's already set to extra foam and everything!
I'm starting to wonder if the espresso machine was a good idea. Is this the only reason anyone visits me in here?
Yes.
MAGNETO AS GOD
Okay, out you go. You want to keep us in almond milk, then I need to get back to work.
Did I just get told off by a teenager?
STORAGE
Careful. She might bite you.
Do you think she can--
Hey, I almost forgot!
What are you guys doing tonight?

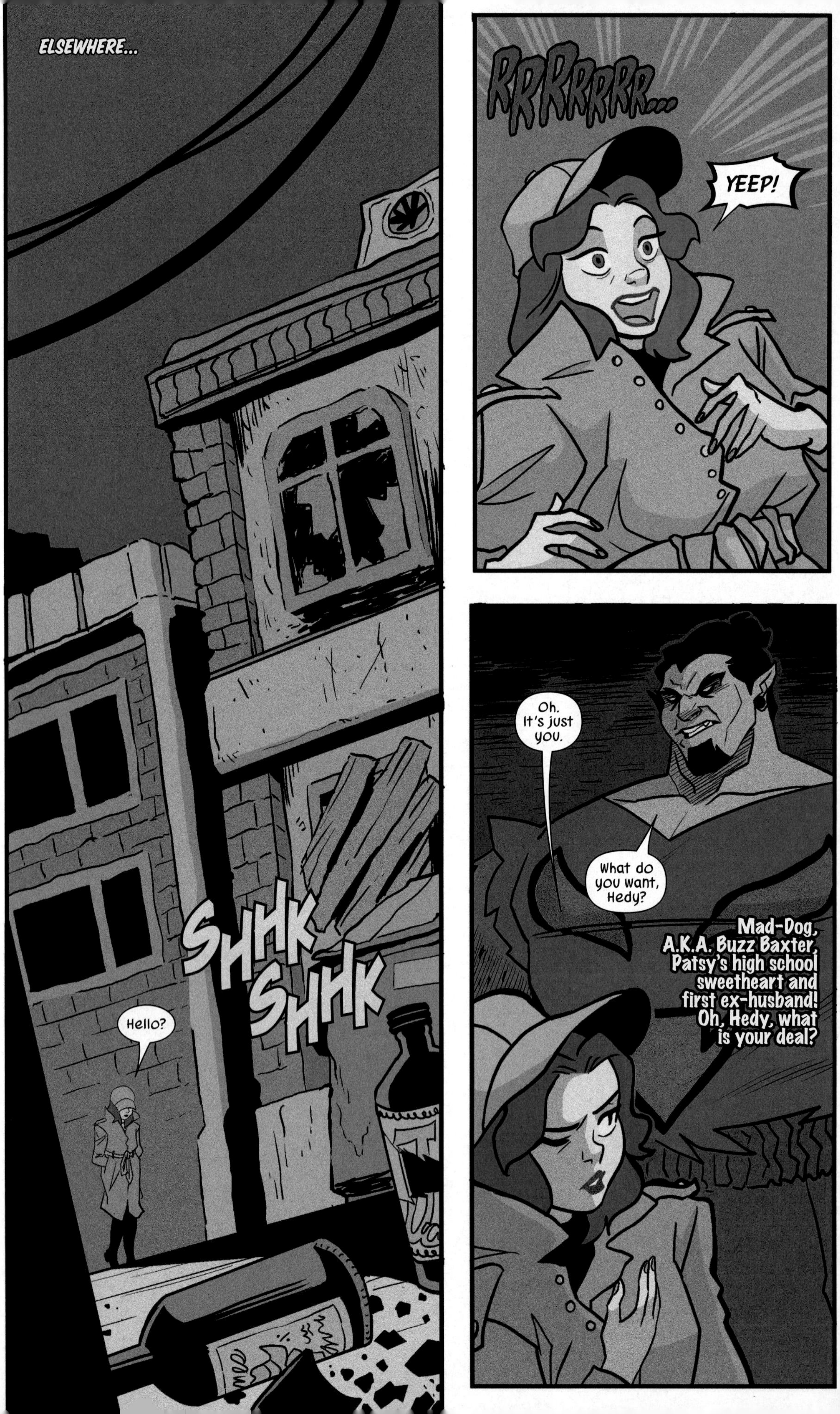

ELSEWHERE...
SHHK
SHHK
Hello?
RRRRRRR...
YEEP!
Oh. It's just you.
What do you want, Hedy?
Mad-Dog, A.K.A. Buzz Baxter, Patsy's high school sweetheart and first ex-husband! Oh, Hedy, what is your deal?

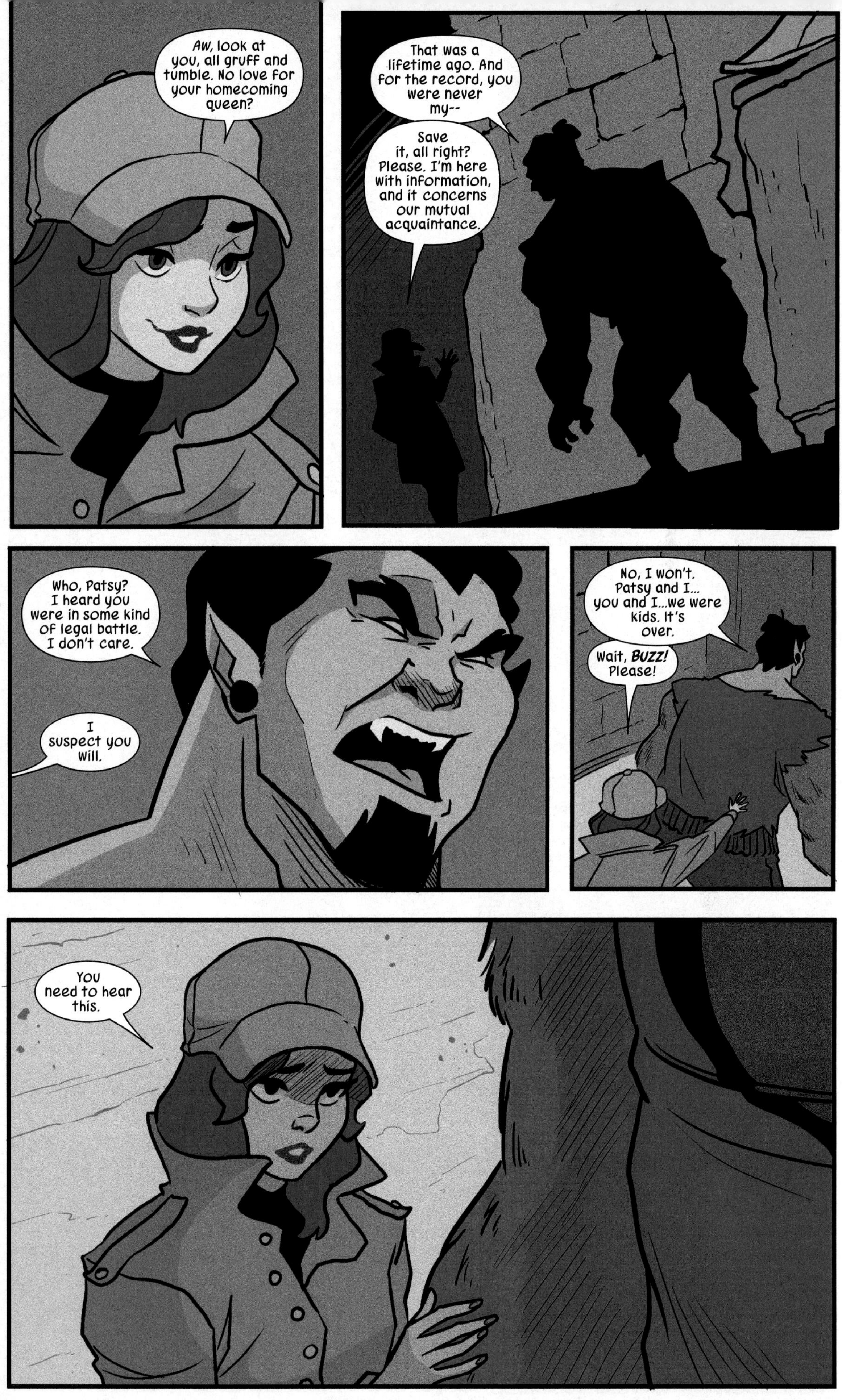
Aw, look at you, all gruff and tumble. No love for your homecoming queen?
That was a lifetime ago. And for the record, you were never my--
Save it, all right? Please. I'm here with information, and it concerns our mutual acquaintance.
Who, Patsy? I heard you were in some kind of legal battle. I don't care.
I suspect you will.
No, I won't. Patsy and I... you and I...we were kids. It's over.
Wait, BUZZ! Please!
You need to hear this.

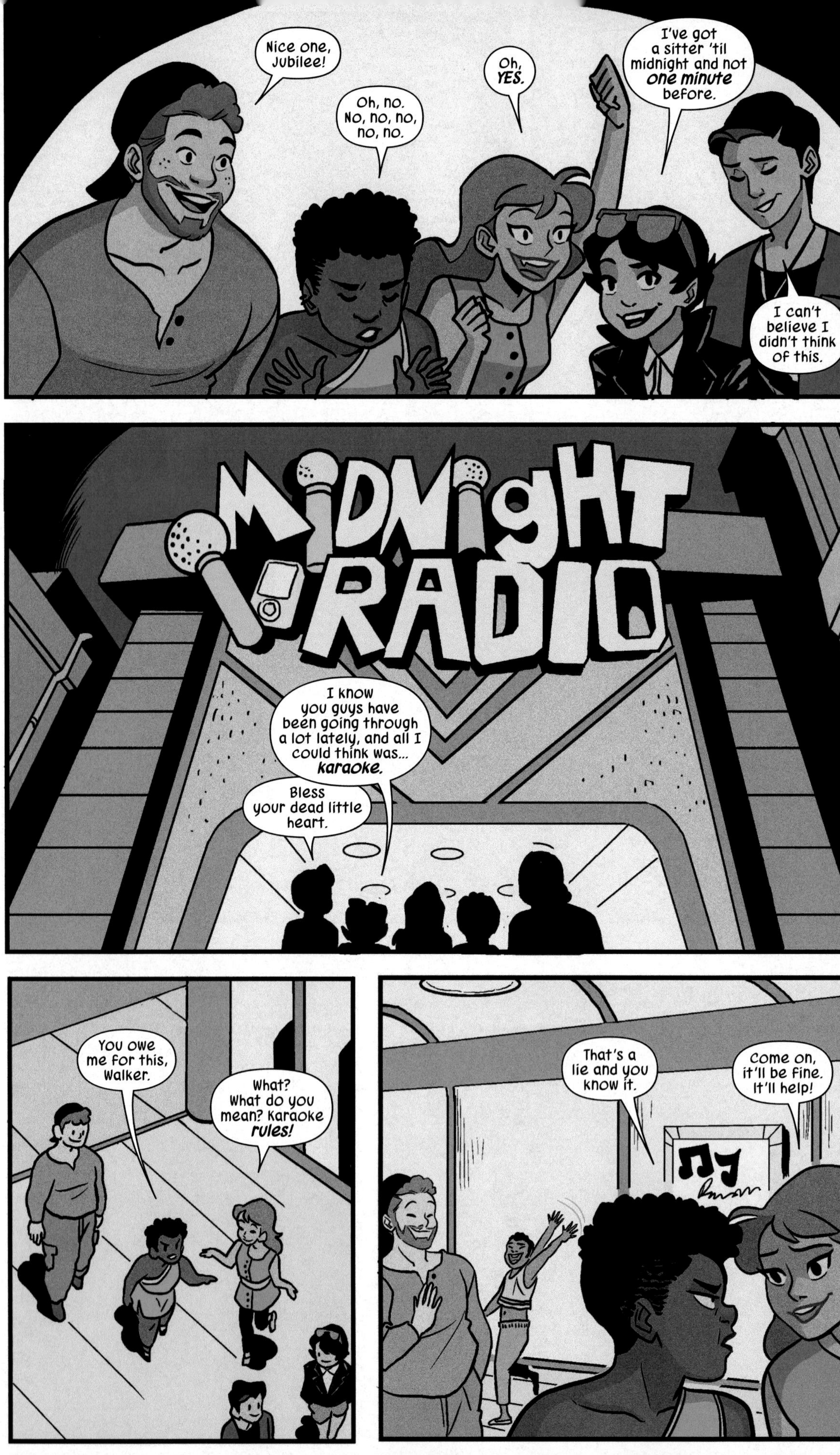
Nice one, Jubilee!
Oh, no. No, no, no, no, no.
Oh, YES.
I've got a sitter 'til midnight and not one minute before.
I can't believe I didn't think of this.
MIDNIGHT RADIO
I know you guys have been going through a lot lately, and all I could think was... karaoke.
Bless your dead little heart.
You owe me for this, Walker.
What? What do you mean? Karaoke rules!
That's a lie and you know it.
Come on, it'll be fine. It'll help!

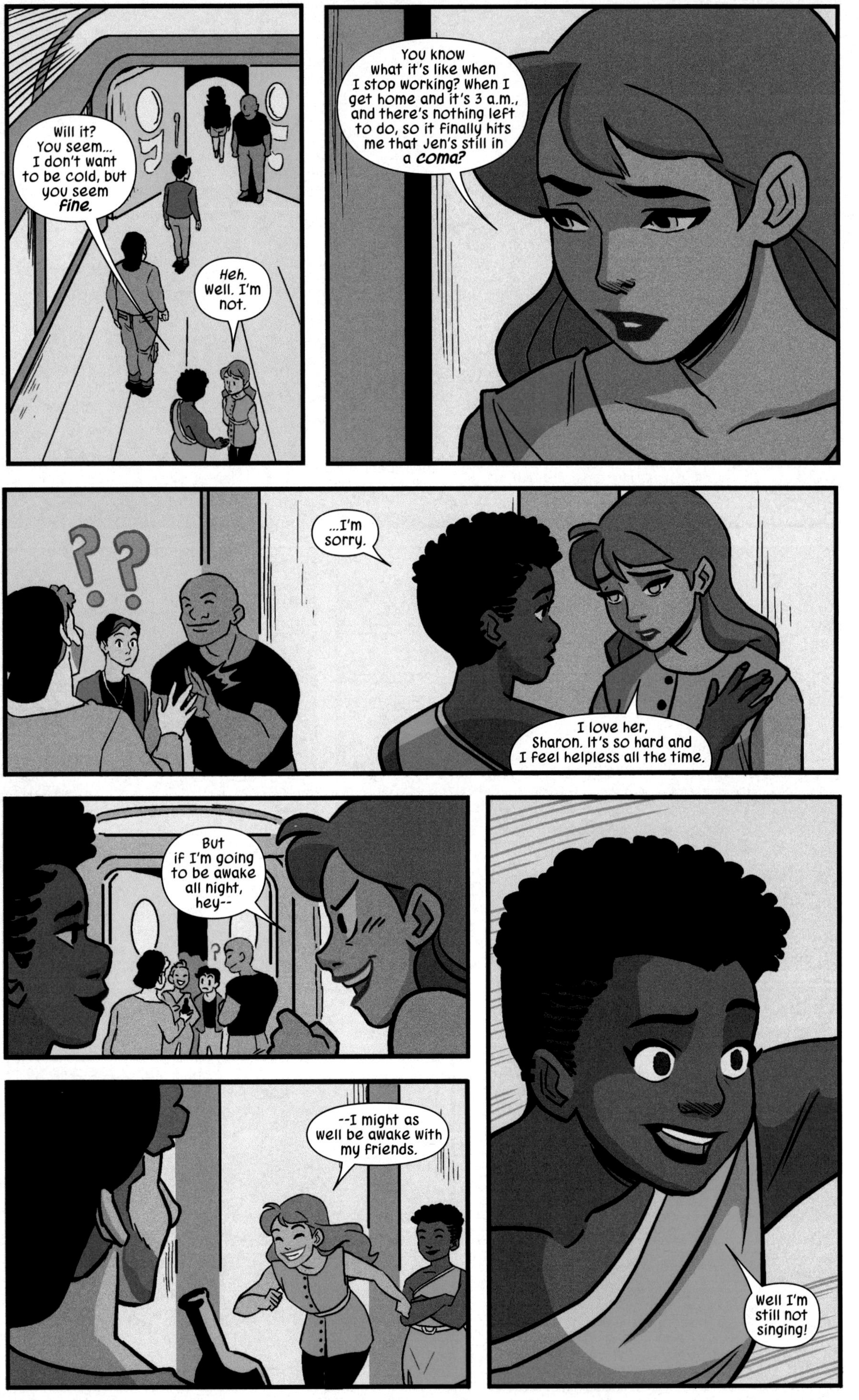
Will it? You seem... I don't want to be cold, but you seem fine.
Heh. Well. I'm not.
You know what it's like when I stop working? When I get home and it's 3 a.m., and there's nothing left to do, so it finally hits me that Jen's still in a coma?
...I'm sorry.
I love her, Sharon. It's so hard and I feel helpless all the time.
But if I'm going to be awake all night, hey--
--I might as well be awake with my friends.
Well I'm still not singing!

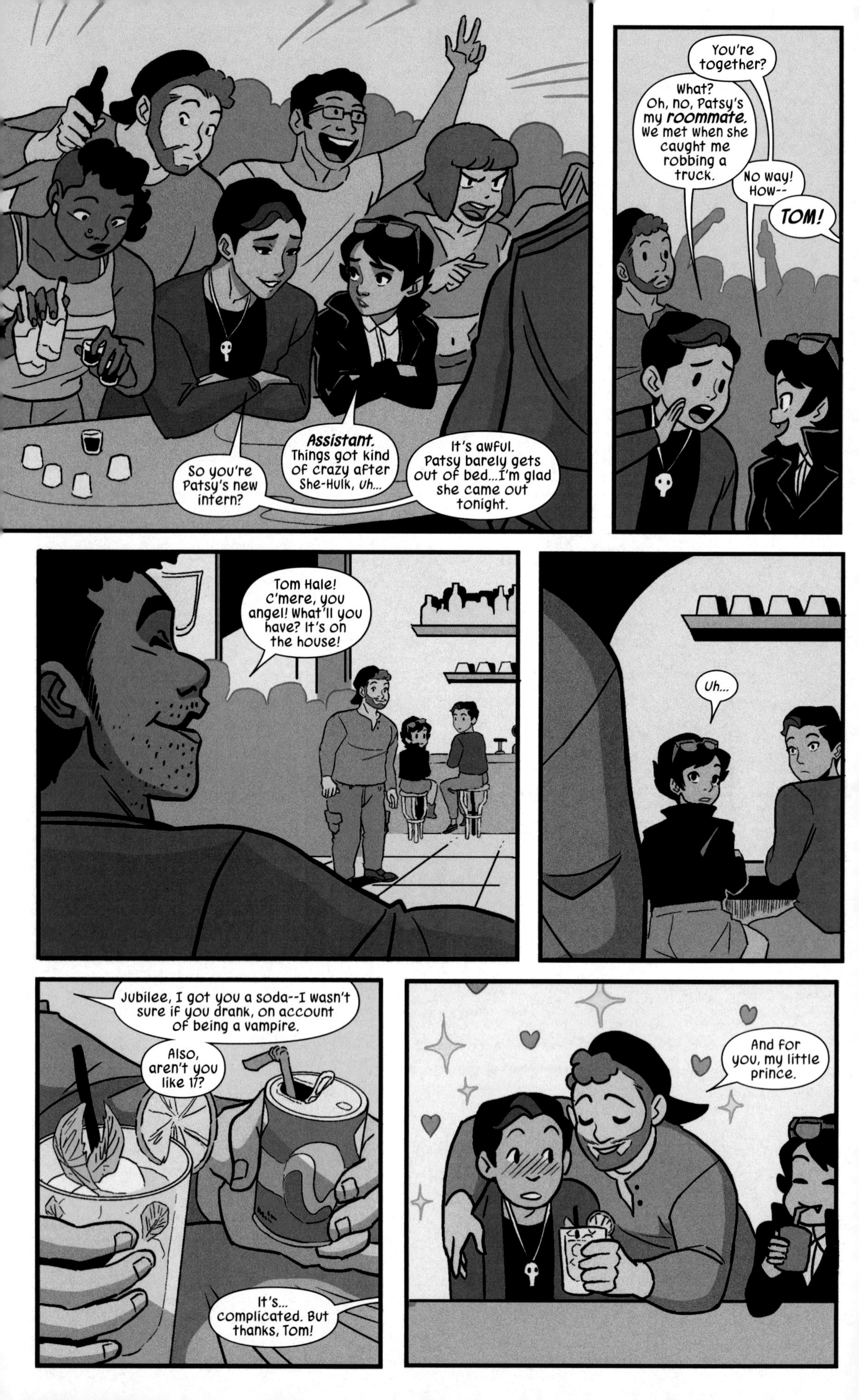

So you're Patsy's new intern?
Assistant. Things got kind of crazy after She-Hulk, uh...
It's awful. Patsy barely gets out of bed...I'm glad she came out tonight.
You're together?
What? Oh, no, Patsy's my roommate. We met when she caught me robbing a truck.
No way! How--
TOM!
Tom Hale! C'mere, you angel! What'll you have? It's on the house!
Uh...
Jubilee, I got you a soda--I wasn't sure if you drank, on account of being a vampire.
Also, aren't you like 17?
It's... complicated. But thanks, Tom!
And for you, my little prince.

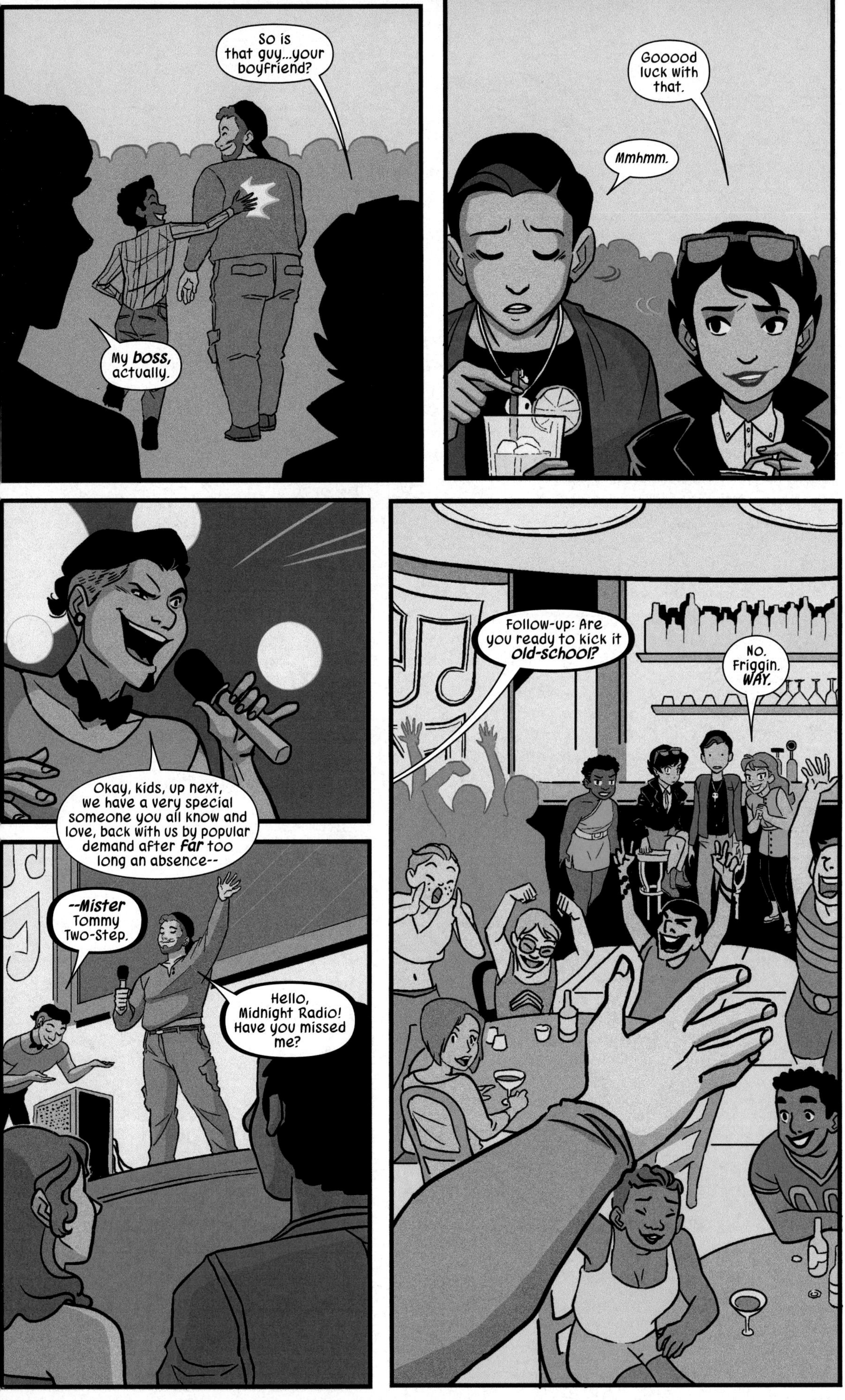

So is that guy...your boyfriend?
My boss, actually.
Gooood luck with that.
Mmhmm.
Okay, kids, up next, we have a very special someone you all know and love, back with us by popular demand after far too long an absence--
--Mister Tommy Two-Step.
Hello, Midnight Radio! Have you missed me?
Follow-up: Are you ready to kick it old-school?
No. Friggin. WAY.

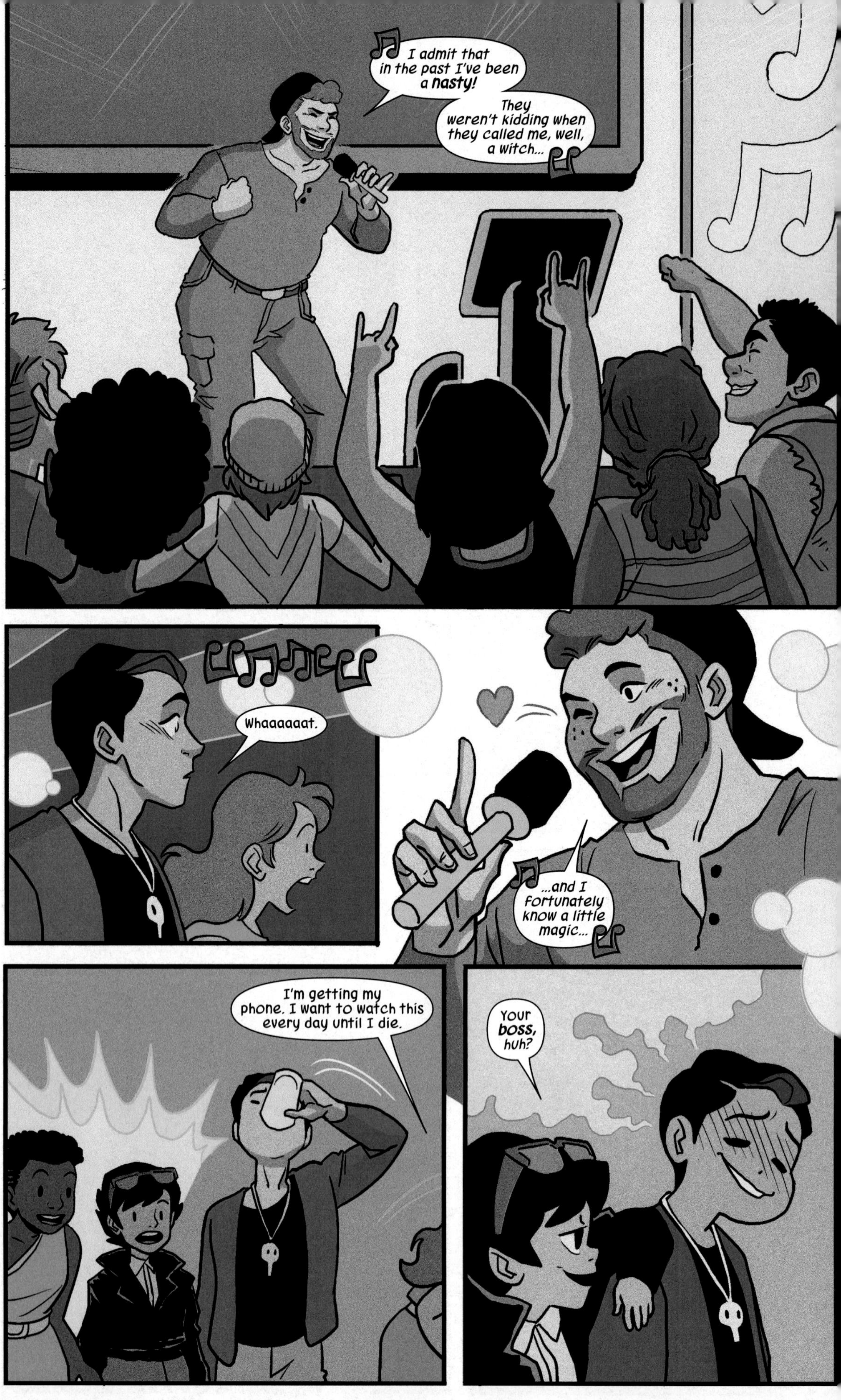
I admit that in the past I've been a **nasty!**
They weren't kidding when they called me, well, a witch...
Whaaaaaat.
...and I fortunately know a little magic...
I'm getting my phone. I want to watch this every day until I die.
Your **boss,** huh?

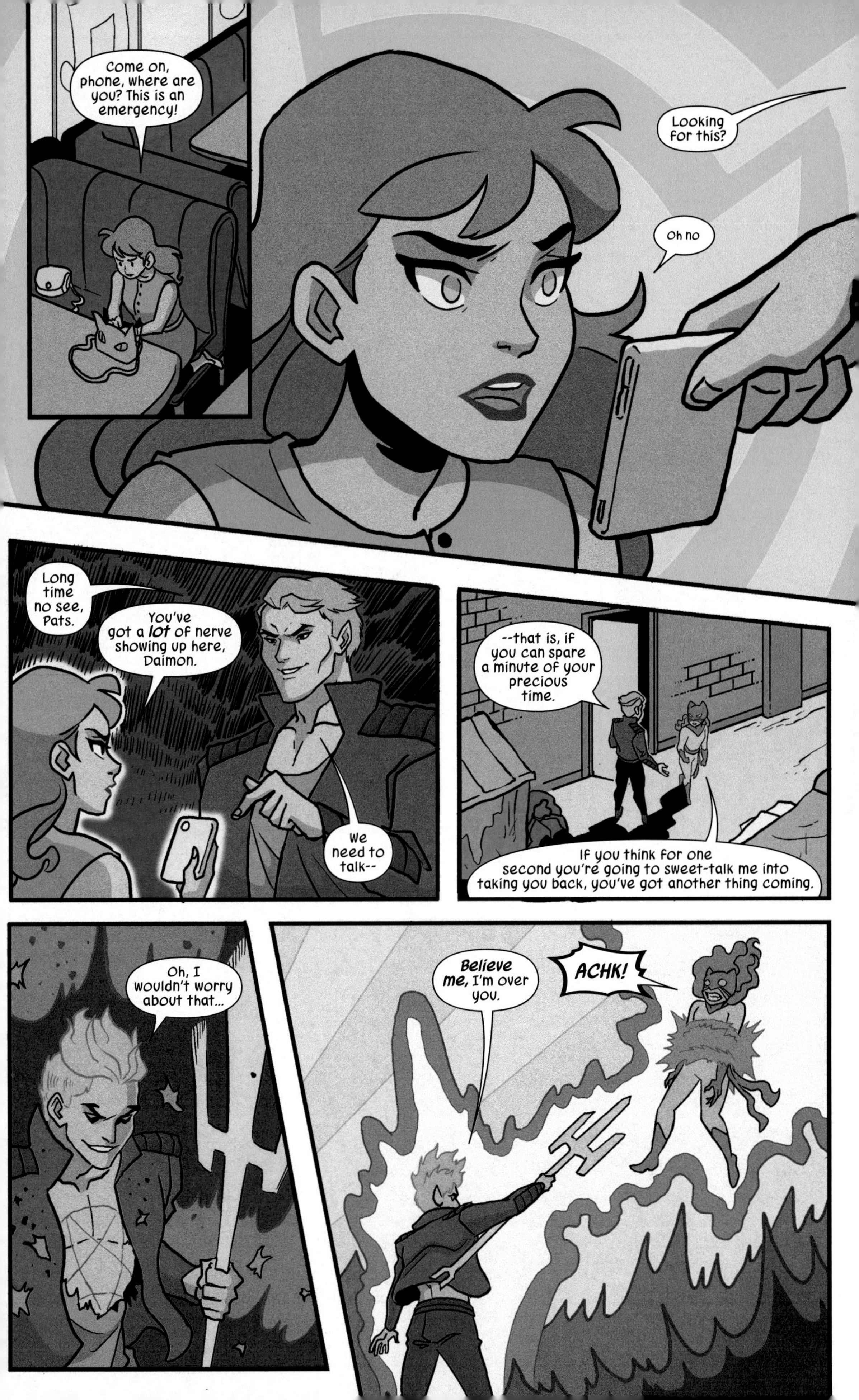

Come on, phone, where are you? This is an emergency!
Looking for this?
Oh no
Long time no see, Pats.
You've got a *lot* of nerve showing up here, Daimon.
We need to talk--
--that is, if you can spare a minute of your precious time.
If you think for one second you're going to sweet-talk me into taking you back, you've got another thing coming.
Oh, I wouldn't worry about that...
Believe me, I'm over you.
ACHK!

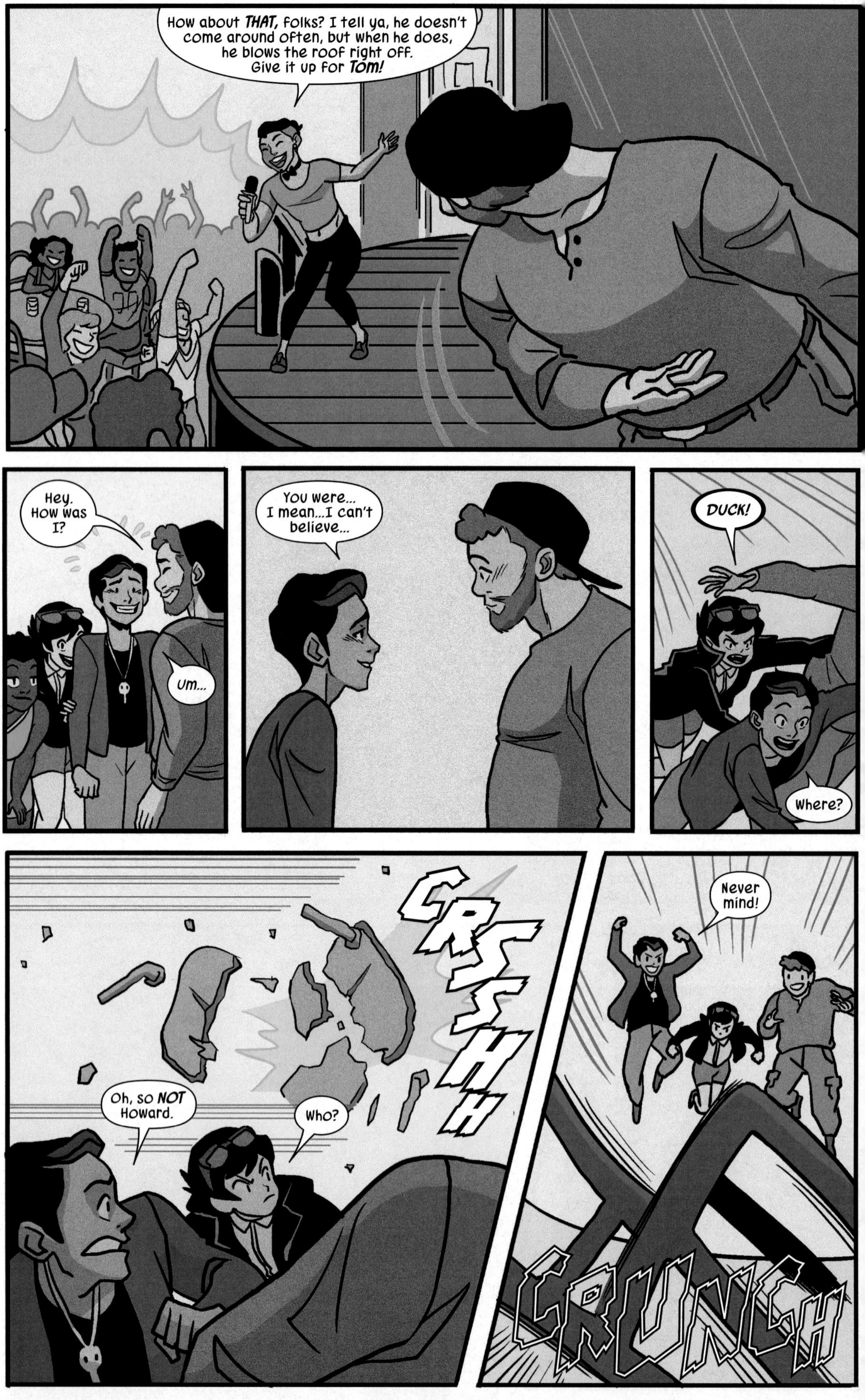
How about *THAT,* folks? I tell ya, he doesn't come around often, but when he does, he blows the roof right off. Give it up for *TOM!*
Hey. How was I?
Um...
You were... I mean...I can't believe...
DUCK!
Where?
CRSSHHH
Oh, so *NOT* Howard.
Who?
Never mind!
CRUNCH

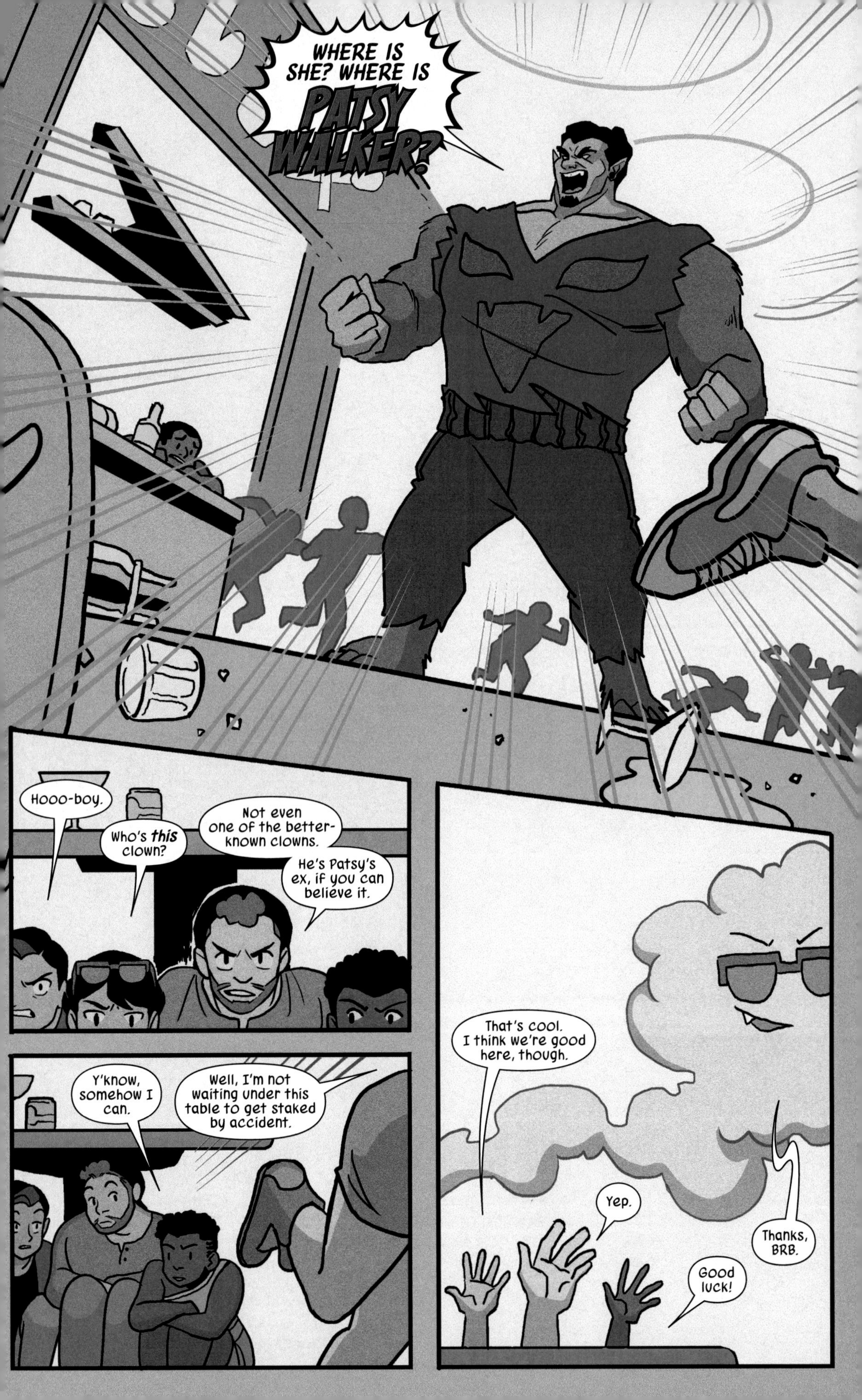
WHERE IS SHE? WHERE IS PATSY WALKER?
Hooo-boy.
Who's *this* clown?
Not even one of the better-known clowns.
He's Patsy's ex, if you can believe it.
Y'know, somehow I can.
Well, I'm not waiting under this table to get staked by accident.
That's cool. I think we're good here, though.
Yep.
Thanks, BRB.
Good luck!

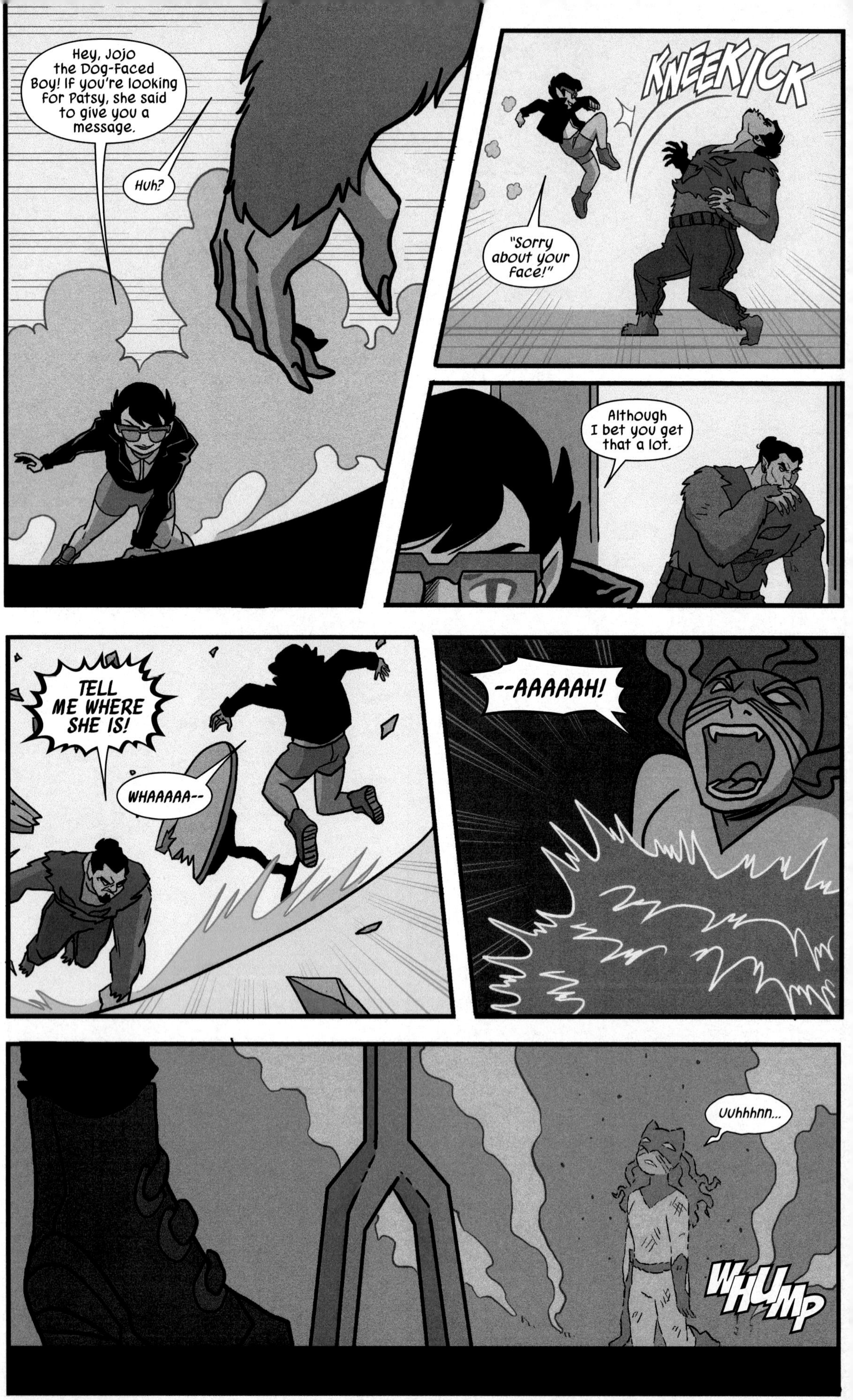
Hey, Jojo the Dog-Faced Boy! If you're looking for Patsy, she said to give you a message.
Huh?
KNEEKICK
"Sorry about your face!"
Although I bet you get that a lot.
TELL ME WHERE SHE IS!
WHAAAAA--
--AAAAAH!
Uuhhhnn...
WHUMP

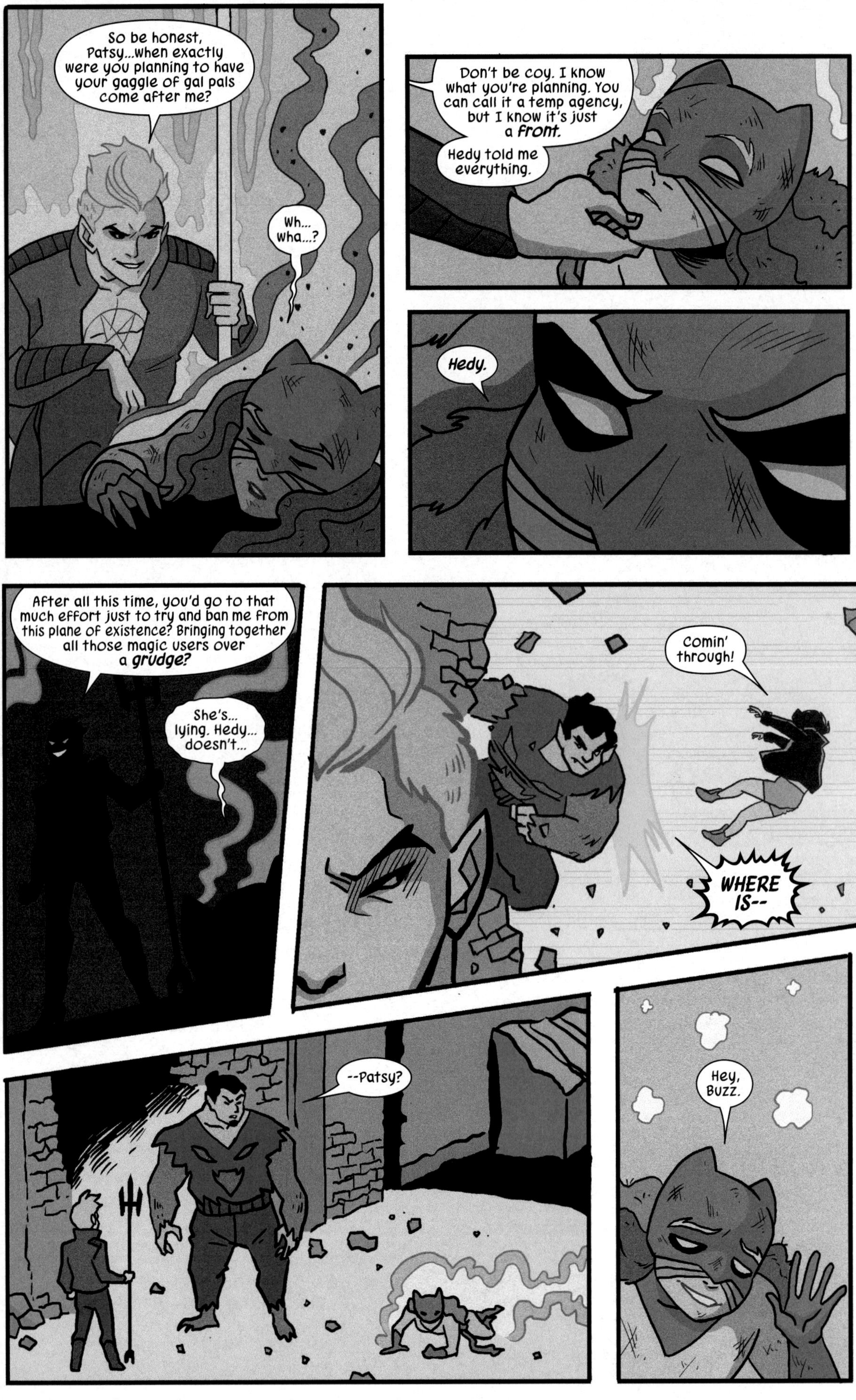
So be honest, Patsy...when exactly were you planning to have your gaggle of gal pals come after me?
Wh... wha...?
Don't be coy. I know what you're planning. You can call it a temp agency, but I know it's just a *front.*
Hedy told me everything.
Hedy.
After all this time, you'd go to that much effort just to try and ban me from this plane of existence? Bringing together all those magic users over a *grudge?*
She's... lying. Hedy... doesn't't...
Comin' through!
WHERE IS--
--Patsy?
Hey, BUZZ.

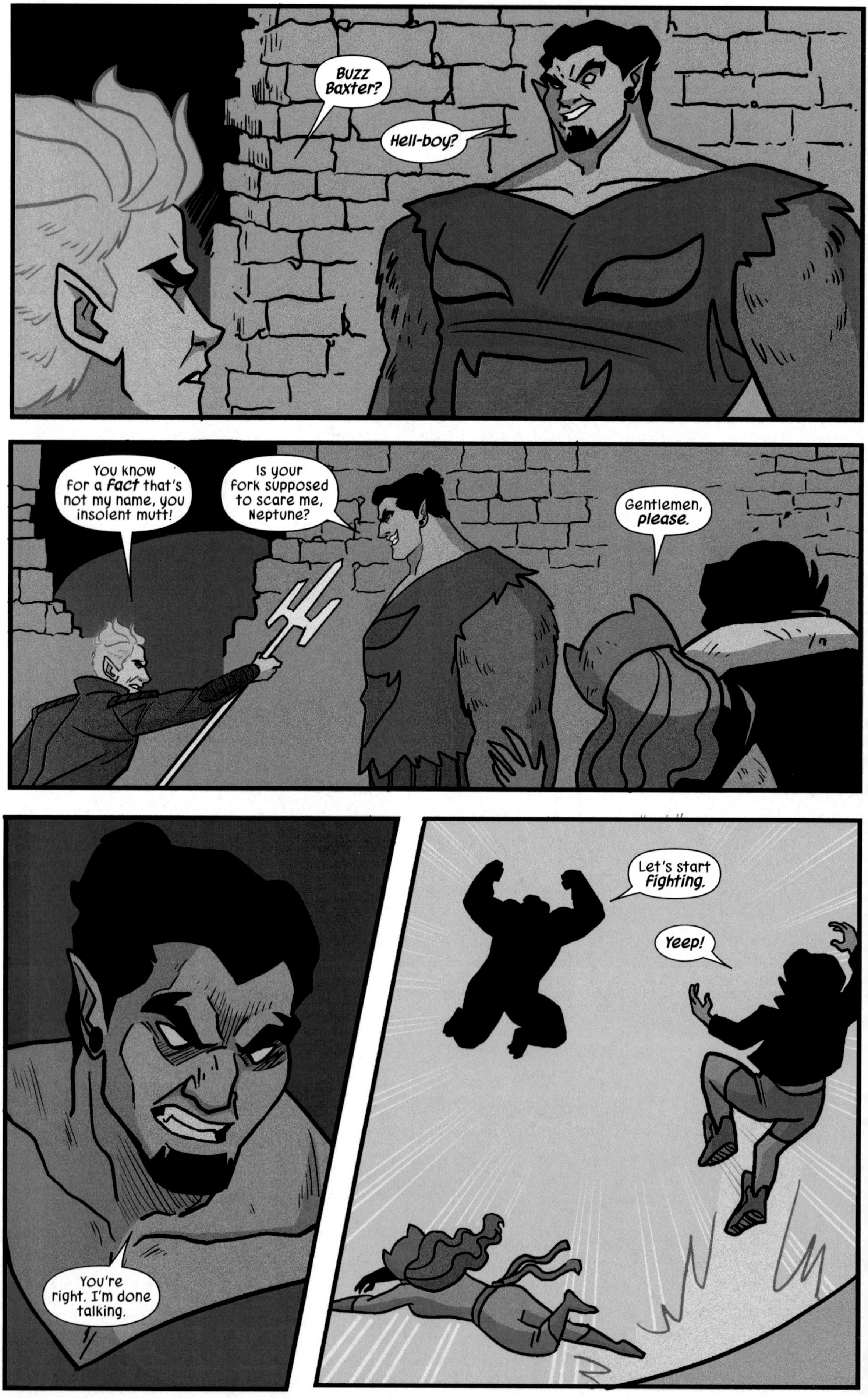
BUZZ Baxter?
Hell-boy?
You know for a fact that's not my name, you insolent mutt!
Is your fork supposed to scare me, Neptune?
Gentlemen, please.
You're right. I'm done talking.
Let's start fighting.
Yeep!

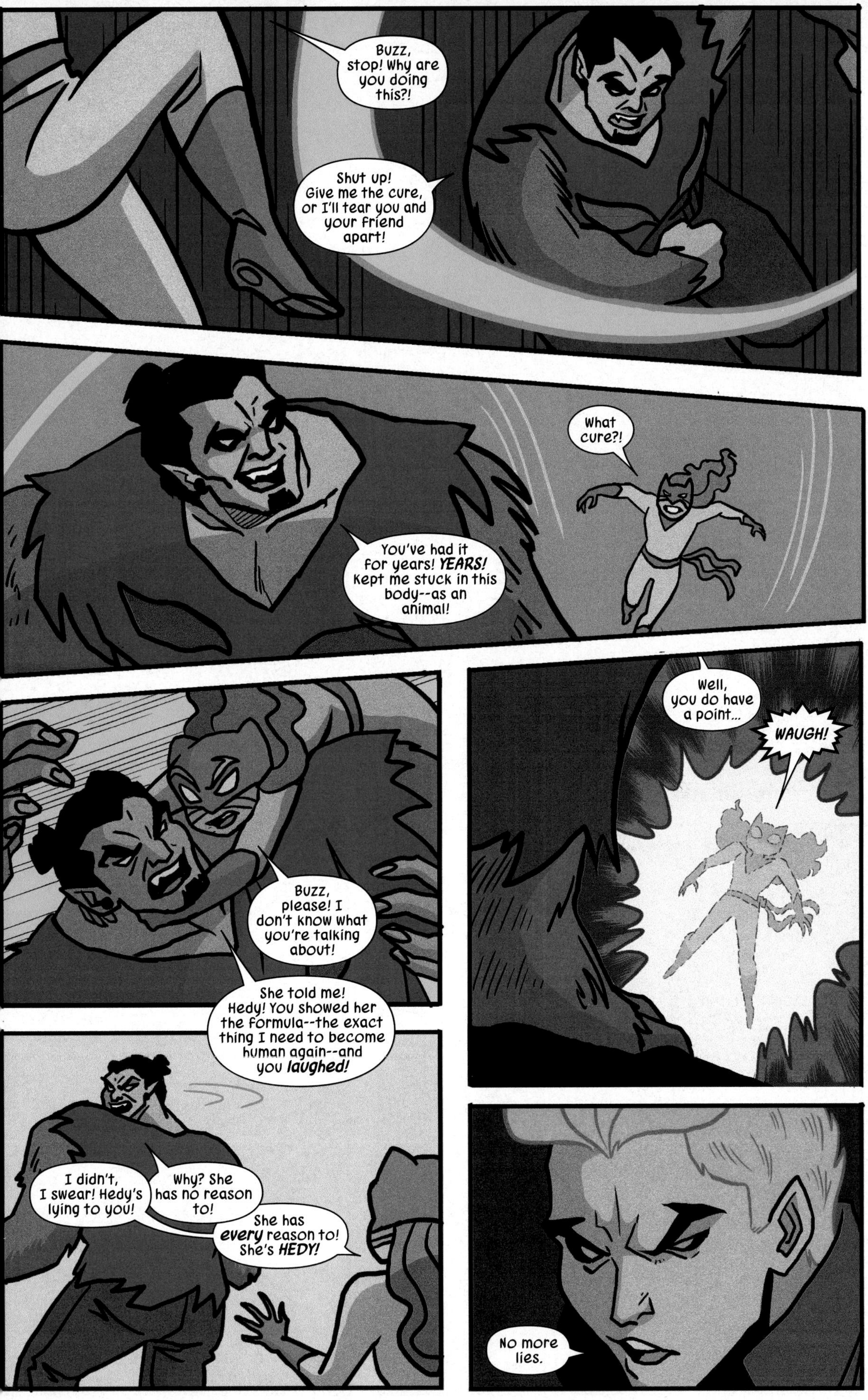
Buzz, stop! Why are you doing this?!
Shut up! Give me the cure, or I'll tear you and your friend apart!
What cure?!
You've had it for years! YEARS! Kept me stuck in this body--as an animal!
Buzz, please! I don't know what you're talking about!
She told me! Hedy! You showed her the formula--the exact thing I need to become human again--and you laughed!
Well, you do have a point...
WAUGH!
I didn't, I swear! Hedy's lying to you!
Why? She has no reason to!
She has every reason to! She's HEDY!
No more lies.

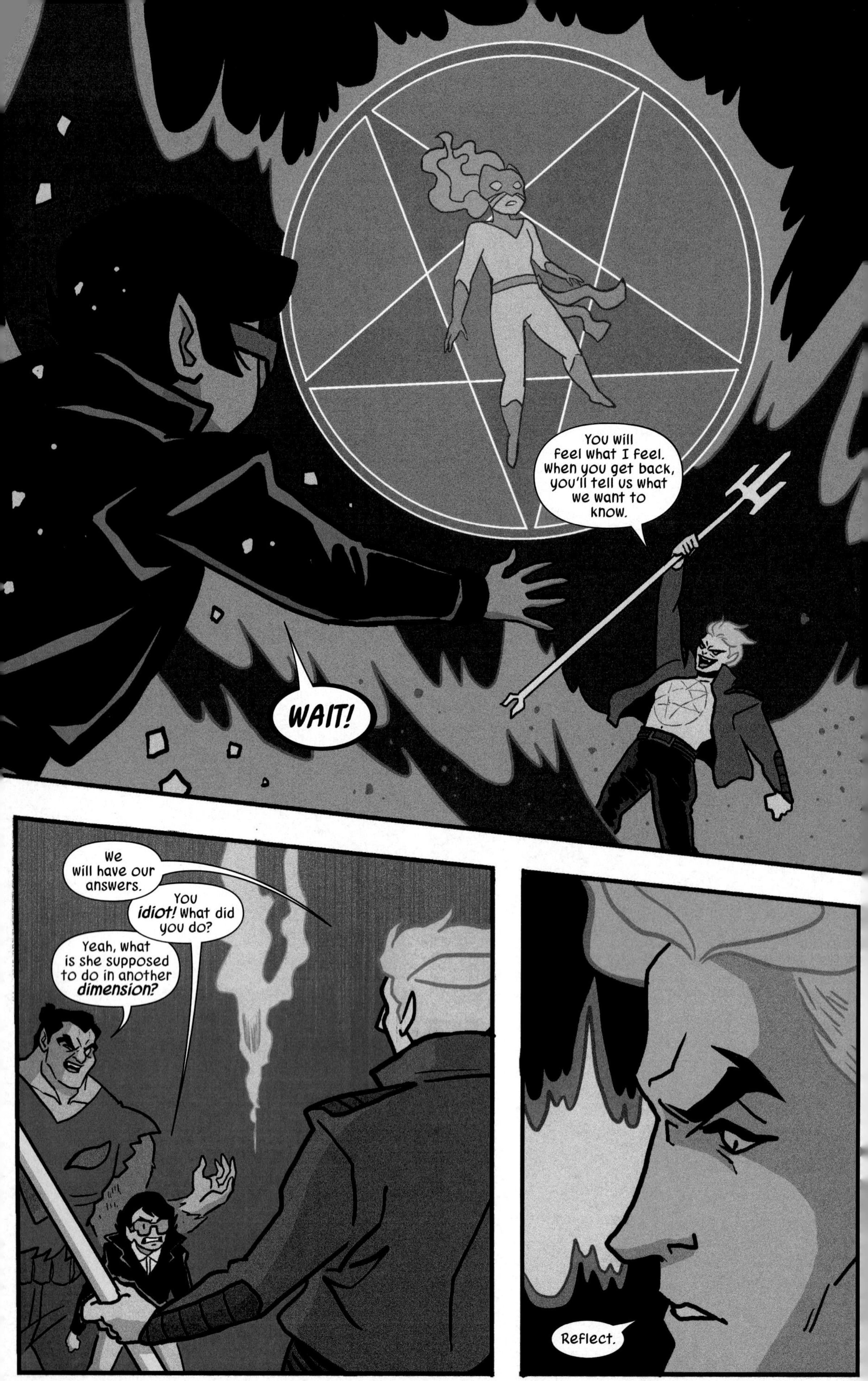
You will feel what I feel. When you get back, you'll tell us what we want to know.
WAIT!
We will have our answers.
You idiot! What did you do?
Yeah, what is she supposed to do in another dimension?
Reflect.

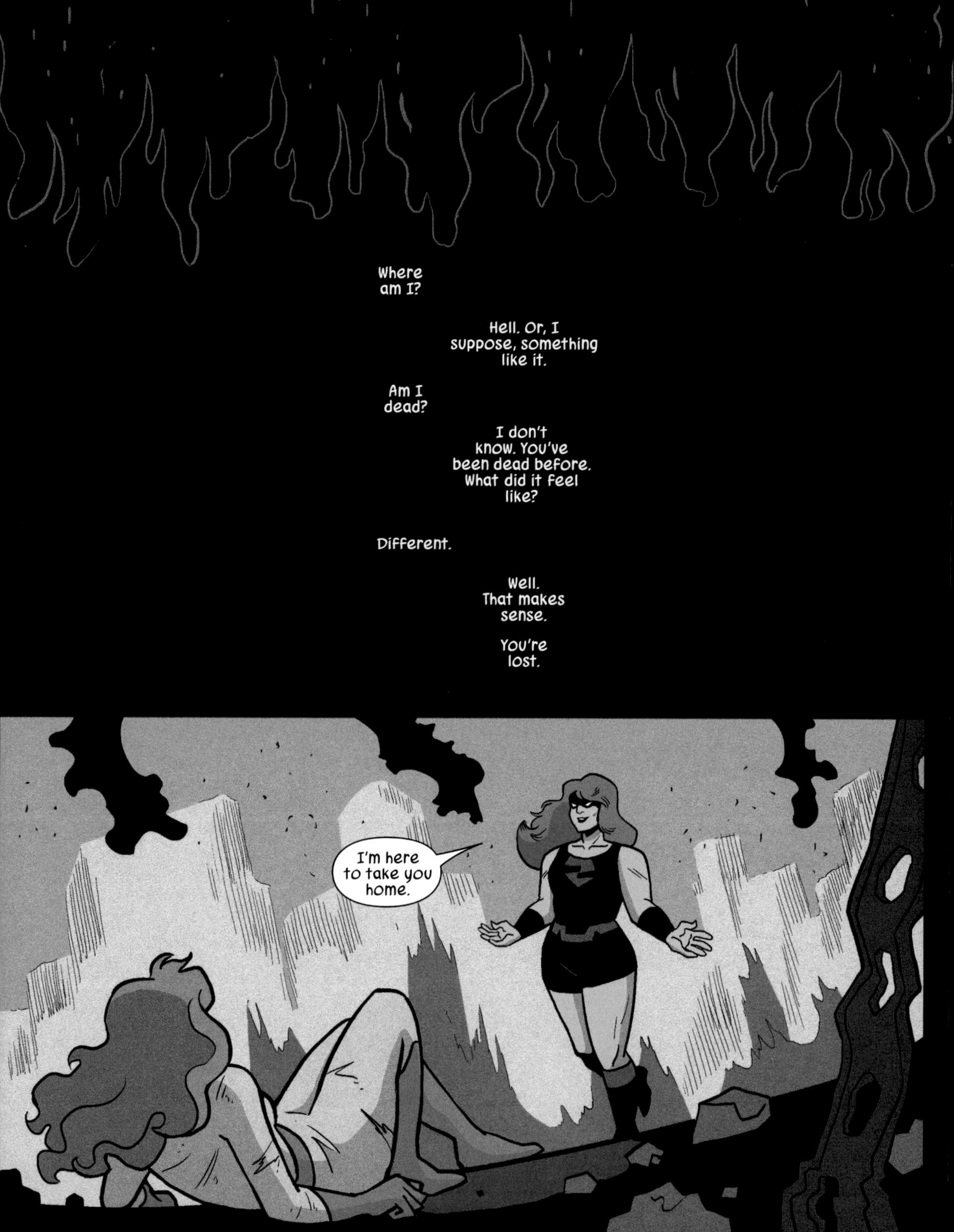
Where am I?
Hell. Or, I suppose, something like it.
Am I dead?
I don't know. You've been dead before. What did it feel like?
Different.
Well. That makes sense.
You're lost.
I'm here to take you home.

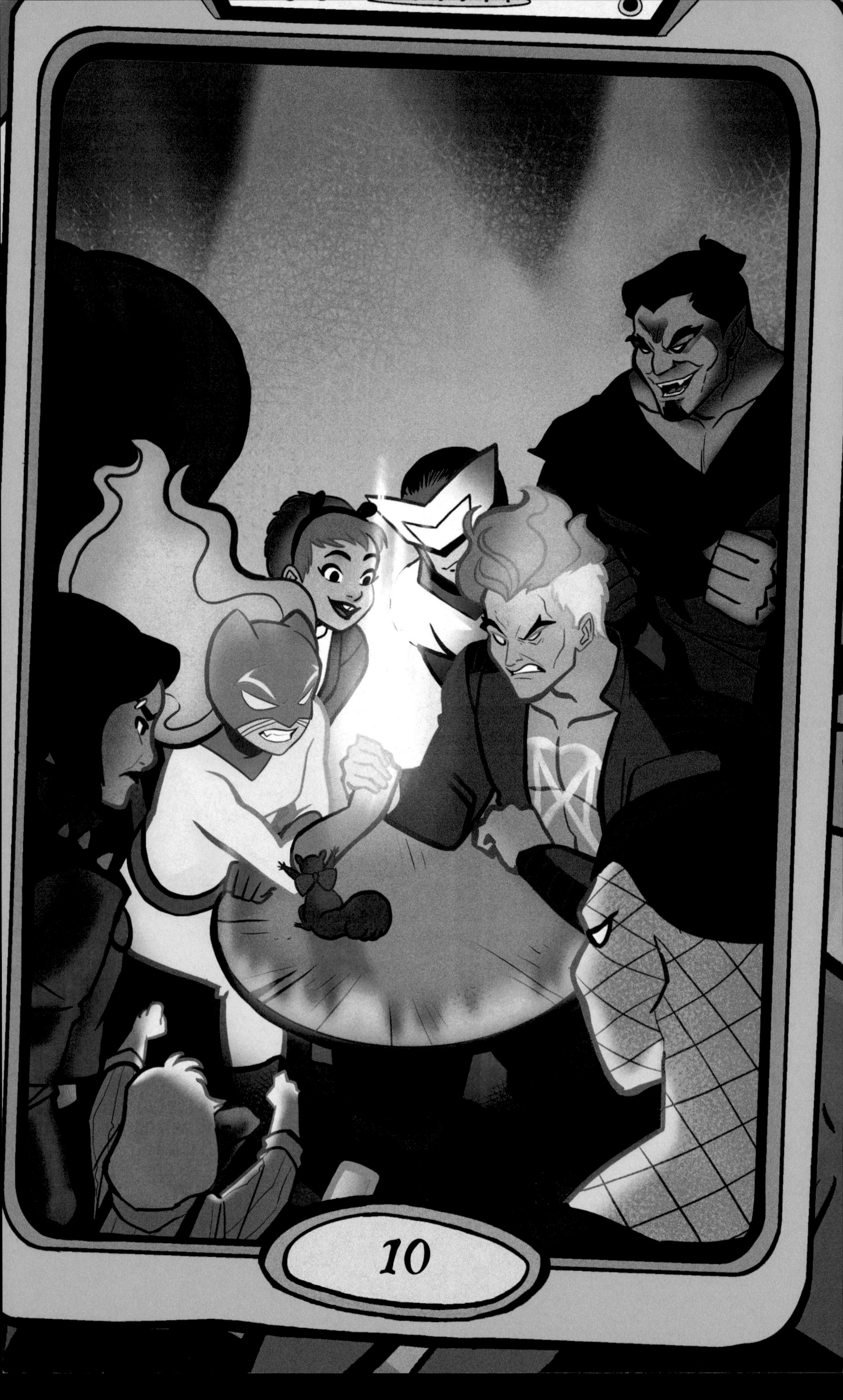
10

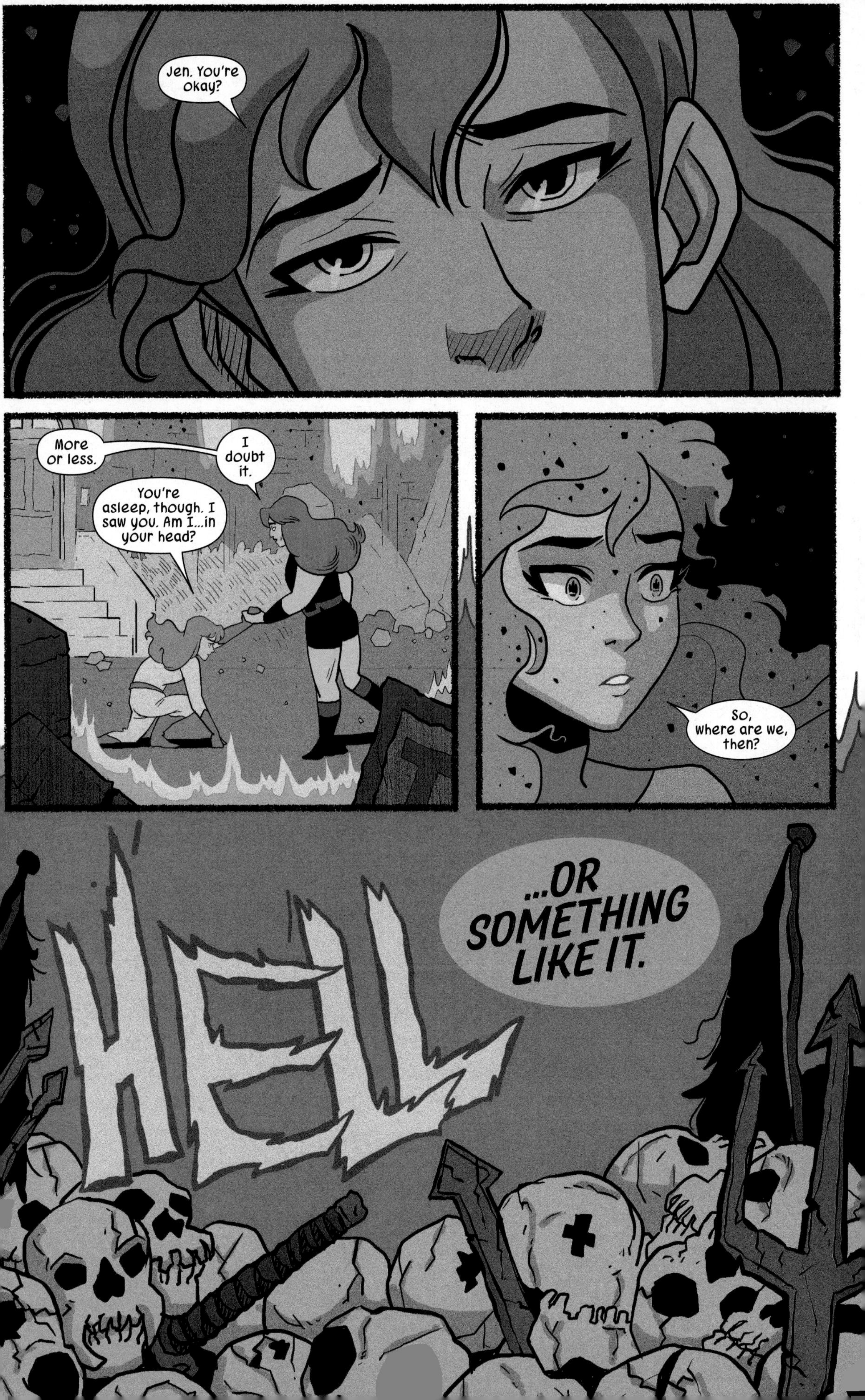
Jen. You're okay?
More or less.
I doubt it.
You're asleep, though. I saw you. Am I...in your head?
So, where are we, then?
HELL
...OR SOMETHING LIKE IT.

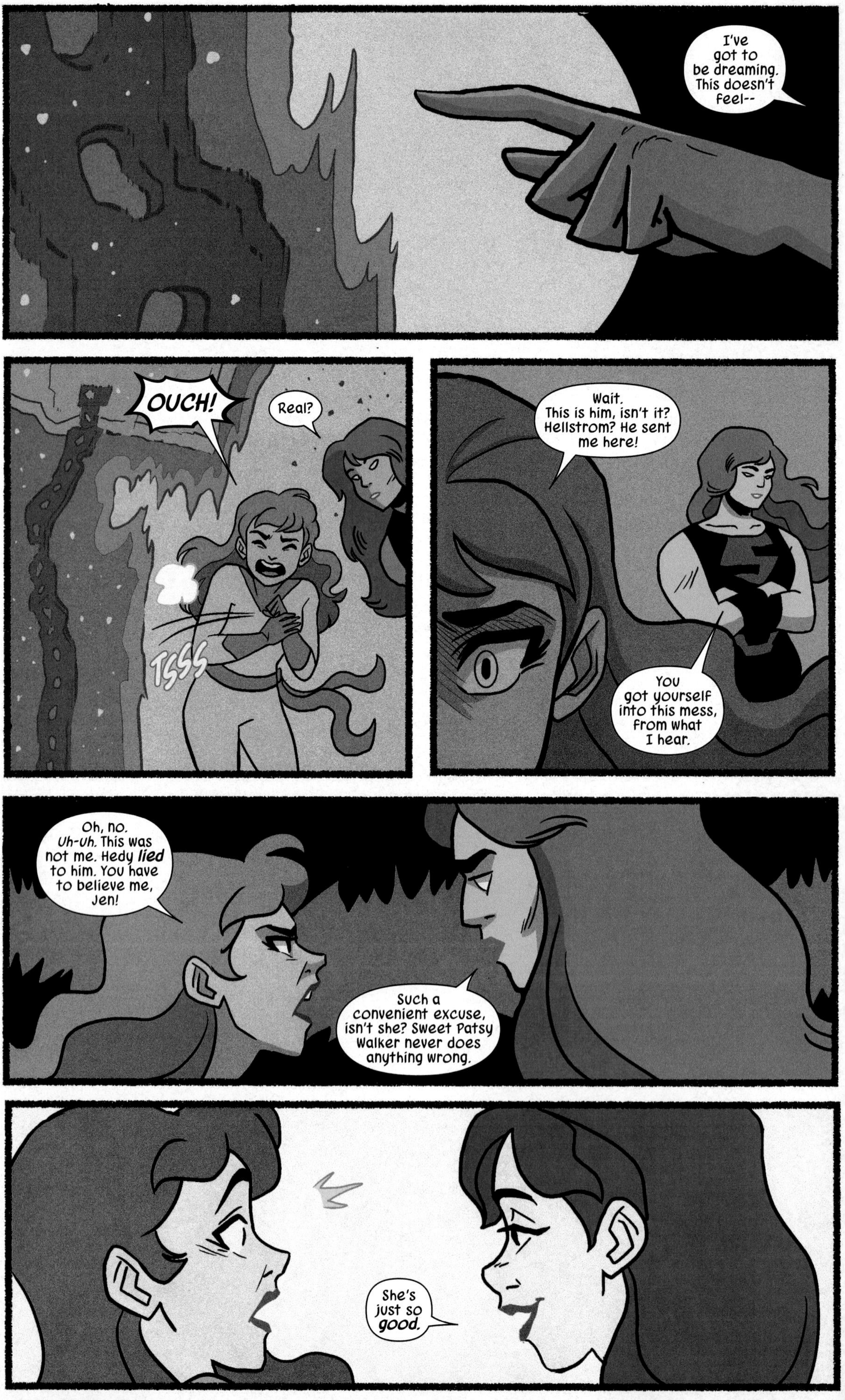
I've got to be dreaming. This doesn't feel--
OUCH!
TSSS
Real?
Wait. This is him, isn't it? Hellstrom? He sent me here!
You got yourself into this mess, from what I hear.
Oh, no. *Uh-uh.* This was not me. Hedy ***lied*** to him. You have to believe me, Jen!
Such a convenient excuse, isn't she? Sweet Patsy Walker never does anything wrong.
She's just so ***good.***

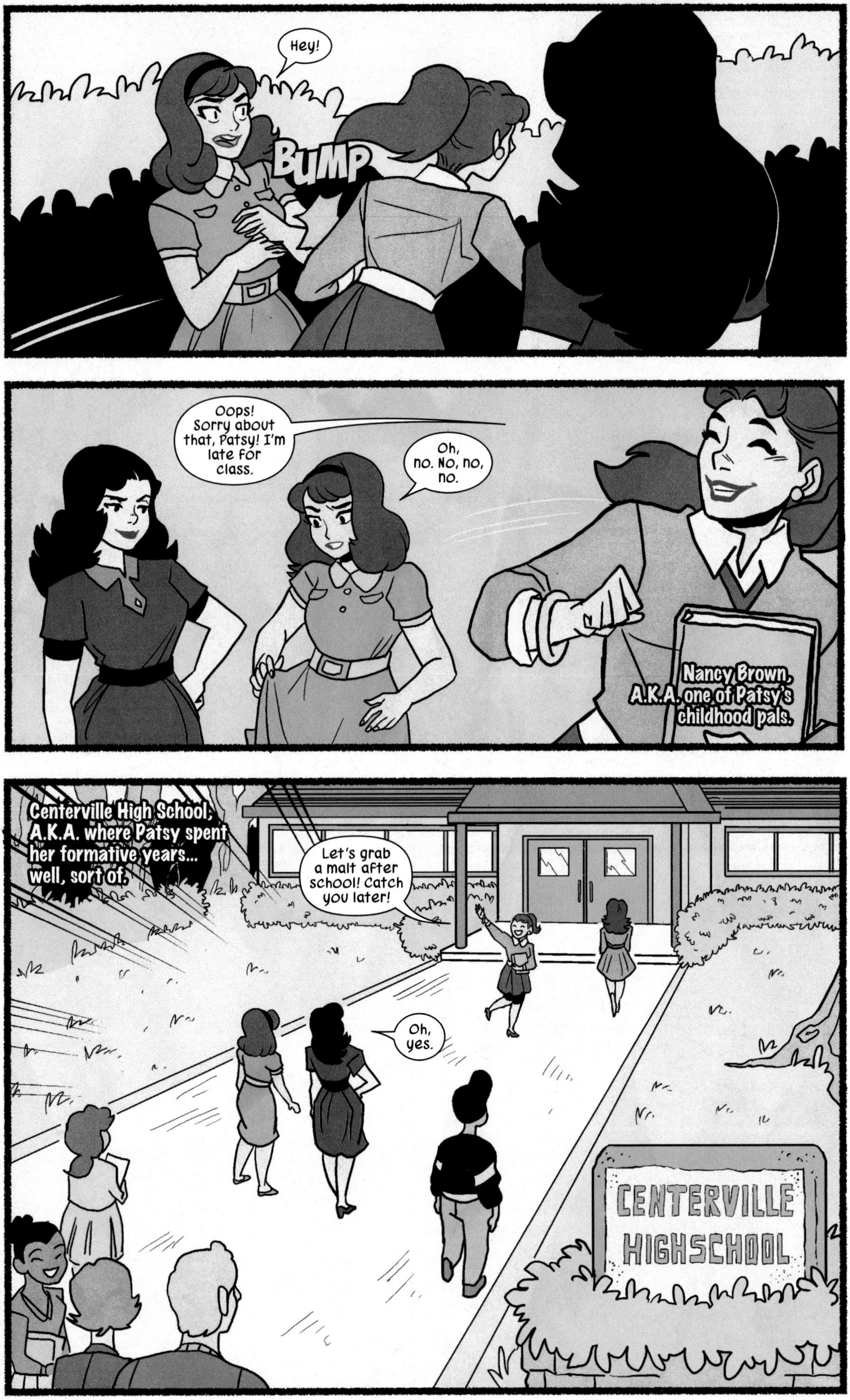
Hey!
BUMP
Oops! Sorry about that, Patsy! I'm late for class.
Oh, no. No, no, no.
Nancy Brown, A.K.A. one of Patsy's childhood pals.
Centerville High School, A.K.A. where Patsy spent her formative years... well, sort of.
Let's grab a malt after school! Catch you later!
Oh, yes.
CENTERVILLE HIGHSCHOOL

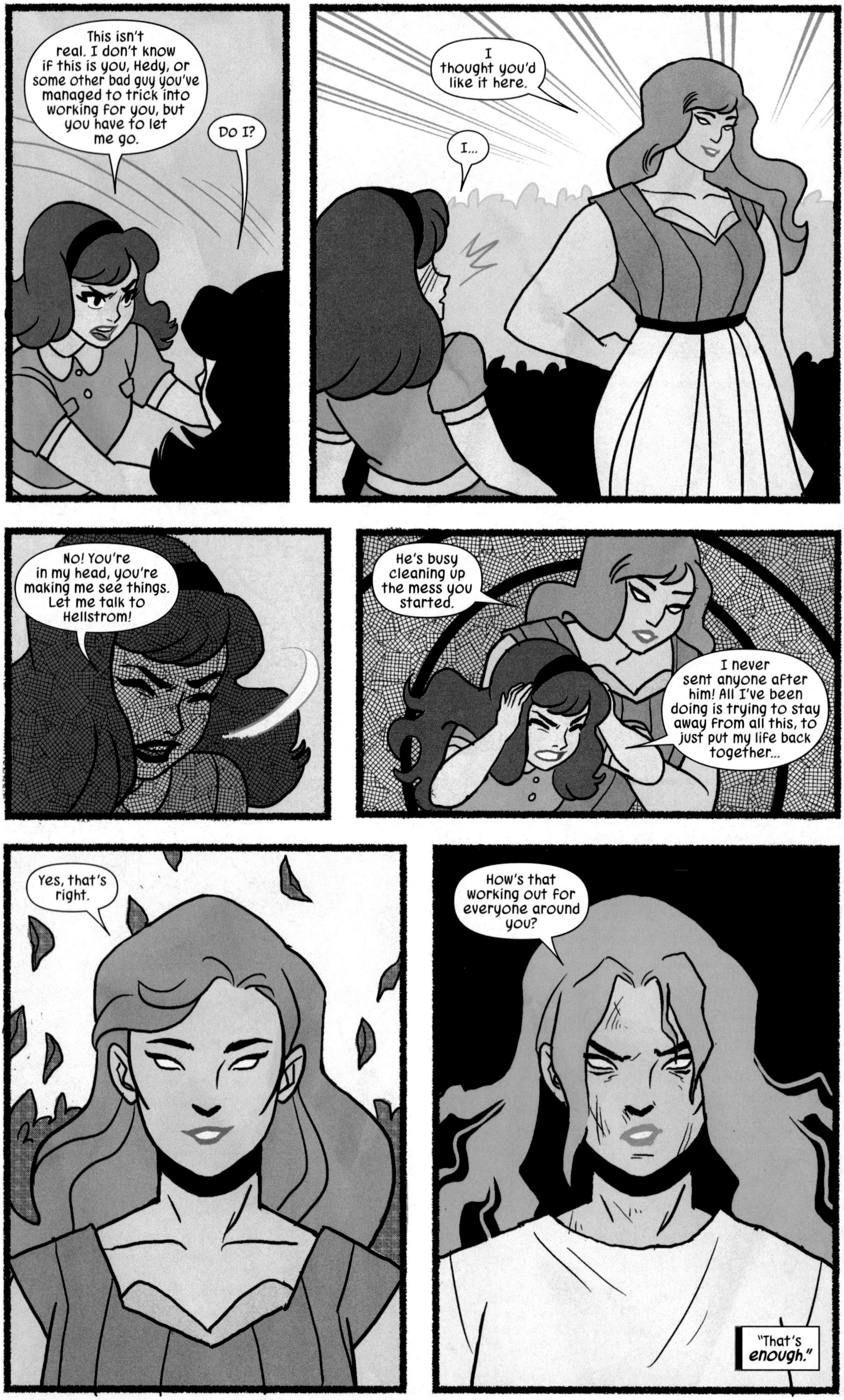
This isn't real. I don't know if this is you, Hedy, or some other bad guy you've managed to trick into working for you, but you have to let me go.
Do I?
I thought you'd like it here.
I...
No! You're in my head, you're making me see things. Let me talk to Hellstrom!
He's busy cleaning up the mess you started.
I never sent anyone after him! All I've been doing is trying to stay away from all this, to just put my life back together...
Yes, that's right.
How's that working out for everyone around you?
"That's enough."

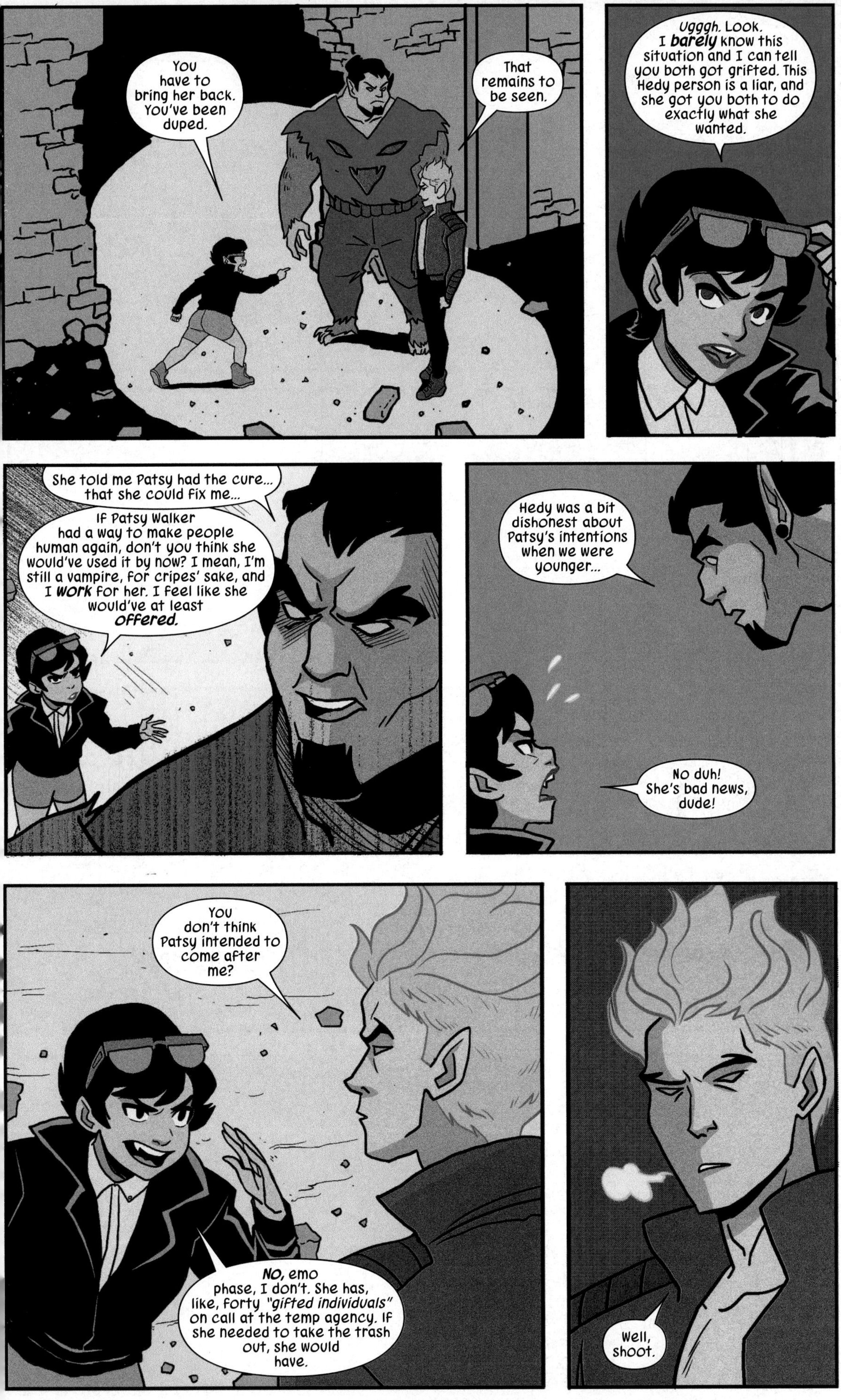

You have to bring her back. You've been duped.
That remains to be seen.
Ugggh. Look. I barely know this situation and I can tell you both got grifted. This Hedy person is a liar, and she got you both to do exactly what she wanted.
She told me Patsy had the cure... that she could fix me...
If Patsy Walker had a way to make people human again, don't you think she would've used it by now? I mean, I'm still a vampire, for cripes' sake, and I WORK for her. I feel like she would've at least offered.
Hedy was a bit dishonest about Patsy's intentions when we were younger...
No duh! She's bad news, dude!
You don't think Patsy intended to come after me?
NO, emo phase, I don't. She has, like, forty "gifted individuals" on call at the temp agency. If she needed to take the trash out, she would have.
Well, shoot.

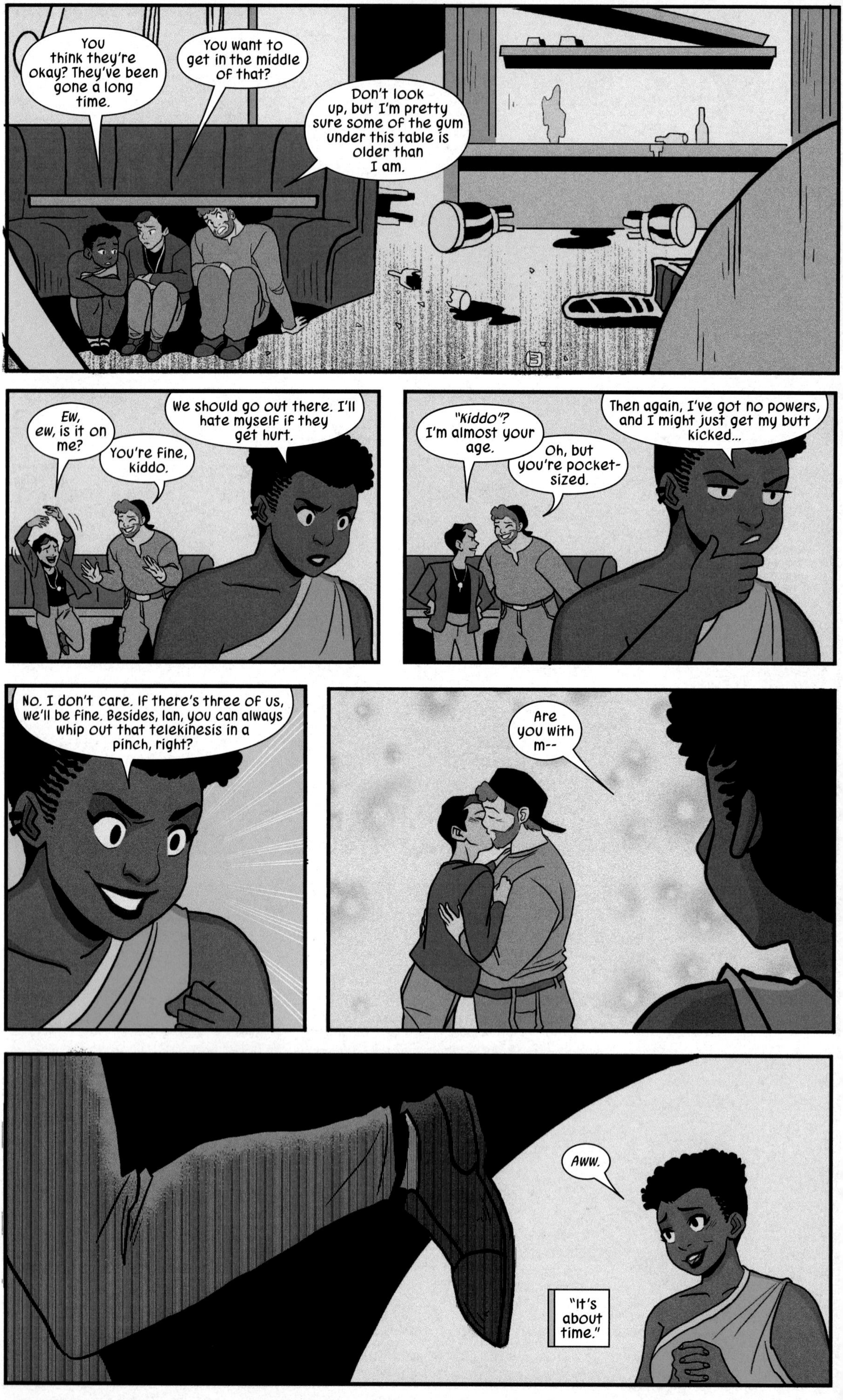

You think they're okay? They've been gone a long time.
You want to get in the middle of that?
Don't look up, but I'm pretty sure some of the gum under this table is older than I am.
Ew, ew, is it on me?
You're fine, kiddo.
We should go out there. I'll hate myself if they get hurt.
"Kiddo"? I'm almost your age.
Oh, but you're pocket-sized.
Then again, I've got no powers, and I might just get my butt kicked...
No. I don't care. If there's three of us, we'll be fine. Besides, Ian, you can always whip out that telekinesis in a pinch, right?
Are you with m--
Aww.
"It's about time."

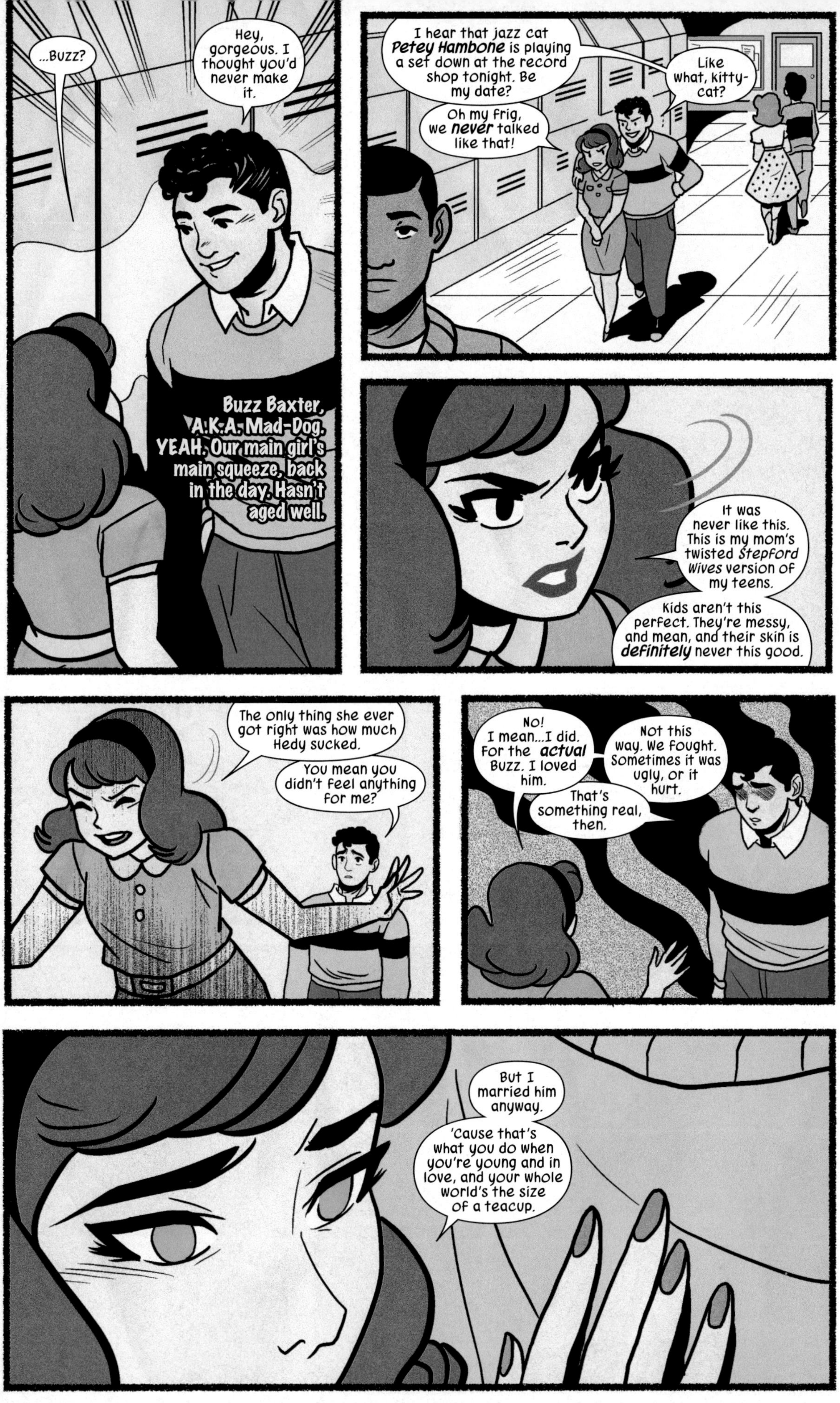
...Buzz?
Hey, gorgeous. I thought you'd never make it.
Buzz Baxter, A.K.A. Mad-Dog. YEAH. Our main girl's main squeeze, back in the day. Hasn't aged well.
I hear that jazz cat Petey Hambone is playing a set down at the record shop tonight. Be my date?
Like what, kitty-cat?
Oh my frig, we never talked like that!
It was never like this. This is my mom's twisted Stepford Wives version of my teens.
Kids aren't this perfect. They're messy, and mean, and their skin is definitely never this good.
The only thing she ever got right was how much Hedy sucked.
You mean you didn't feel anything for me?
No! I mean...I did. For the actual Buzz. I loved him.
Not this way. We fought. Sometimes it was ugly, or it hurt.
That's something real, then.
But I married him anyway.
'Cause that's what you do when you're young and in love, and your whole world's the size of a teacup.

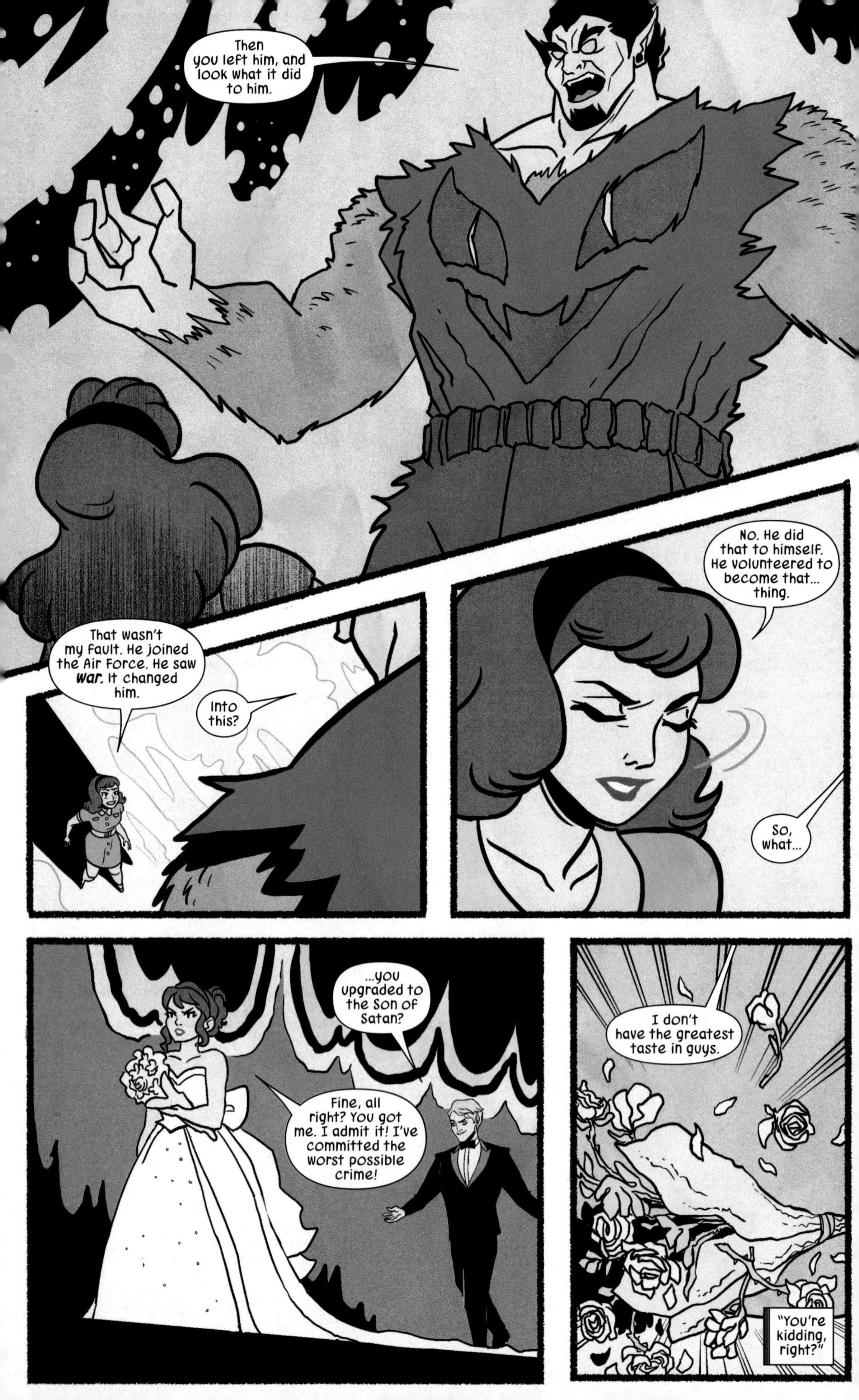
Then you left him, and look what it did to him.
That wasn't my fault. He joined the Air Force. He saw war. It changed him.
Into this?
No. He did that to himself. He volunteered to become that... thing.
So, what...
...you upgraded to the Son of Satan?
Fine, all right? You got me. I admit it! I've committed the worst possible crime!
I don't have the greatest taste in guys.
"You're kidding, right?"

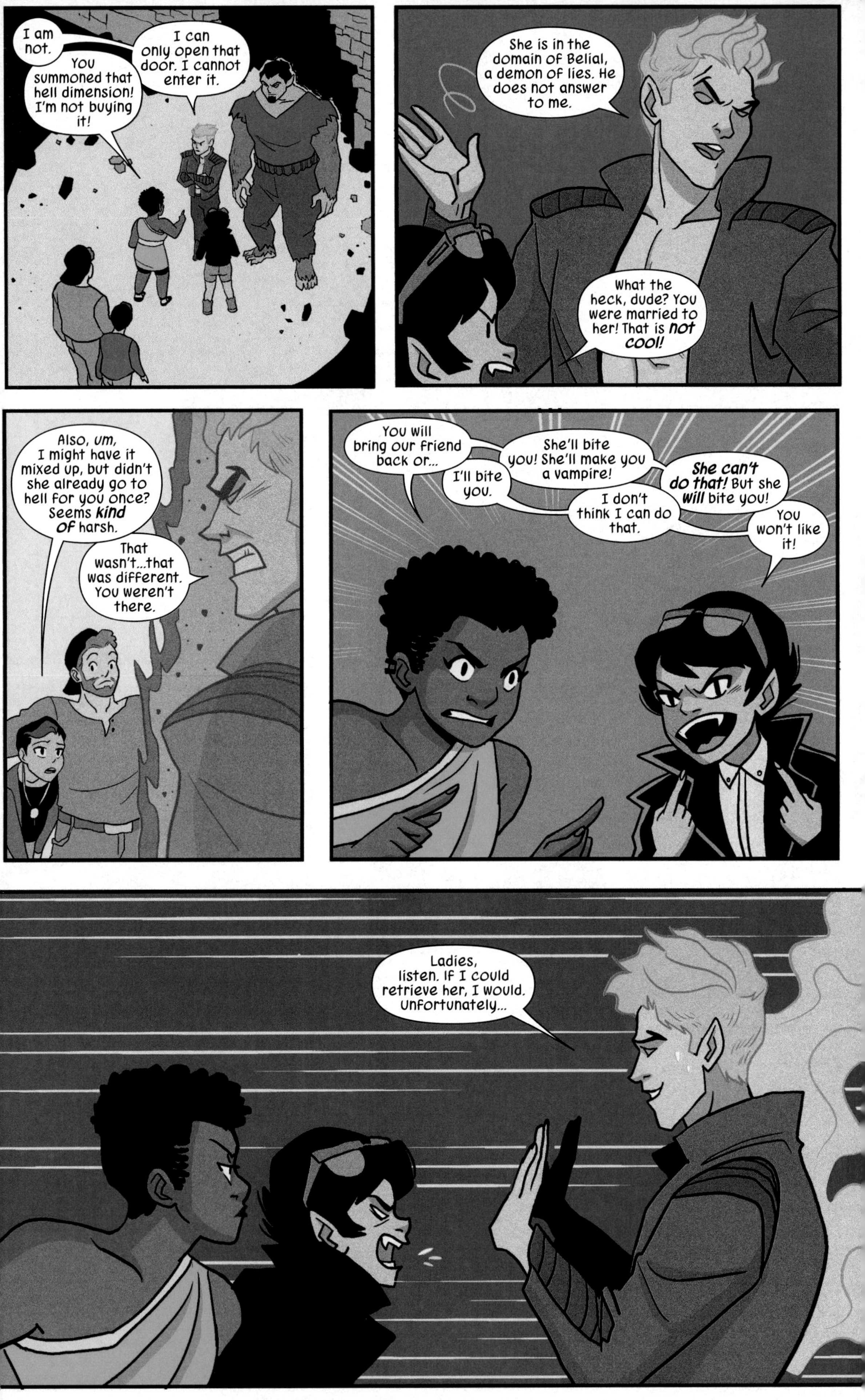
I am not.
I can only open that door. I cannot enter it.
You summoned that hell dimension! I'm not buying it!
She is in the domain of Belial, a demon of lies. He does not answer to me.
What the heck, dude? You were married to her! That is **not cool!**
Also, um, I might have it mixed up, but didn't she already go to hell for you once? Seems **kind of** harsh.
That wasn't...that was different. You weren't there.
You will bring our friend back or...
She'll bite you! She'll make you a vampire!
I'll bite you.
She can't do that! But she **will** bite you!
I don't think I can do that.
You won't like it!
Ladies, listen. If I could retrieve her, I would. Unfortunately...

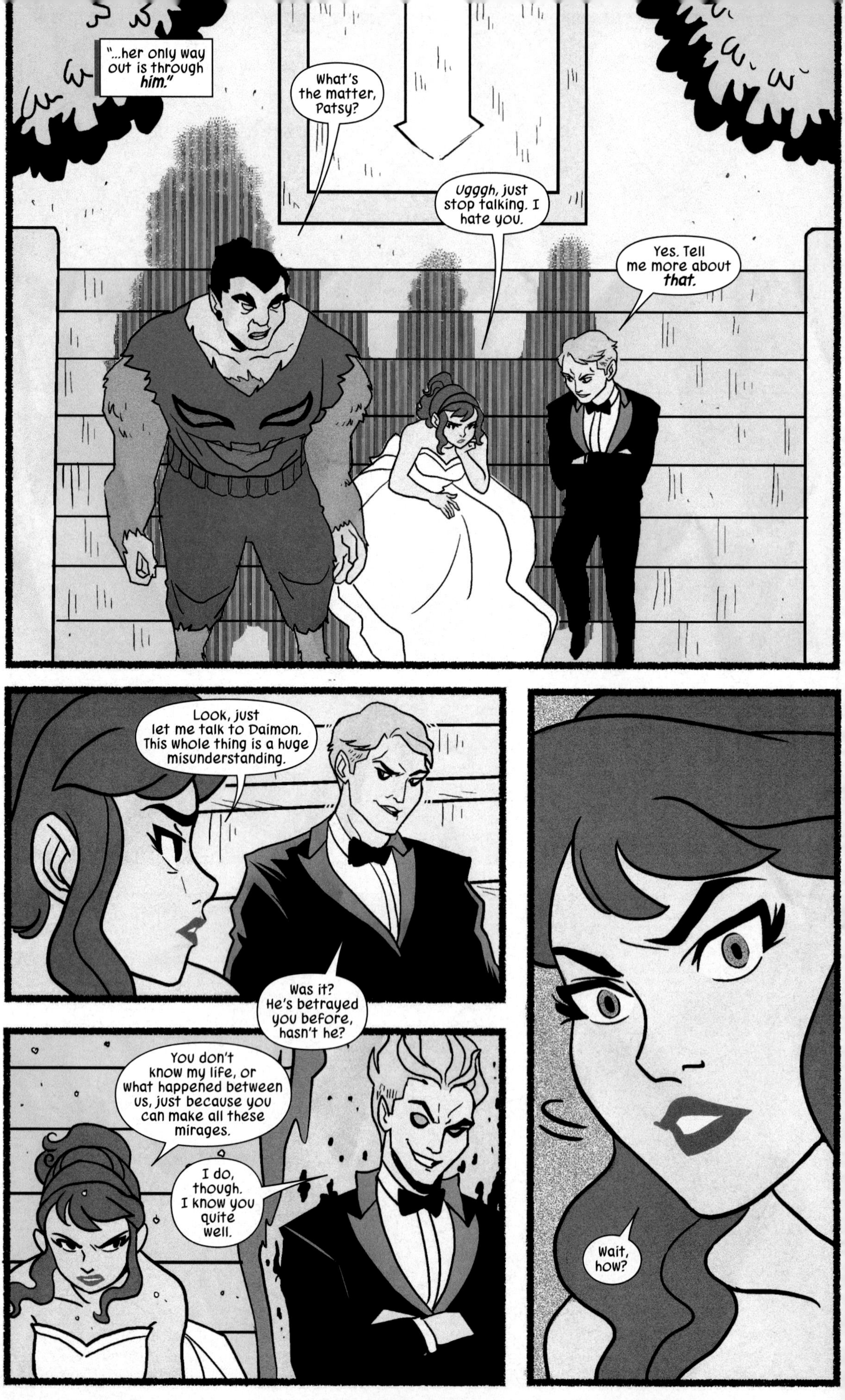
"...her only way out is through *him.*"
What's the matter, Patsy?
Ugggh, just stop talking. I hate you.
Yes. Tell me more about *that.*
Look, just let me talk to Daimon. This whole thing is a huge misunderstanding.
Was it? He's betrayed you before, hasn't he?
You don't know my life, or what happened between us, just because you can make all these mirages.
I do, though. I know you quite well.
Wait, how?

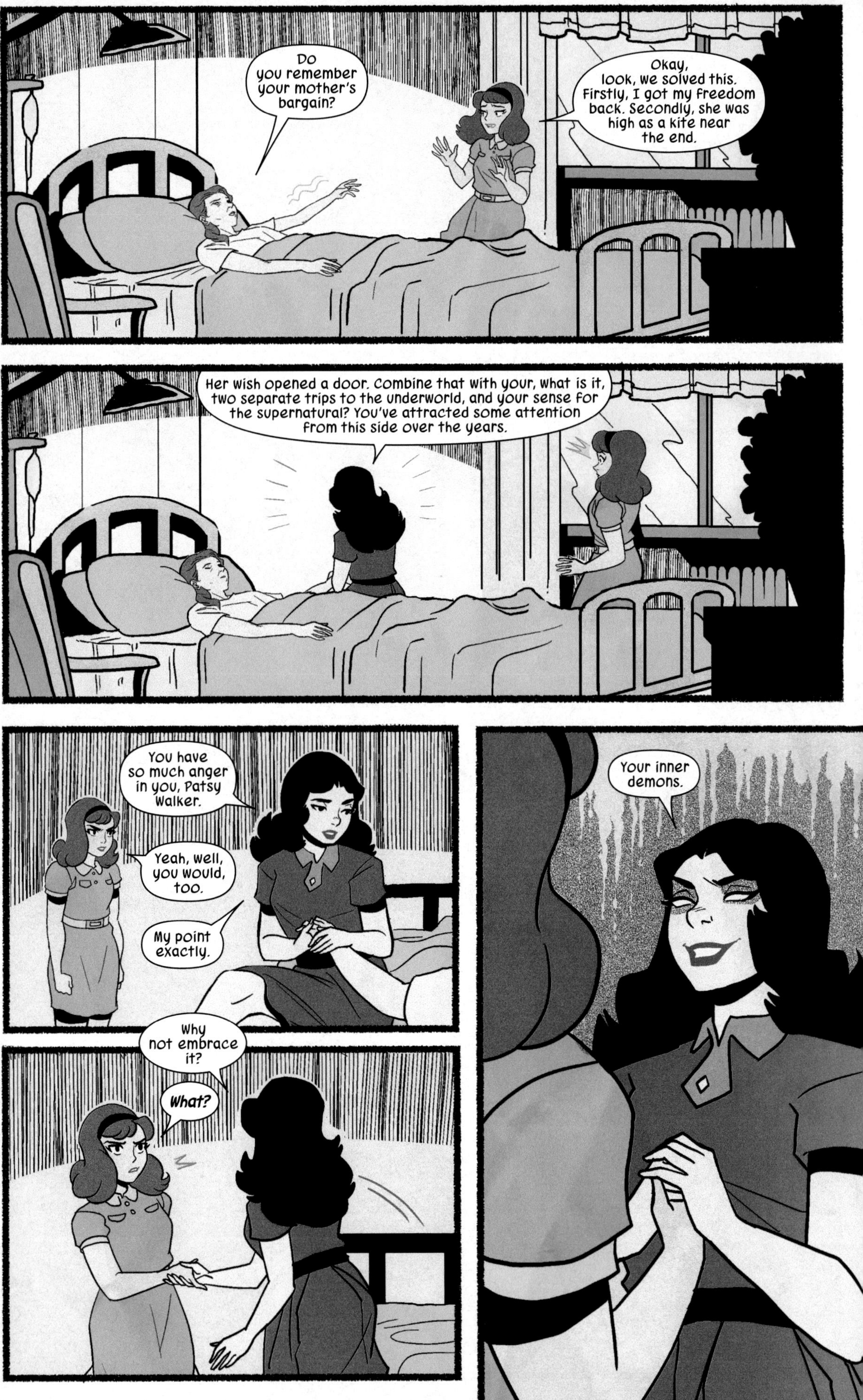
Do you remember your mother's bargain?
Okay, look, we solved this. Firstly, I got my freedom back. Secondly, she was high as a kite near the end.
Her wish opened a door. Combine that with your, what is it, two separate trips to the underworld, and your sense for the supernatural? You've attracted some attention from this side over the years.
You have so much anger in you, Patsy Walker.
Yeah, well, you would, too.
My point exactly.
Why not embrace it?
What?
Your inner demons.

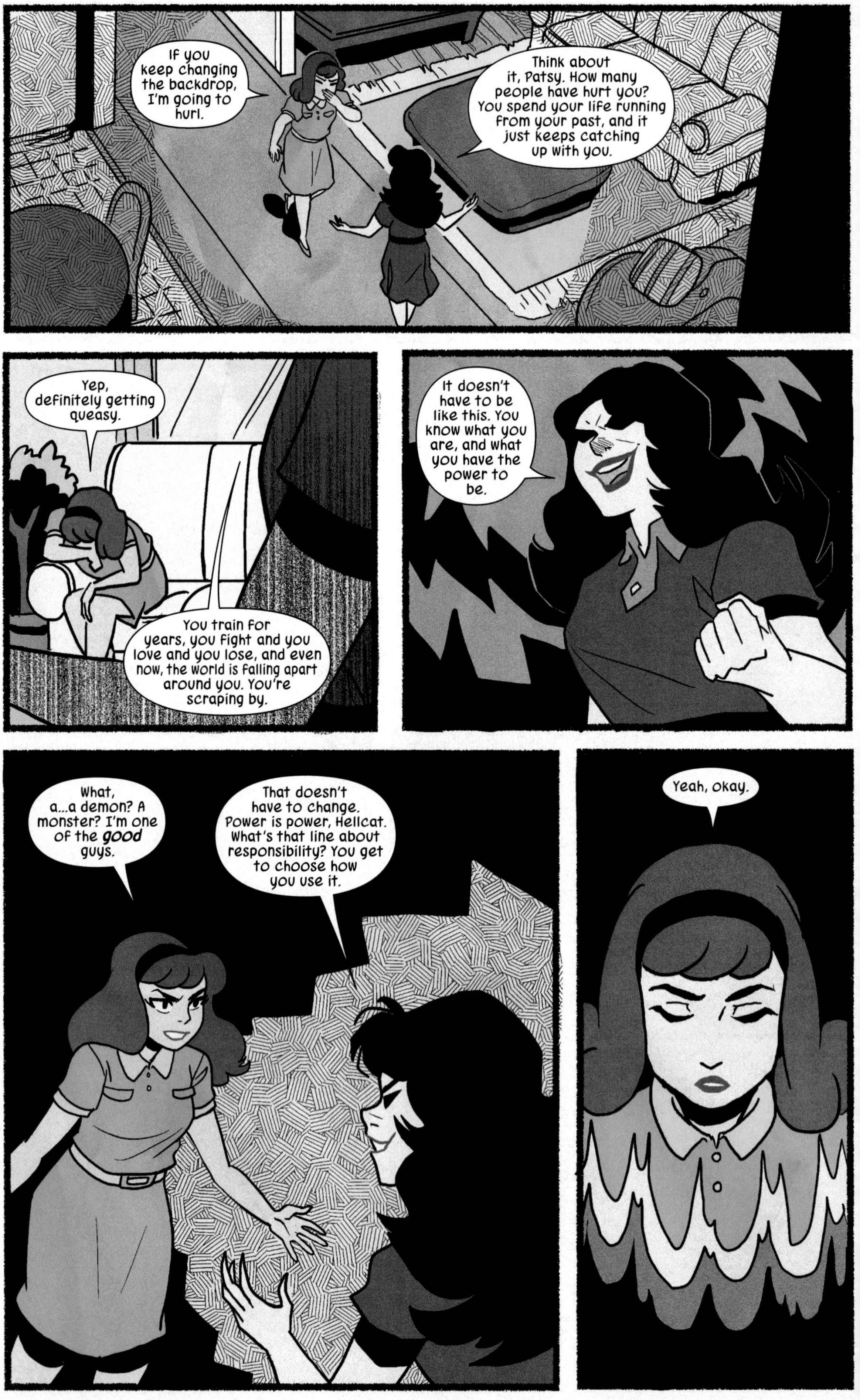
If you keep changing the backdrop, I'm going to hurl.
Think about it, Patsy. How many people have hurt you? You spend your life running from your past, and it just keeps catching up with you.
Yep, definitely getting queasy.
You train for years, you fight and you love and you lose, and even now, the world is falling apart around you. You're scraping by.
It doesn't have to be like this. You know what you are, and what you have the power to be.
What, a...a demon? A monster? I'm one of the good guys.
That doesn't have to change. Power is power, Hellcat. What's that line about responsibility? You get to choose how you use it.
Yeah, okay.

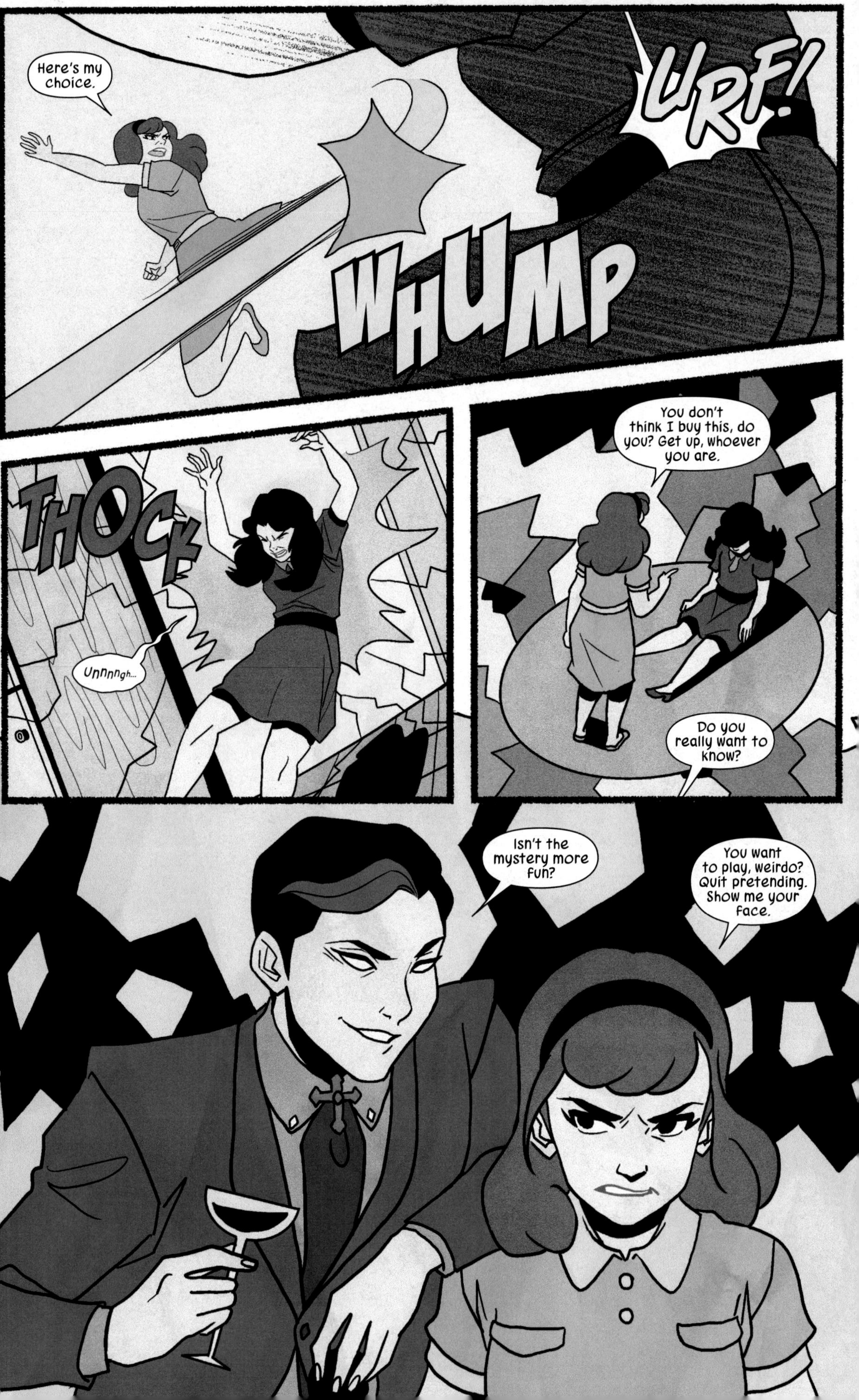
Here's my choice.
URF!
WHUMP
THOCK
Unnnngh...
You don't think I buy this, do you? Get up, whoever you are.
Do you really want to know?
Isn't the mystery more fun?
You want to play, weirdo? Quit pretending. Show me your face.

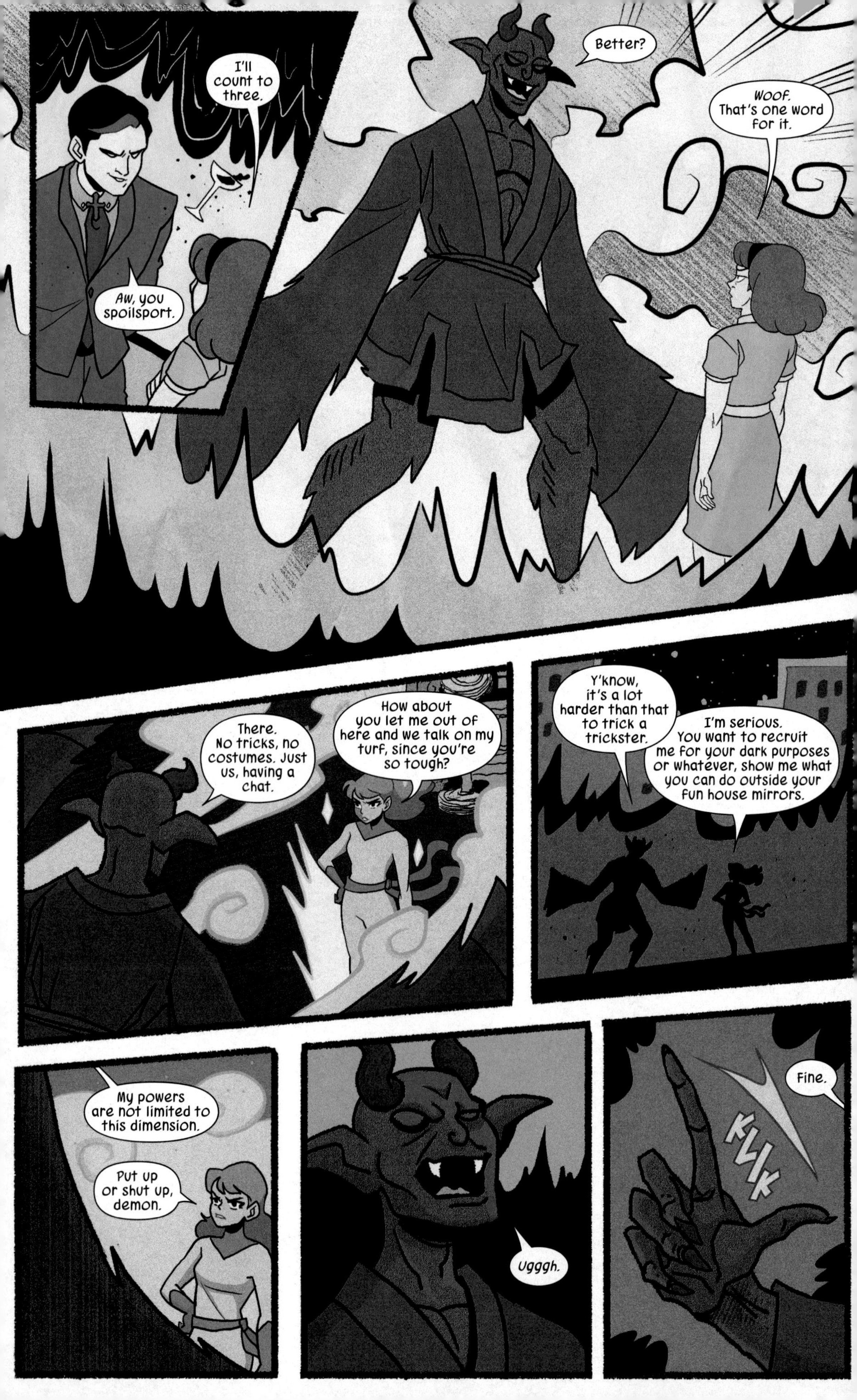
I'll count to three.
Aw, you spoilsport.
Better?
WOOF. That's one word for it.
There. No tricks, no costumes. Just us, having a chat.
How about you let me out of here and we talk on my turf, since you're so tough?
Y'know, it's a lot harder than that to trick a trickster.
I'm serious. You want to recruit me for your dark purposes or whatever, show me what you can do outside your fun house mirrors.
My powers are not limited to this dimension.
Put up or shut up, demon.
Ugggh.
Fine.
KLIK

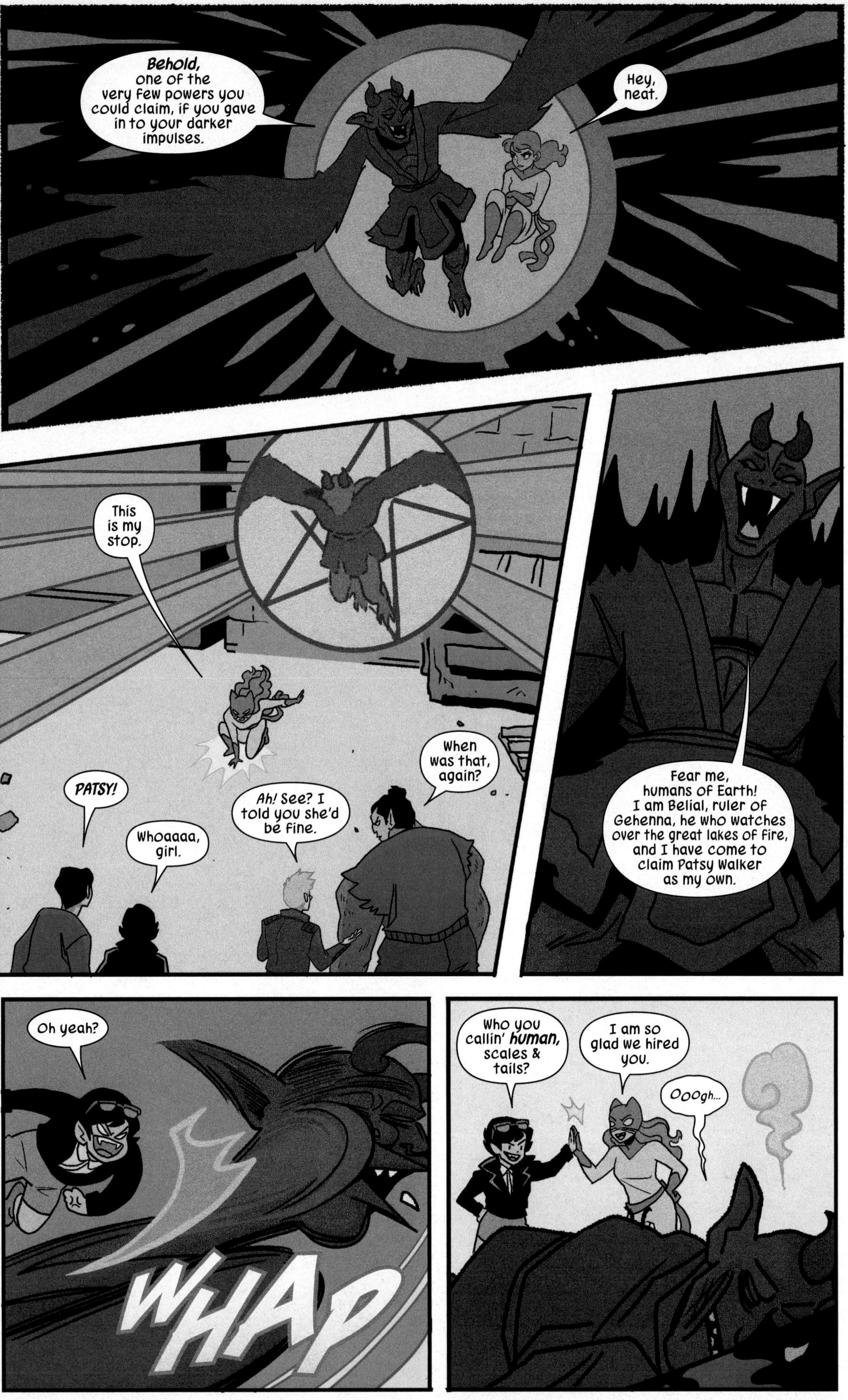
Behold, one of the very few powers you could claim, if you gave in to your darker impulses.
Hey, neat.
This is my stop.
PATSY!
Whoaaaa, girl.
Ah! See? I told you she'd be fine.
When was that, again?
Fear me, humans of Earth! I am Belial, ruler of Gehenna, he who watches over the great lakes of fire, and I have come to claim Patsy Walker as my own.
Oh yeah?
WHAP
Who you callin' human, scales & tails?
I am so glad we hired you.
Ooogh...

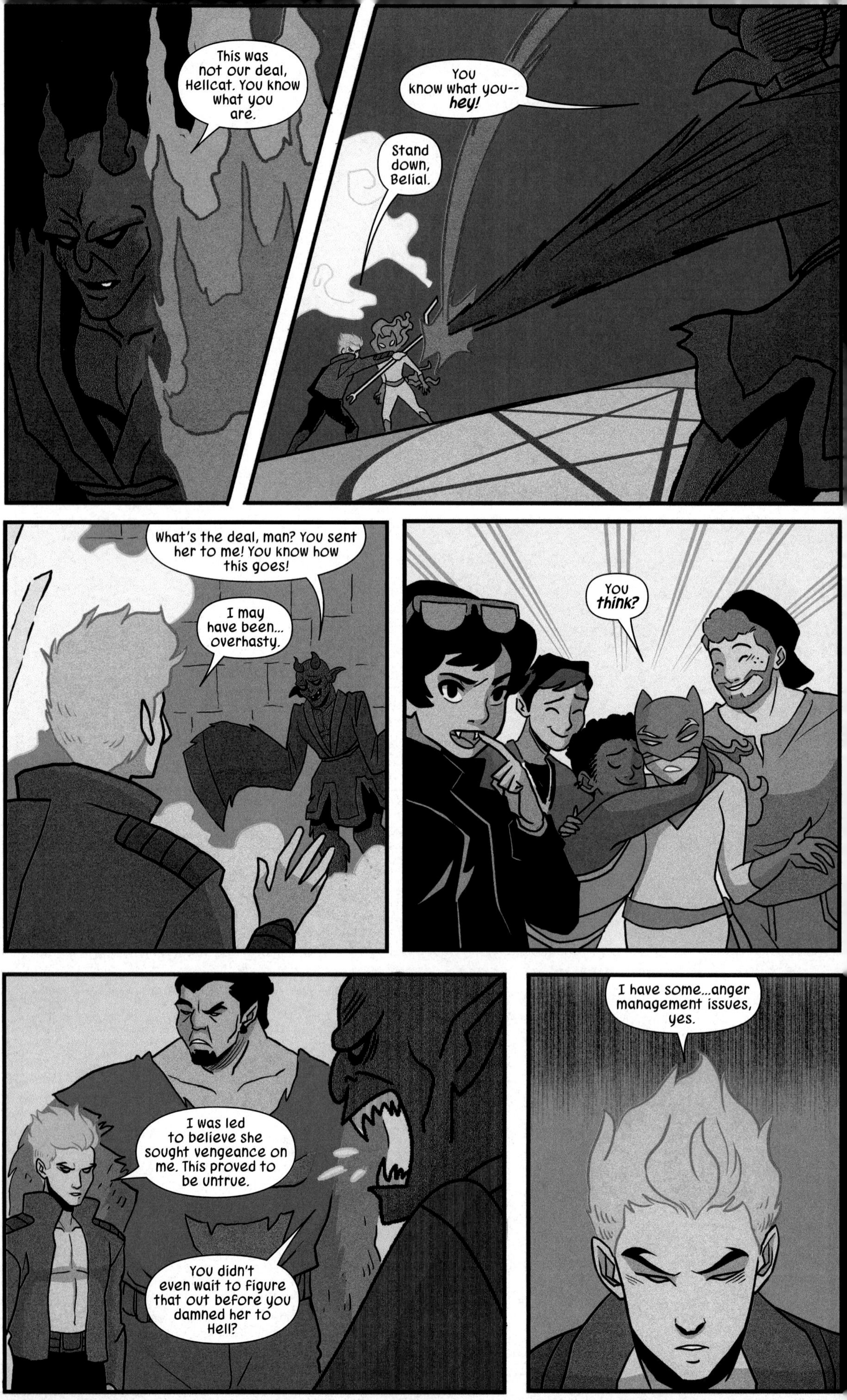

This was not our deal, Hellcat. You know what you are.
You know what you-- *hey!*
Stand down, Belial.
What's the deal, man? You sent her to me! You know how this goes!
I may have been... overhasty.
You *think?*
I was led to believe she sought vengeance on me. This proved to be untrue.
You didn't even wait to figure that out before you damned her to Hell?
I have some...anger management issues, yes.

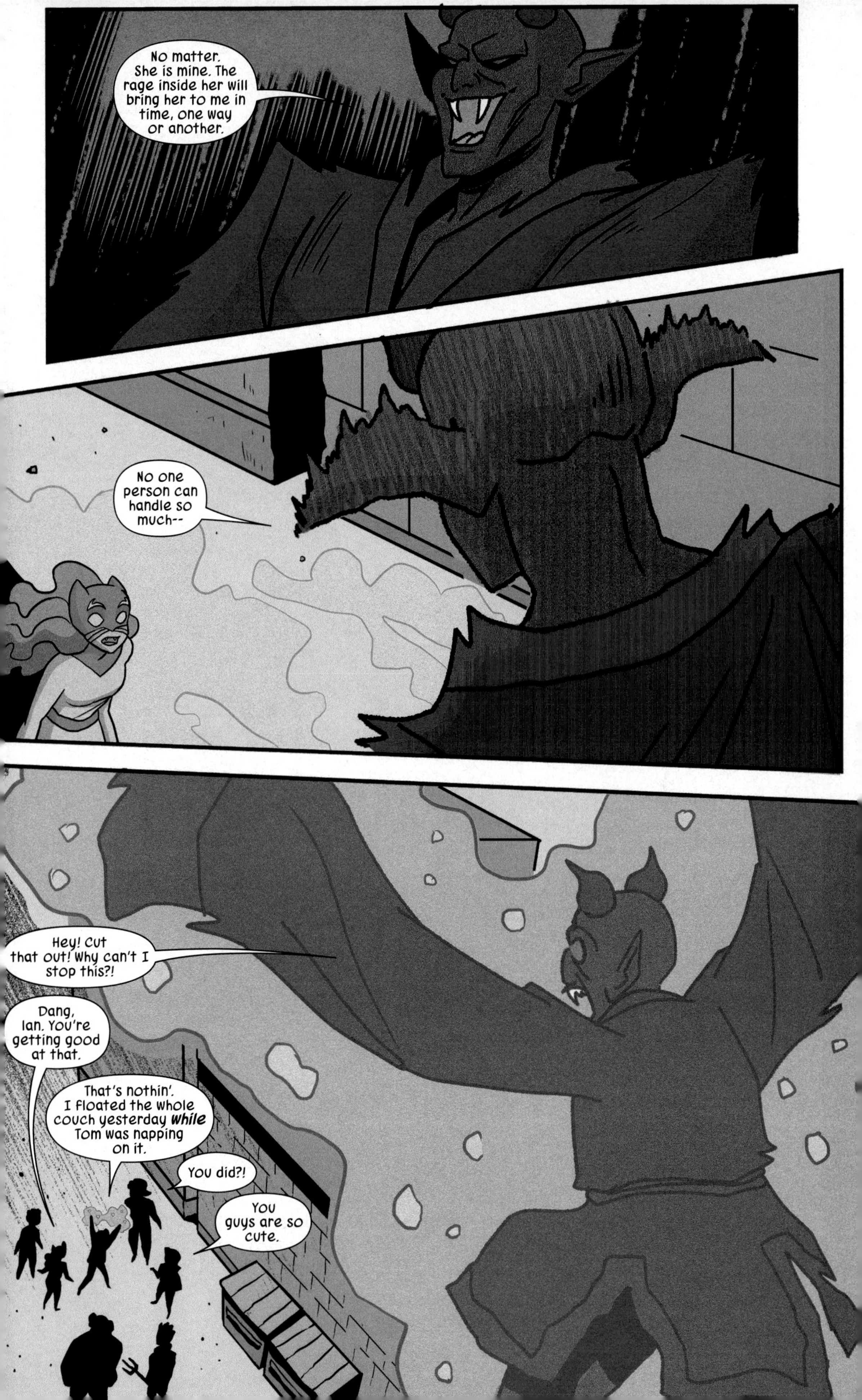
No matter. She is mine. The rage inside her will bring her to me in time, one way or another.
No one person can handle so much--
Hey! Cut that out! Why can't I stop this?!
Dang, Ian. You're getting good at that.
That's nothin'. I floated the whole couch yesterday *while* Tom was napping on it.
You did?!
You guys are so cute.

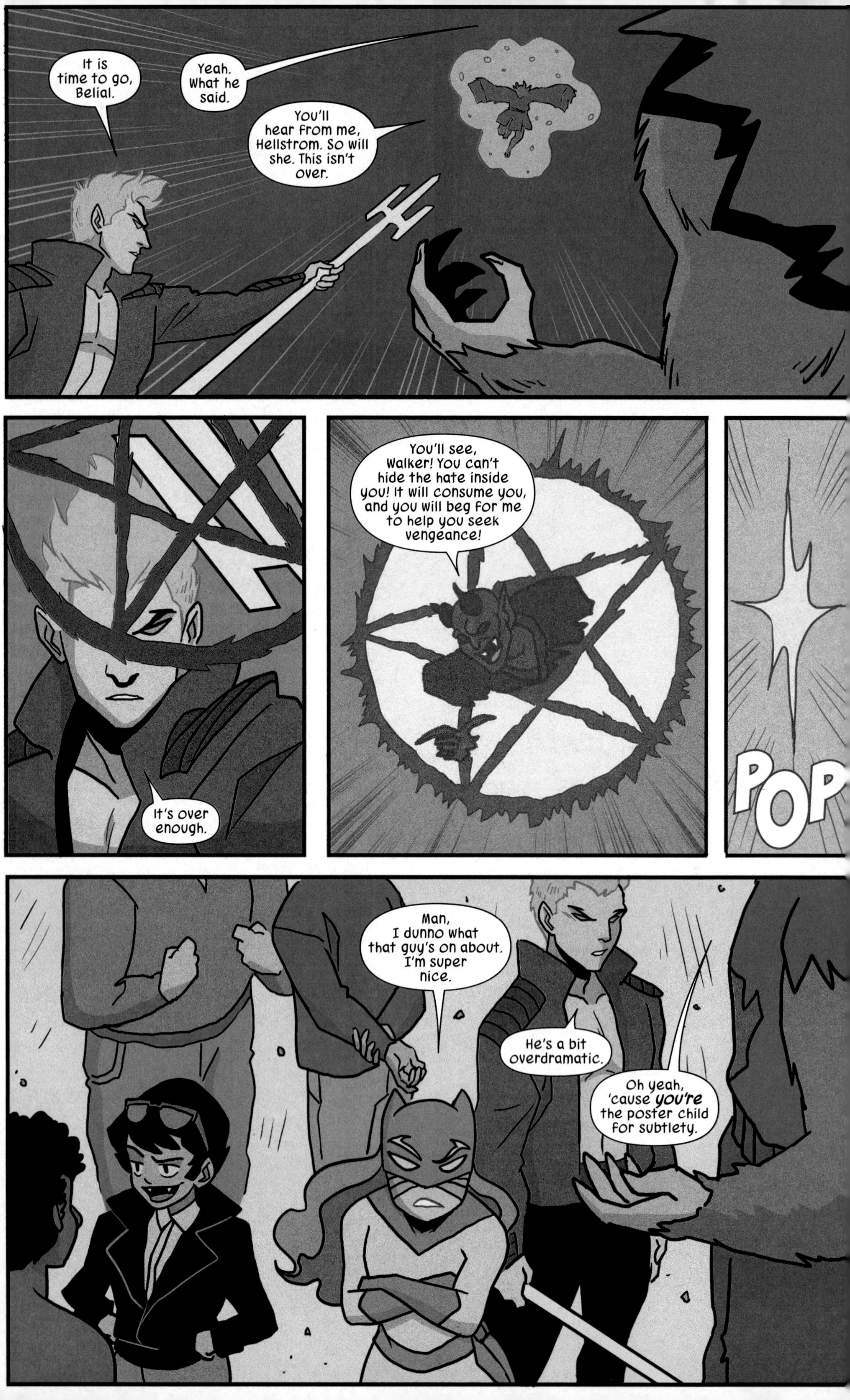
It is time to go, Belial.
Yeah. What he said.
You'll hear from me, Hellstrom. So will she. This isn't over.
It's over enough.
You'll see, Walker! You can't hide the hate inside you! It will consume you, and you will beg for me to help you seek vengeance!
POP
Man, I dunno what that guy's on about. I'm super nice.
He's a bit overdramatic.
Oh yeah, 'cause *you're* the poster child for subtlety.

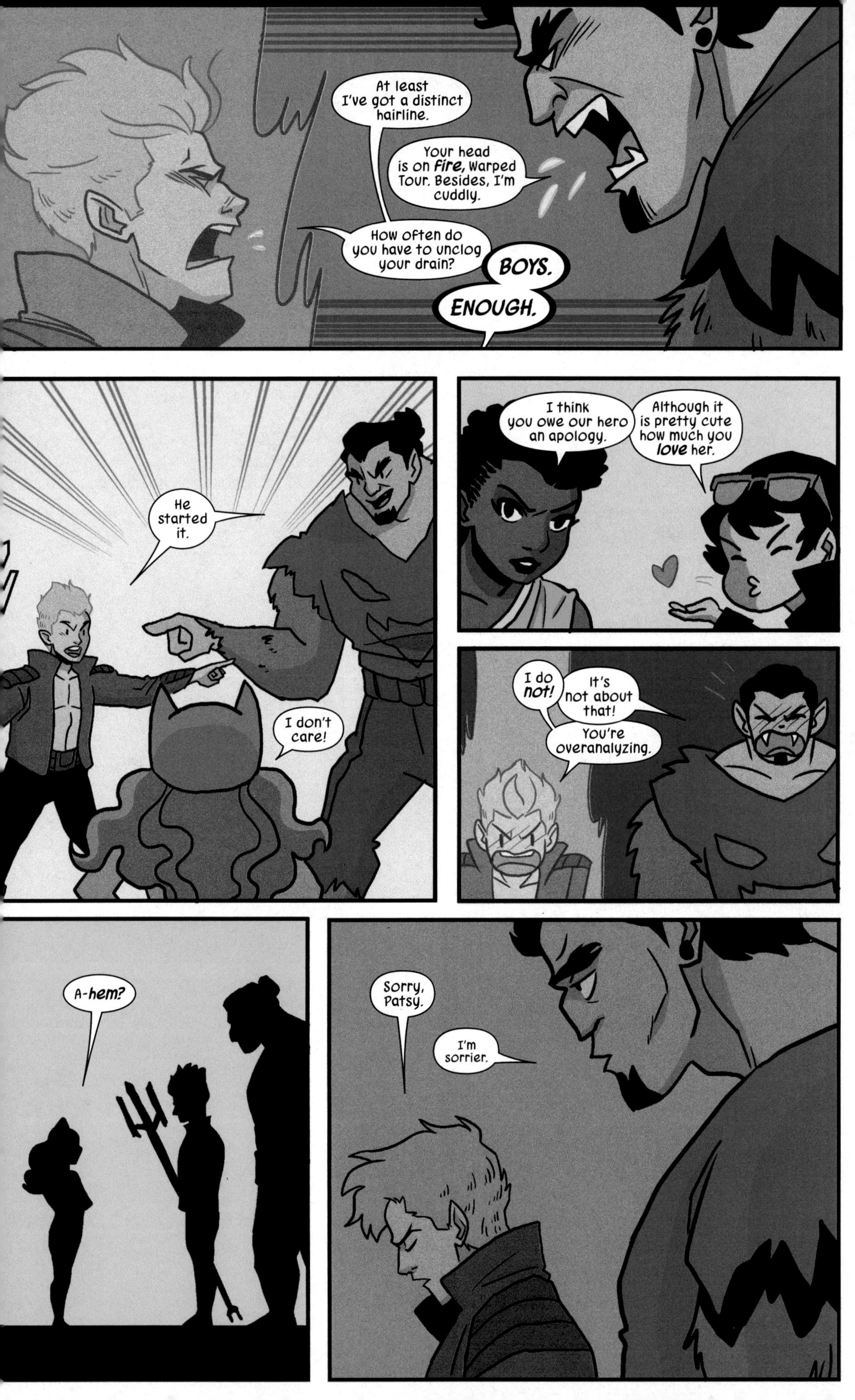
At least I've got a distinct hairline.
Your head is on fire, Warped Tour. Besides, I'm cuddly.
How often do you have to unclog your drain?
BOYS.
ENOUGH.
He started it.
I don't care!
I think you owe our hero an apology.
Although it is pretty cute how much you love her.
I do not!
It's not about that!
You're overanalyzing.
A-hem?
Sorry, Patsy.
I'm sorrier.

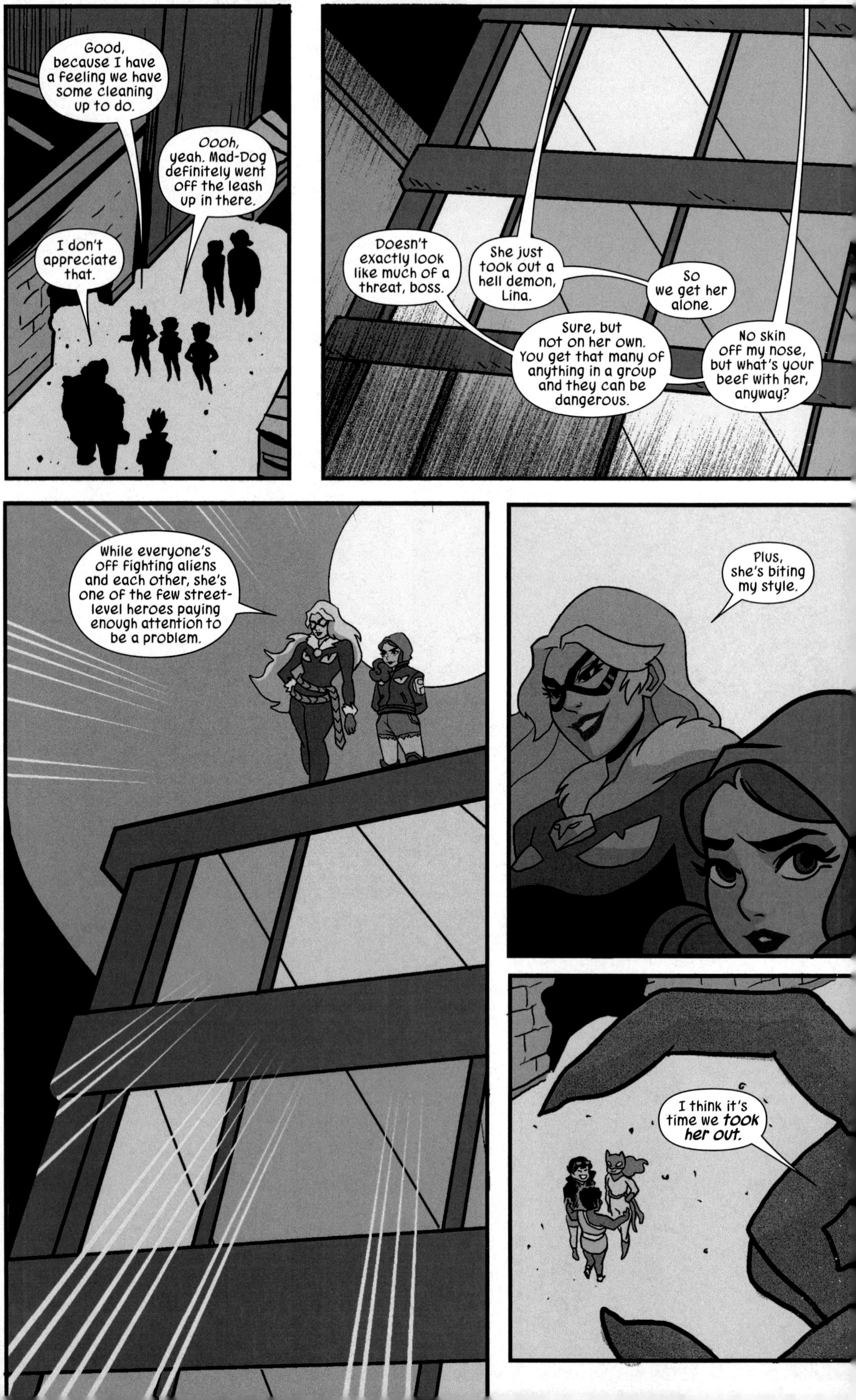
Good, because I have a feeling we have some cleaning up to do.
Oooh, yeah. Mad-Dog definitely went off the leash up in there.
I don't appreciate that.
Doesn't exactly look like much of a threat, boss.
She just took out a hell demon, Lina.
Sure, but not on her own. You get that many of anything in a group and they can be dangerous.
So we get her alone.
No skin off my nose, but what's your beef with her, anyway?
While everyone's off fighting aliens and each other, she's one of the few street-level heroes paying enough attention to be a problem.
Plus, she's biting my style.
I think it's time we took her out.

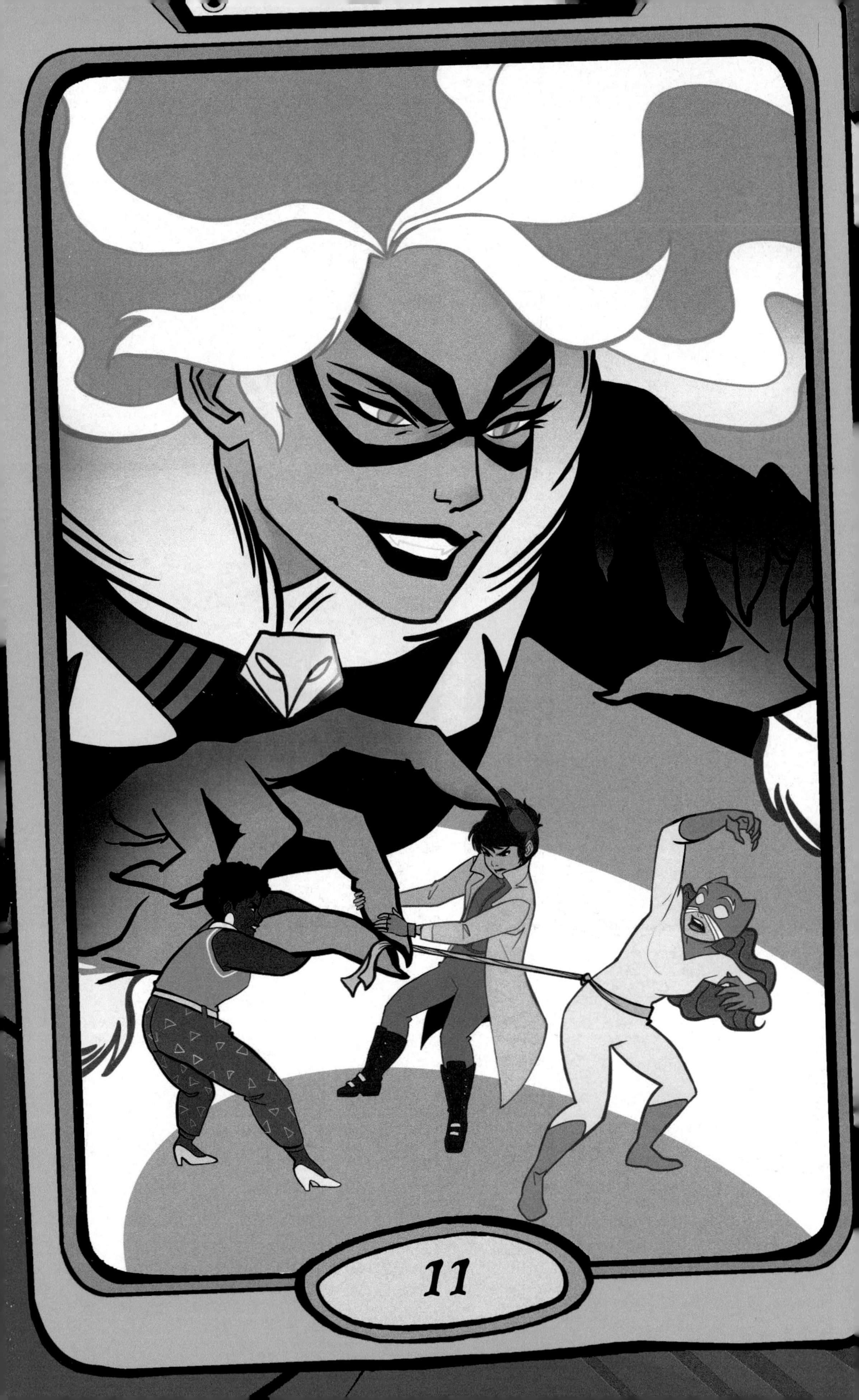
11

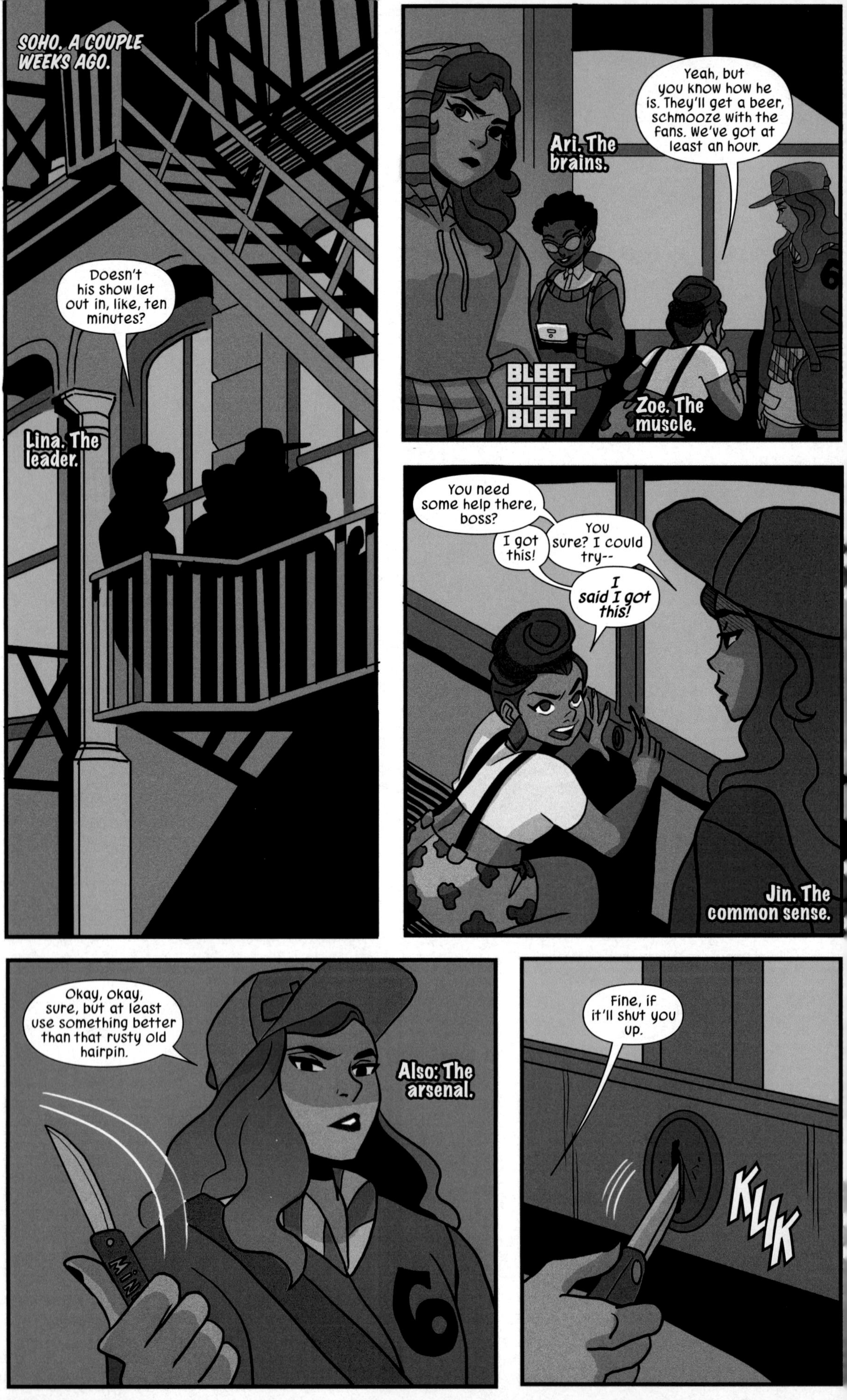
SOHO. A COUPLE WEEKS AGO.
Doesn't his show let out in, like, ten minutes?
Lina. The leader.
Ari. The brains.
Yeah, but you know how he is. They'll get a beer, schmooze with the fans. We've got at least an hour.
BLEET BLEET BLEET
Zoe. The muscle.
You need some help there, boss?
I got this!
You sure? I could try--
I said I got this!
Jin. The common sense.
Okay, okay, sure, but at least use something better than that rusty old hairpin.
Also: The arsenal.
Fine, if it'll shut you up.
KLIK

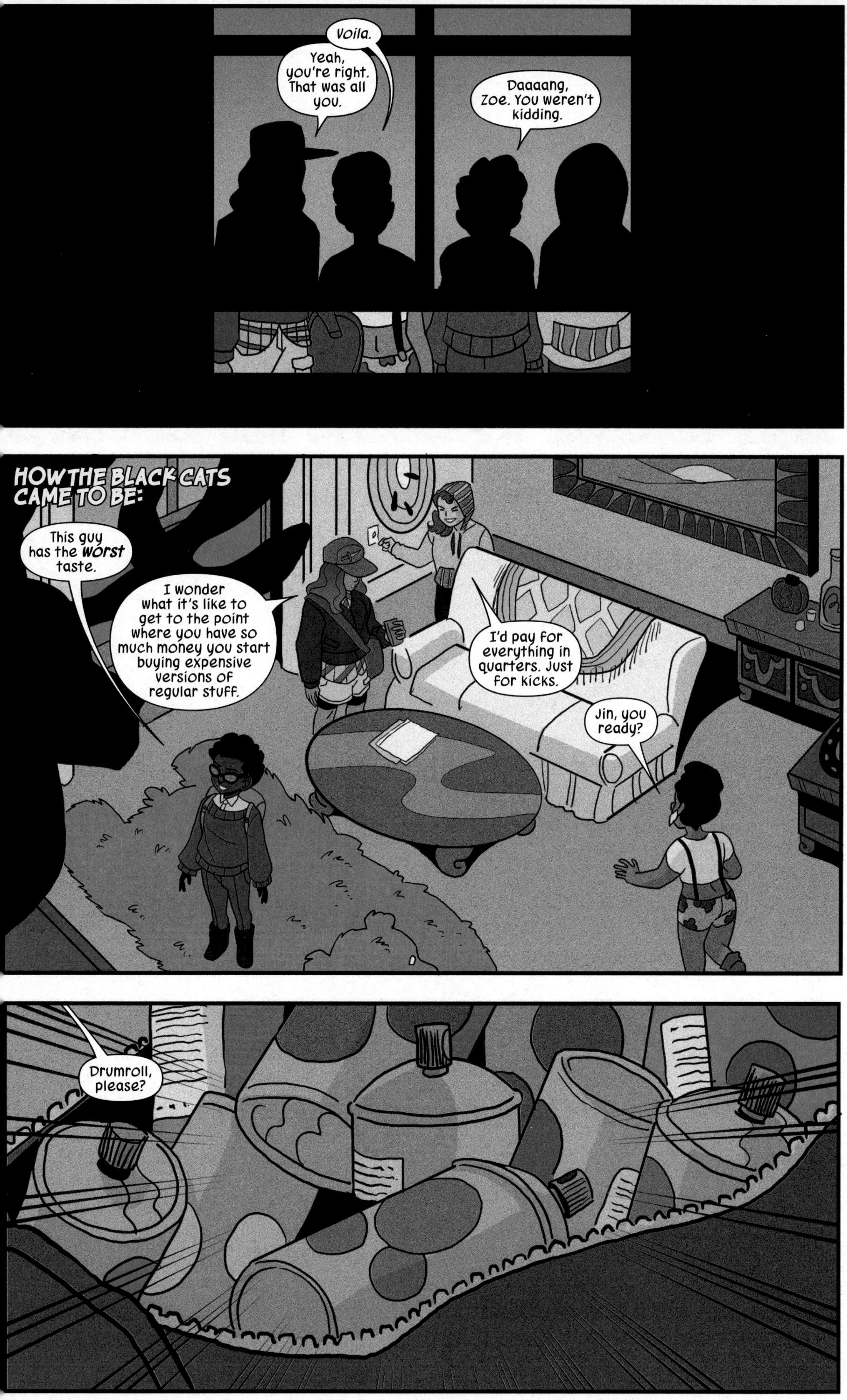
Yeah, you're right. That was all you.
Voila.
Daaaang, Zoe. You weren't kidding.
HOW THE BLACK CATS CAME TO BE:
This guy has the *worst* taste.
I wonder what it's like to get to the point where you have so much money you start buying expensive versions of regular stuff.
I'd pay for everything in quarters. Just for kicks.
Jin, you ready?
Drumroll, please?

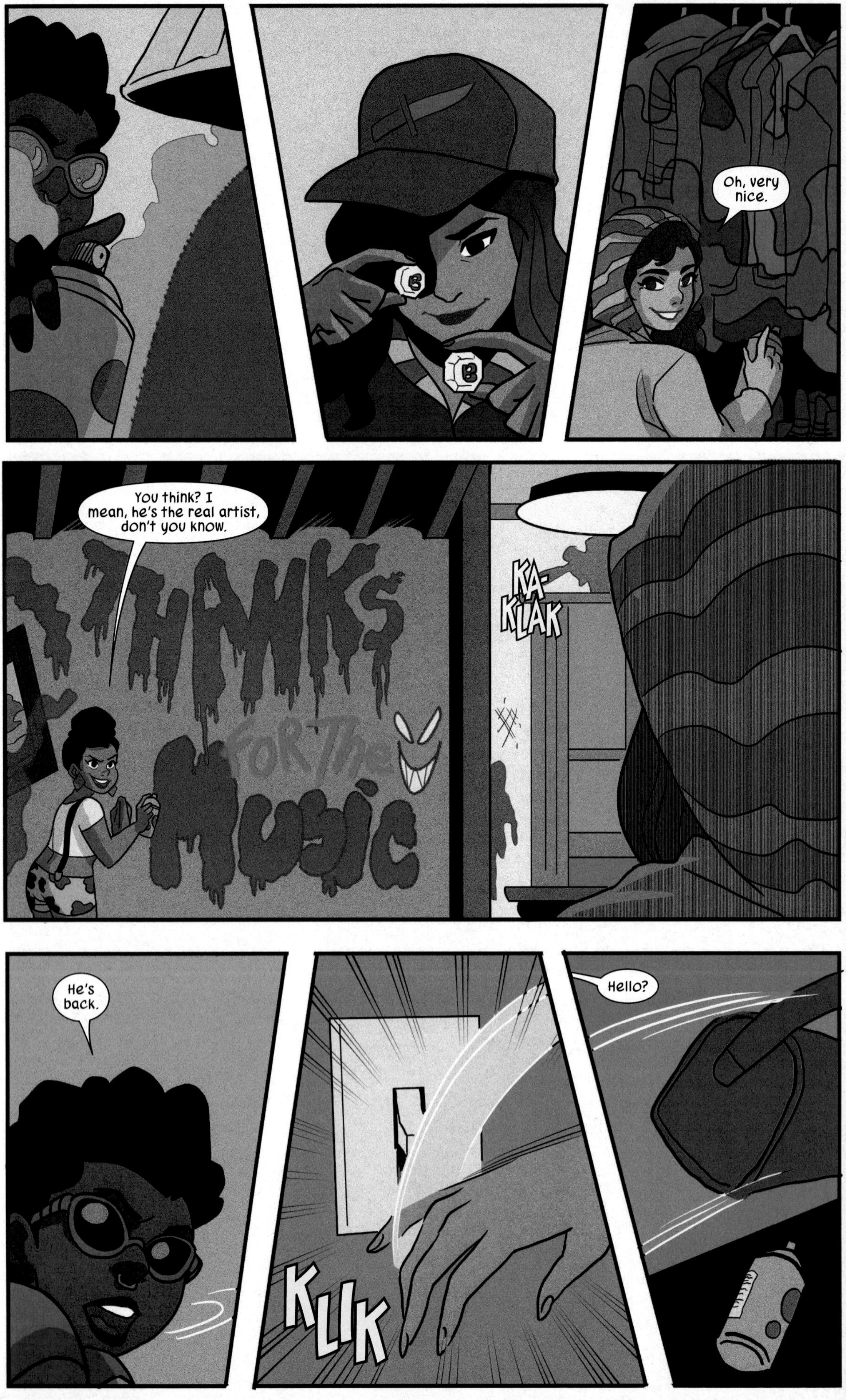
Oh, very nice.
You think? I mean, he's the real artist, don't you know.
THANKS FOR THE MUSIC
KA-KLAK
He's back.
KLIK
Hello?

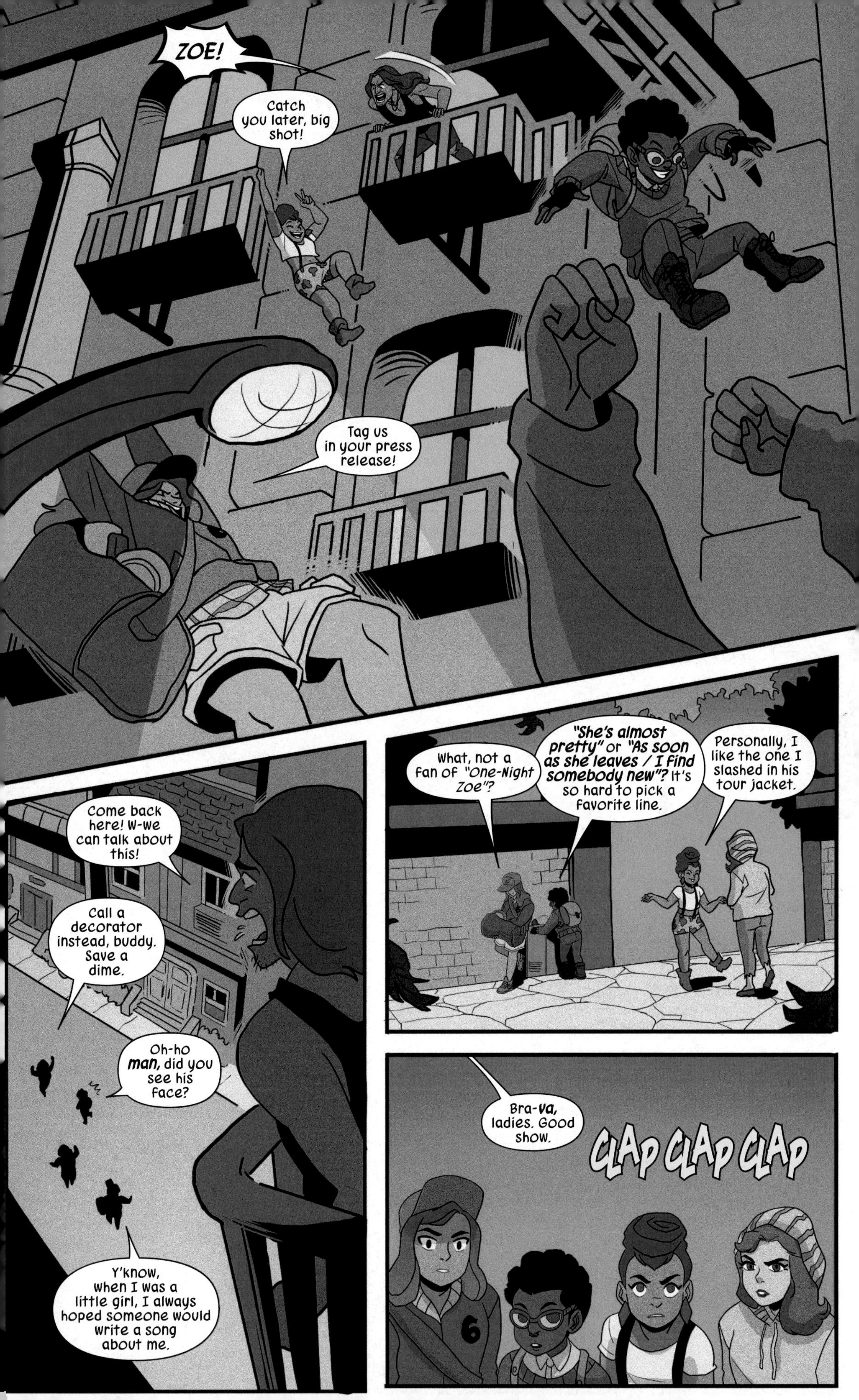
ZOE!
Catch you later, big shot!
Tag us in your press release!
Come back here! W-we can talk about this!
Call a decorator instead, buddy. Save a dime.
Oh-ho man, did you see his face?
Y'know, when I was a little girl, I always hoped someone would write a song about me.
What, not a fan of "One-Night Zoe"?
"She's almost pretty" or "As soon as she leaves / I find somebody new"? It's so hard to pick a favorite line.
Personally, I like the one I slashed in his tour jacket.
Bra-va, ladies. Good show.
CLAP CLAP CLAP

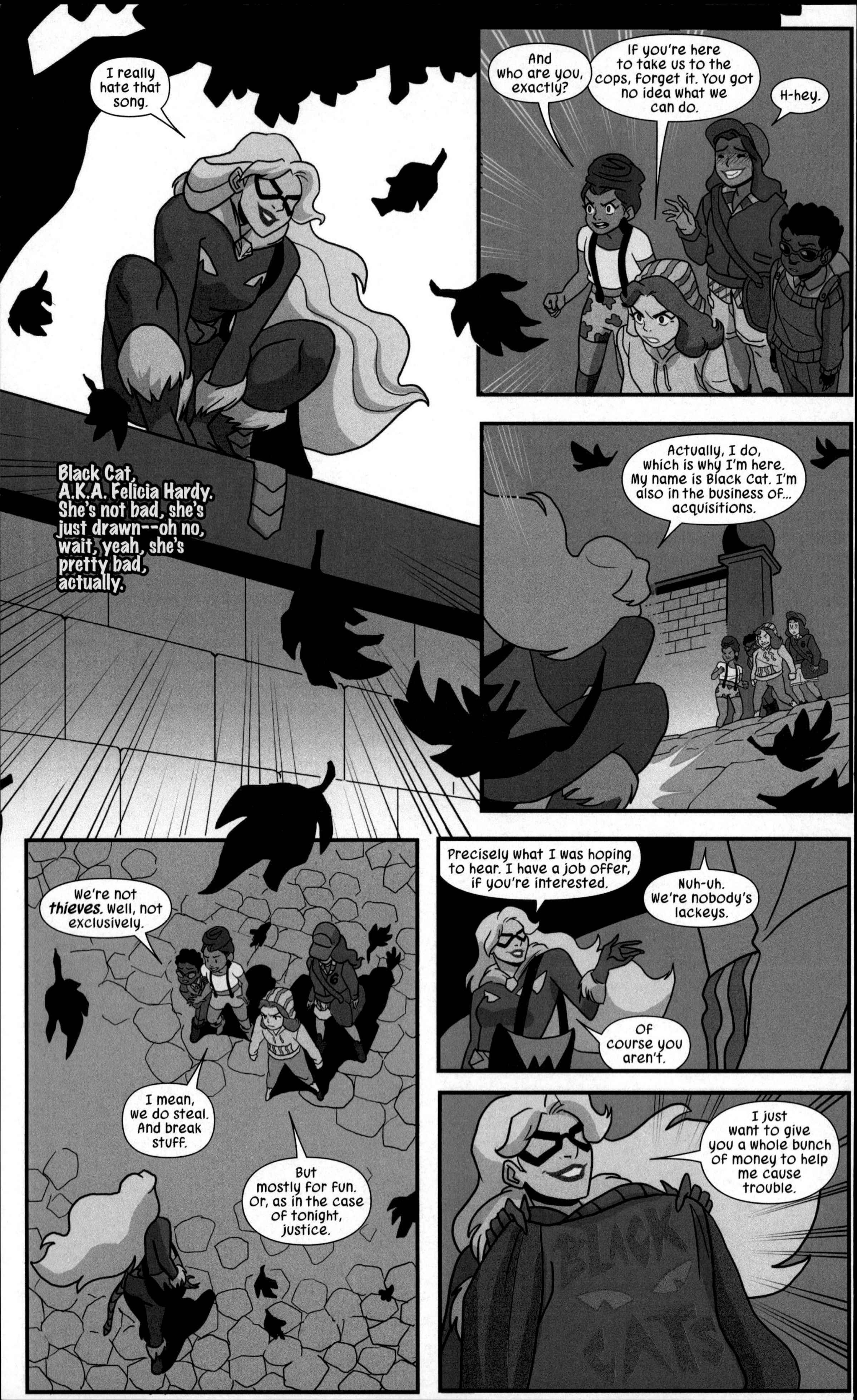
I really hate that song.
And who are you, exactly?
If you're here to take us to the cops, forget it. You got no idea what we can do.
H-hey.
Black Cat, A.K.A. Felicia Hardy. She's not bad, she's just drawn--oh no, wait, yeah, she's pretty bad, actually.
Actually, I do, which is why I'm here. My name is Black Cat. I'm also in the business of... acquisitions.
We're not *thieves.* Well, not exclusively.
I mean, we do steal. And break stuff.
But mostly for fun. Or, as in the case of tonight, justice.
Precisely what I was hoping to hear. I have a job offer, if you're interested.
Nuh-uh. We're nobody's lackeys.
Of course you aren't.
I just want to give you a whole bunch of money to help me cause trouble.
BLACK CATS

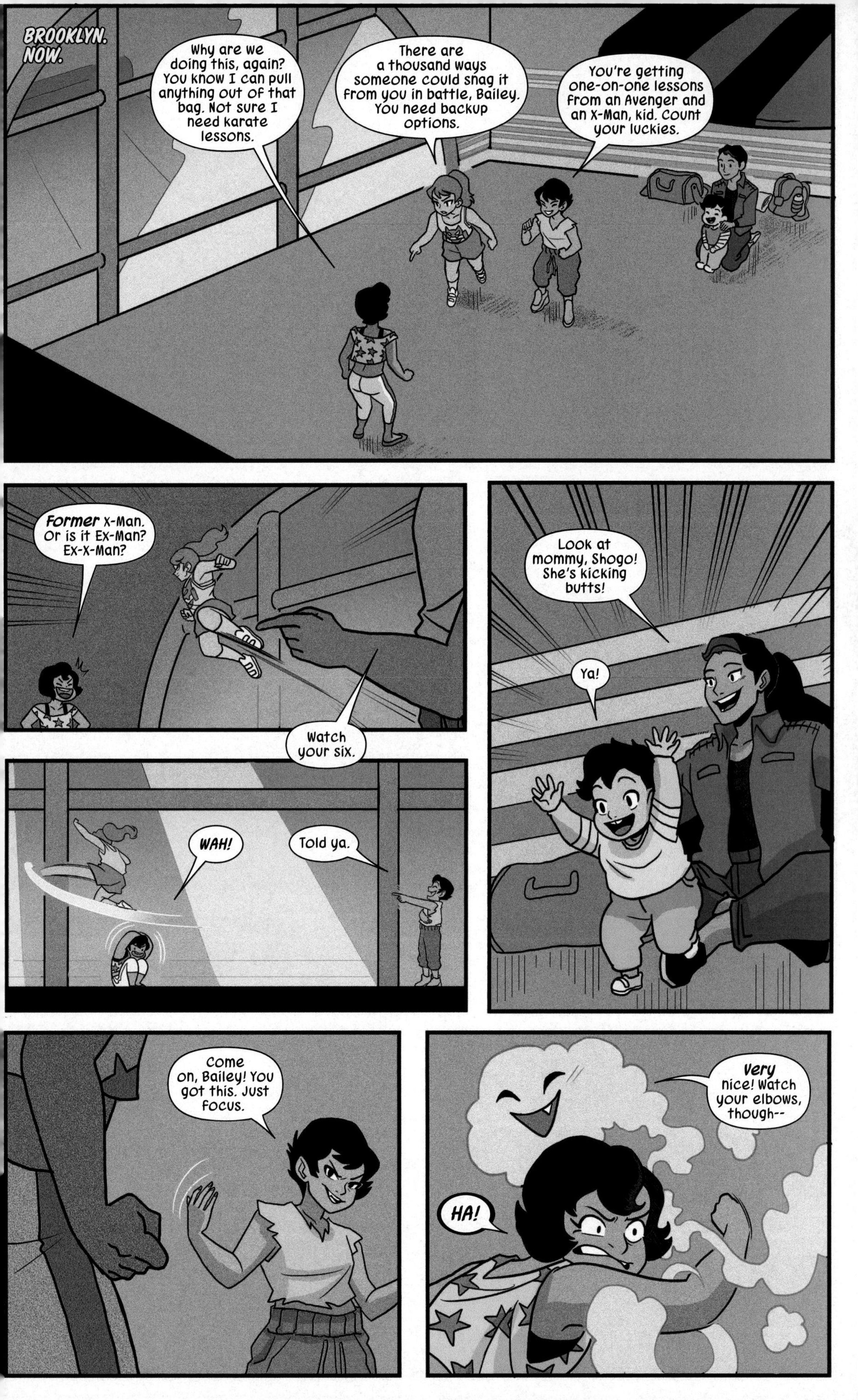
BROOKLYN. NOW.
Why are we doing this, again? You know I can pull anything out of that bag. Not sure I need karate lessons.
There are a thousand ways someone could snag it from you in battle, Bailey. You need backup options.
You're getting one-on-one lessons from an Avenger and an X-Man, kid. Count your luckies.
Former X-Man. Or is it Ex-Man? Ex-X-Man?
Watch your six.
Look at mommy, Shogo! She's kicking butts!
Ya!
WAH!
Told ya.
Come on, Bailey! You got this. Just focus.
Very nice! Watch your elbows, though--
HA!

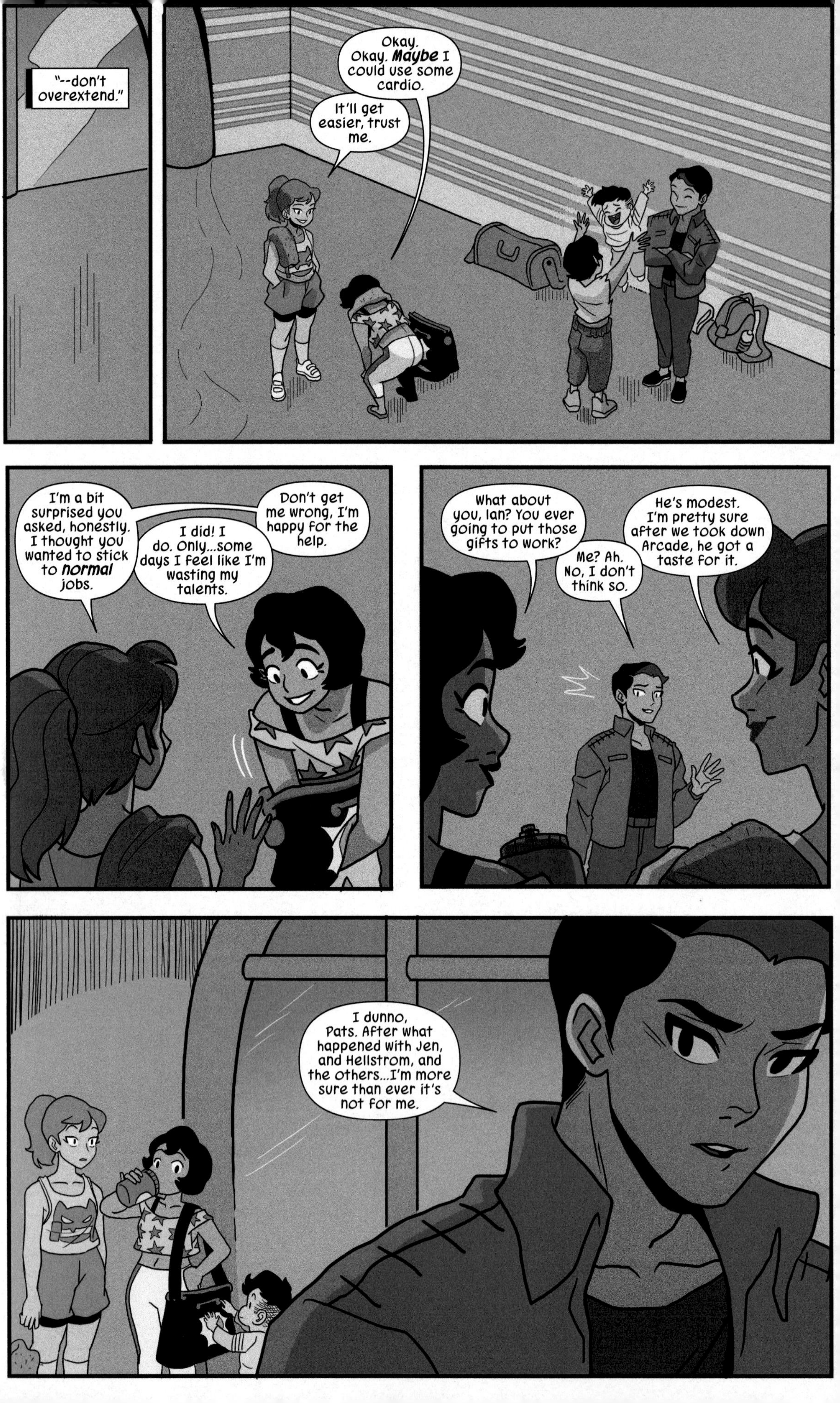
"--don't overextend."
Okay. Okay. *Maybe* I could use some cardio.
It'll get easier, trust me.
I'm a bit surprised you asked, honestly. I thought you wanted to stick to *normal* jobs.
Don't get me wrong, I'm happy for the help.
I did! I do. Only...some days I feel like I'm wasting my talents.
What about you, Ian? You ever going to put those gifts to work?
Me? Ah. No, I don't think so.
He's modest. I'm pretty sure after we took down Arcade, he got a taste for it.
I dunno, Pats. After what happened with Jen, and Hellstrom, and the others...I'm more sure than ever it's not for me.

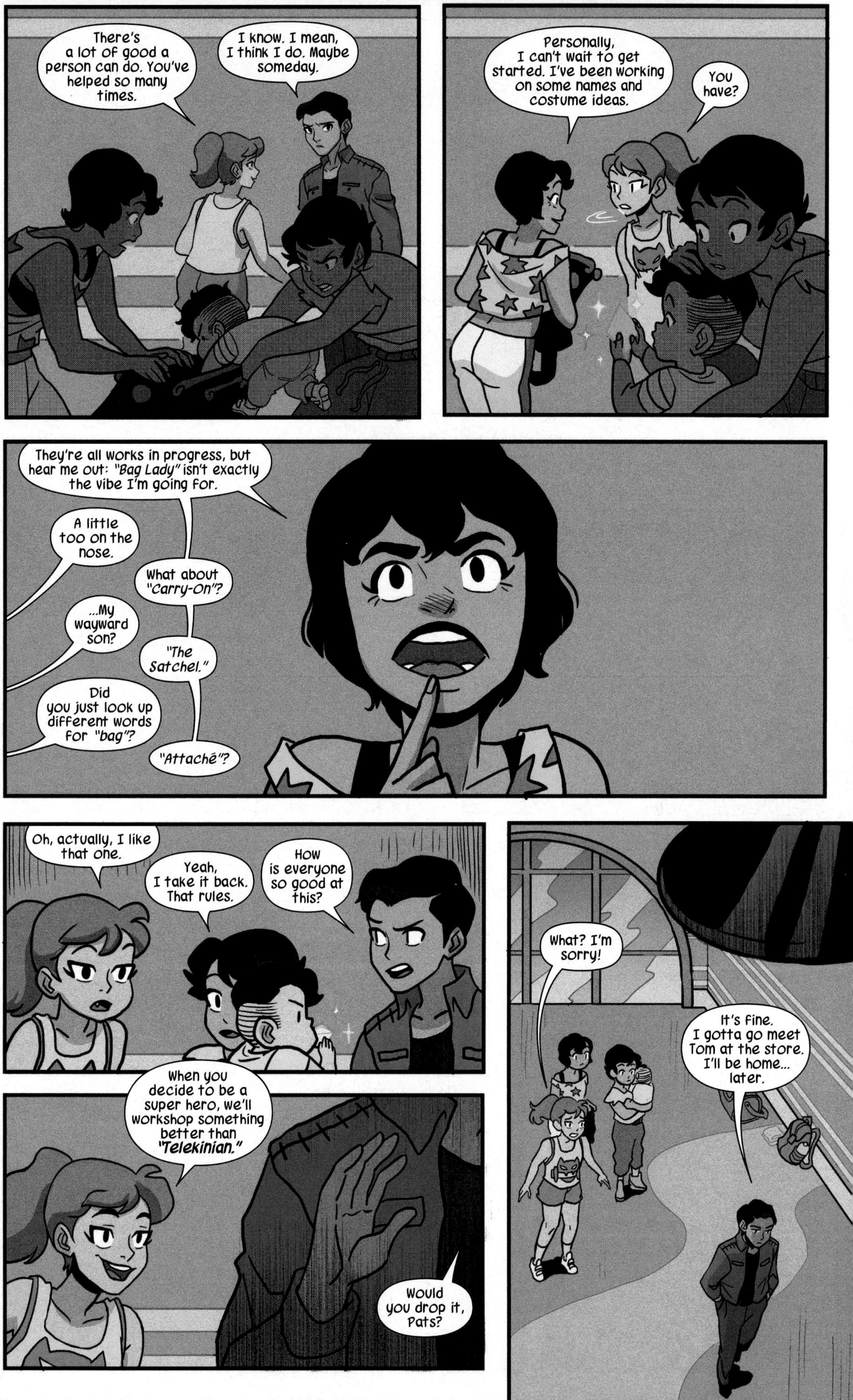
There's a lot of good a person can do. You've helped so many times.
I know. I mean, I think I do. Maybe someday.
Personally, I can't wait to get started. I've been working on some names and costume ideas.
You have?
They're all works in progress, but hear me out: "Bag Lady" isn't exactly the vibe I'm going for.
A little too on the nose.
What about "Carry-On"?
...My wayward son?
"The Satchel."
Did you just look up different words for "bag"?
"Attaché"?
Oh, actually, I like that one.
Yeah, I take it back. That rules.
How is everyone so good at this?
When you decide to be a super hero, we'll workshop something better than "Telekinian."
Would you drop it, Pats?
What? I'm sorry!
It's fine. I gotta go meet Tom at the store. I'll be home... later.

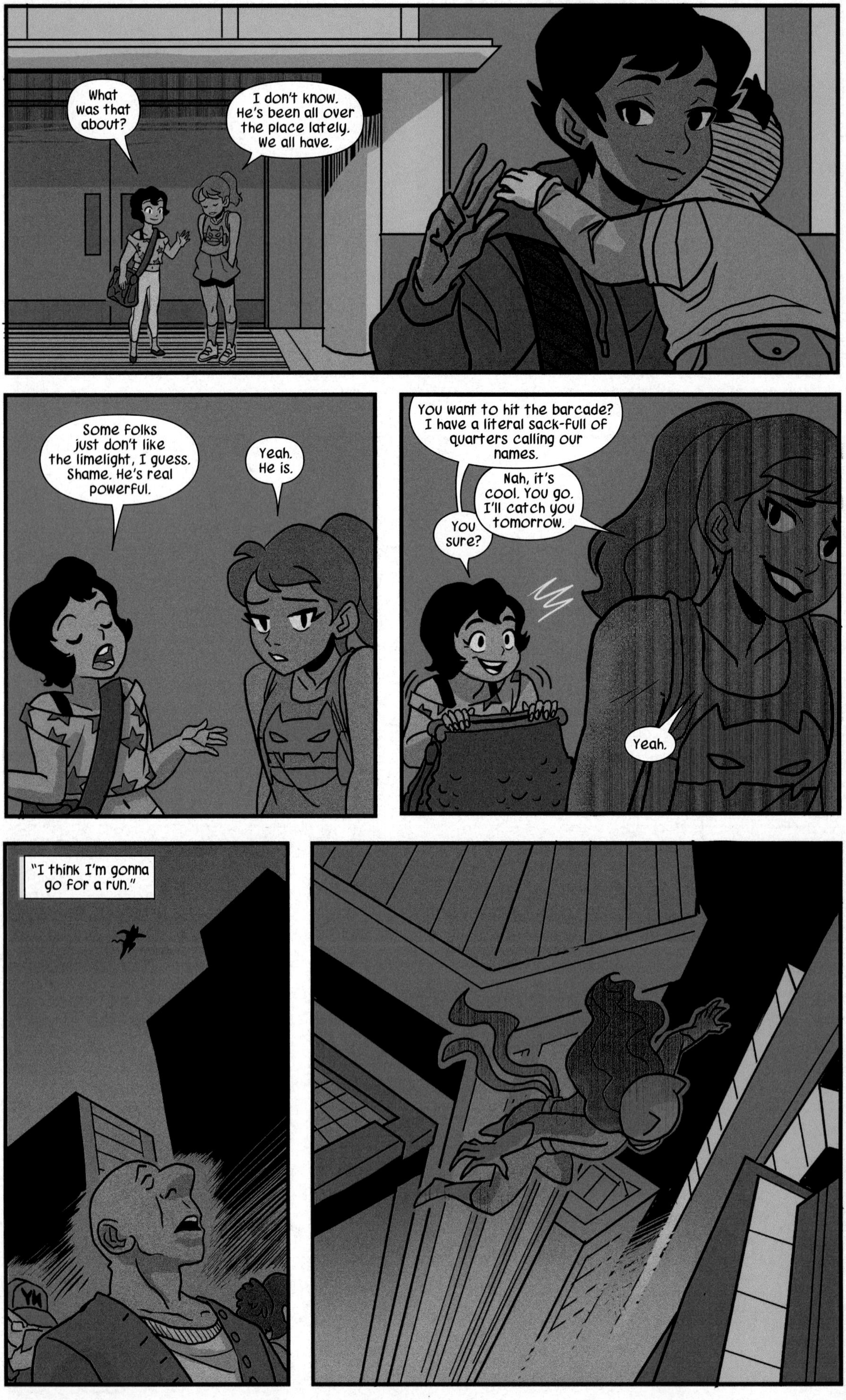
What was that about?
I don't know. He's been all over the place lately. We all have.
Some folks just don't like the limelight, I guess. Shame. He's real powerful.
Yeah. He is.
You want to hit the barcade? I have a literal sack-full of quarters calling our names.
You sure?
Nah, it's cool. You go. I'll catch you tomorrow.
Yeah.
"I think I'm gonna go for a run."

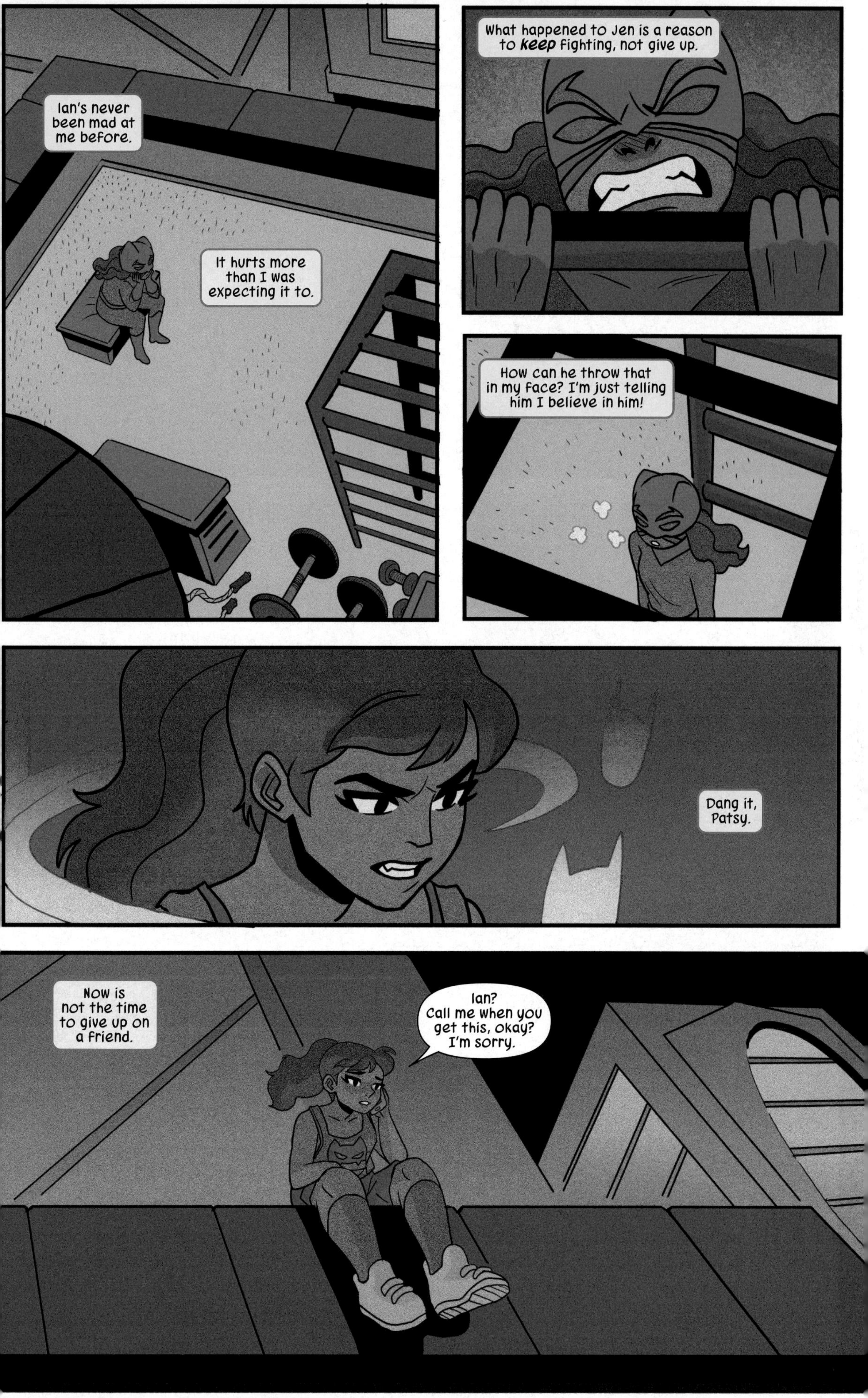
Ian's never been mad at me before.
It hurts more than I was expecting it to.
What happened to Jen is a reason to *keep* fighting, not give up.
How can he throw that in my face? I'm just telling him I believe in him!
Dang it, Patsy.
Now is not the time to give up on a friend.
Ian? Call me when you get this, okay? I'm sorry.

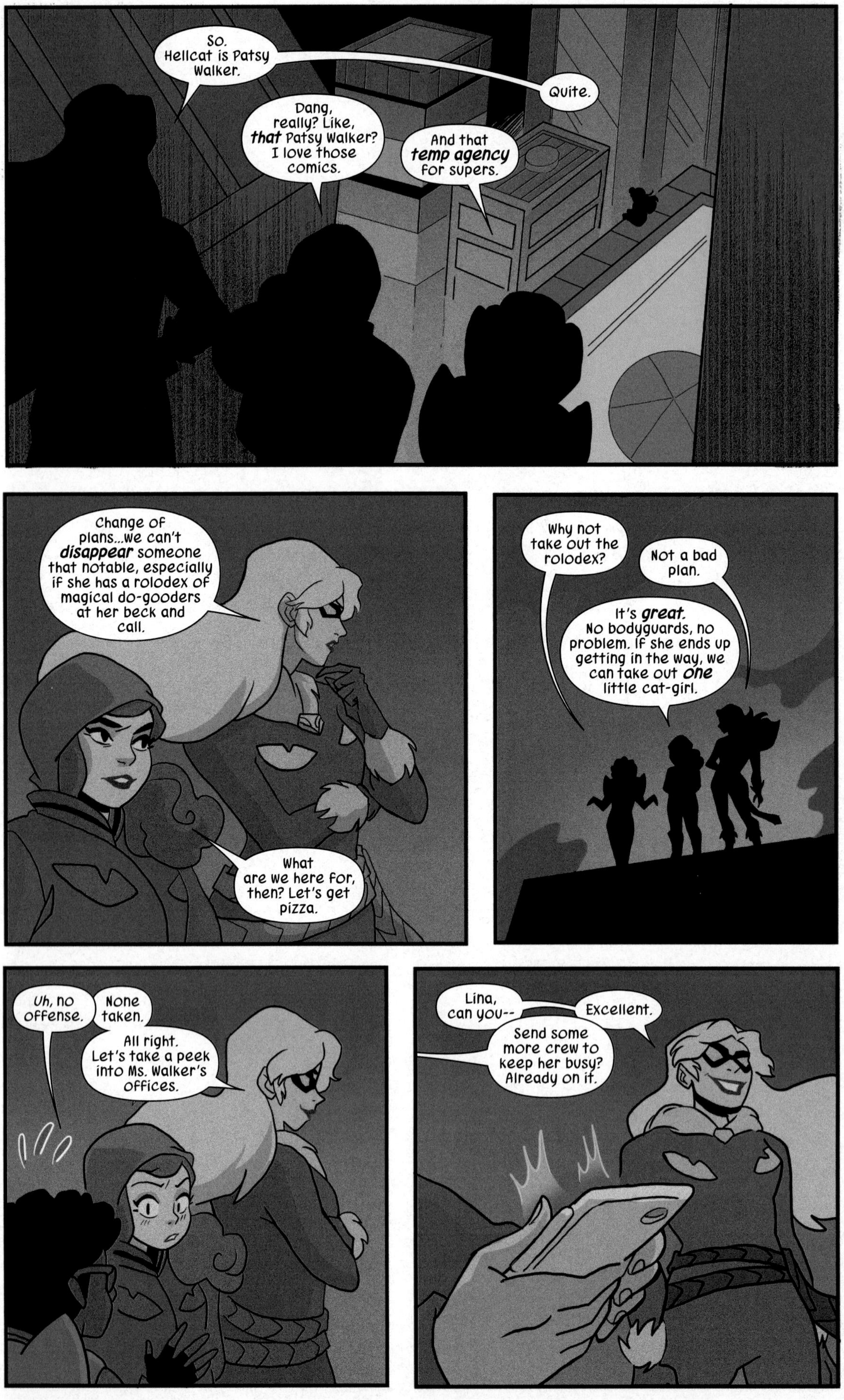
So. Hellcat is Patsy Walker.
Quite.
Dang, really? Like, *that* Patsy Walker? I love those comics.
And that *temp agency* for supers.
Change of plans...we can't *disappear* someone that notable, especially if she has a rolodex of magical do-gooders at her beck and call.
What are we here for, then? Let's get pizza.
Why not take out the rolodex?
Not a bad plan.
It's *great.* No bodyguards, no problem. If she ends up getting in the way, we can take out *one* little cat-girl.
Uh, no offense.
None taken.
All right. Let's take a peek into Ms. Walker's offices.
Lina, can you--
Excellent.
Send some more crew to keep her busy? Already on it.

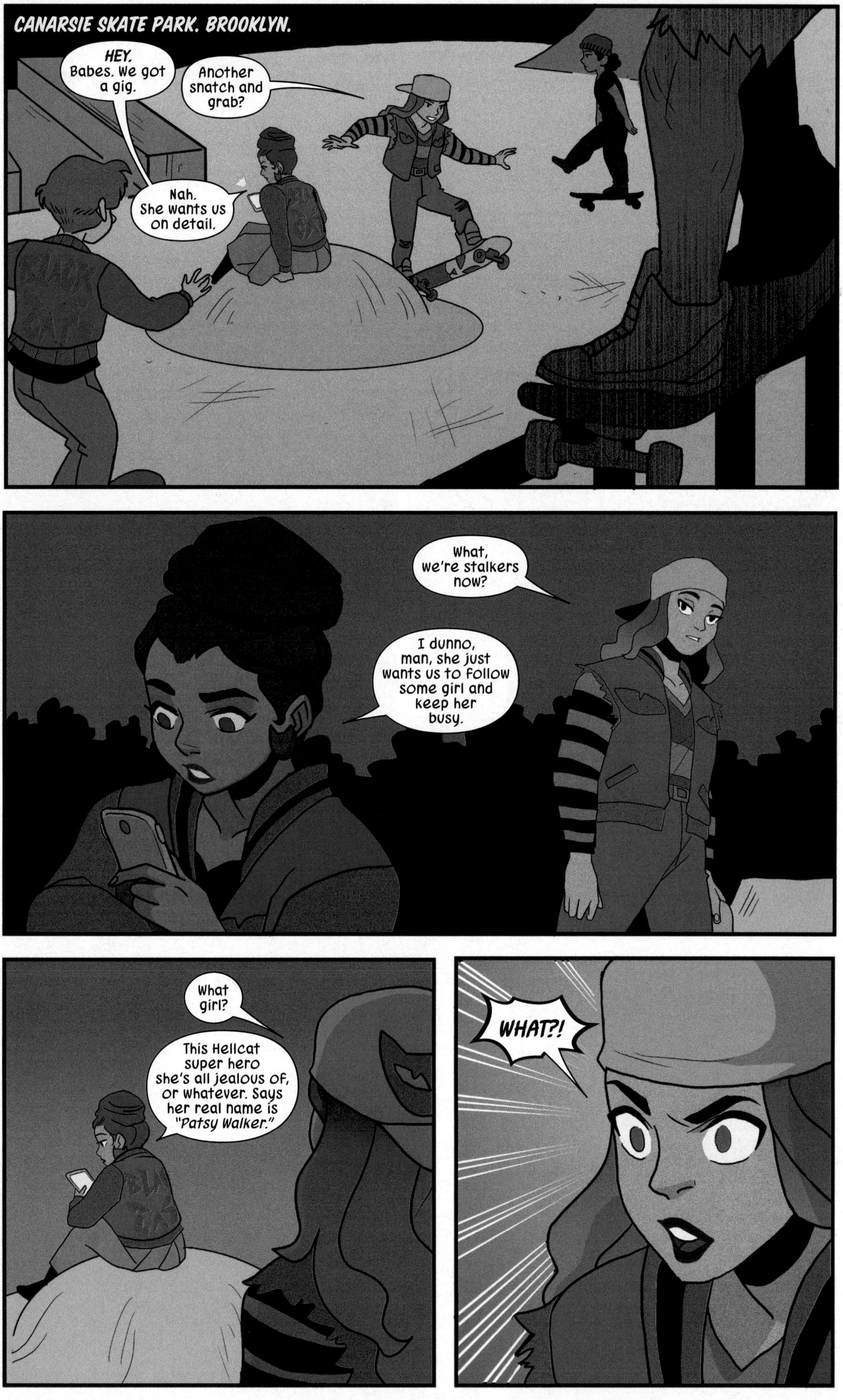
CANARSIE SKATE PARK. BROOKLYN.
HEY. Babes. We got a gig.
Another snatch and grab?
Nah. She wants us on detail.
What, we're stalkers now?
I dunno, man, she just wants us to follow some girl and keep her busy.
What girl?
This Hellcat super hero she's all jealous of, or whatever. Says her real name is "Patsy Walker."
WHAT?!

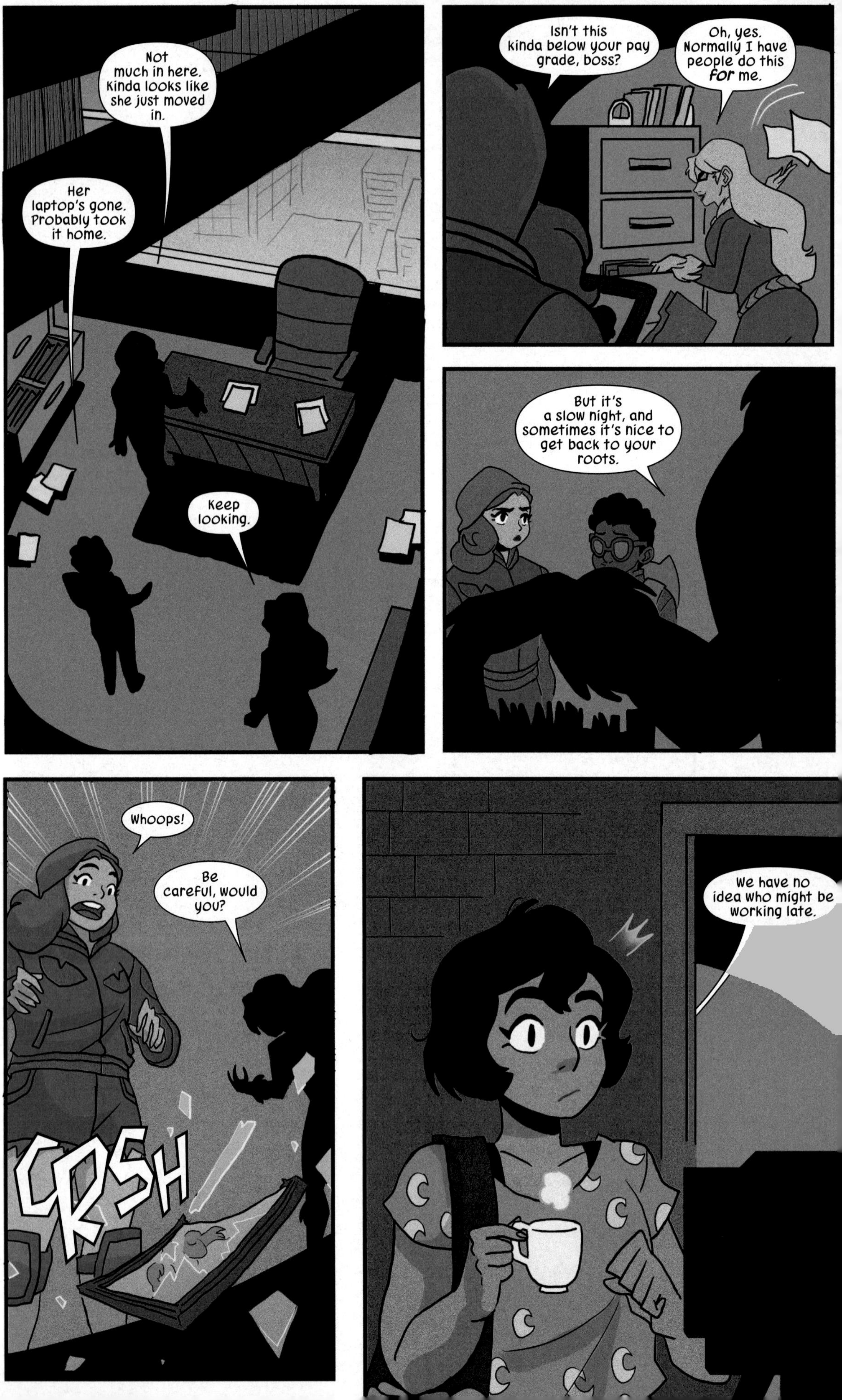
Not much in here. Kinda looks like she just moved in.
Her laptop's gone. Probably took it home.
Keep looking.
Isn't this kinda below your pay grade, boss?
Oh, yes. Normally I have people do this for me.
But it's a slow night, and sometimes it's nice to get back to your roots.
Whoops!
Be careful, would you?
CRSH
We have no idea who might be working late.

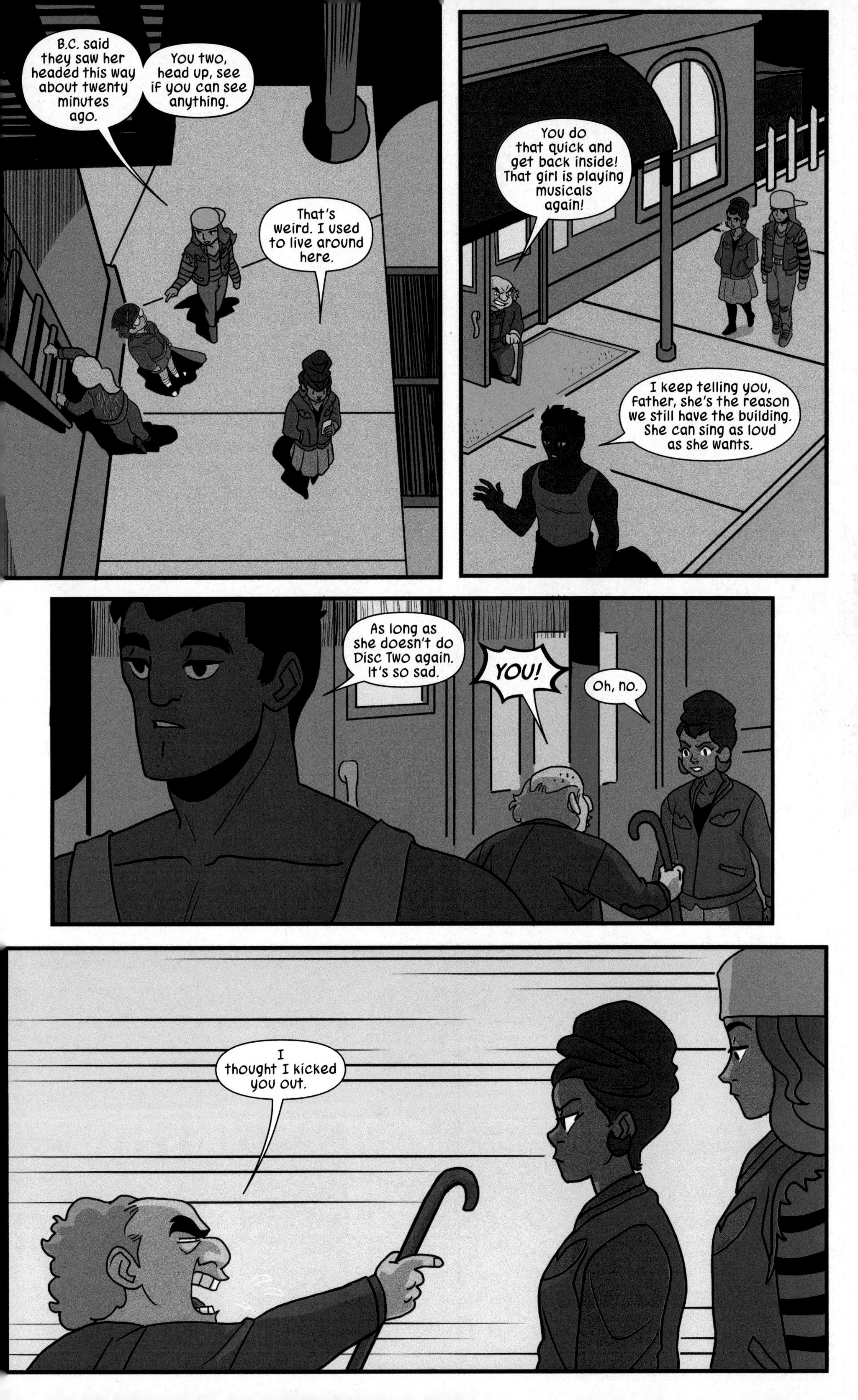
B.C. said they saw her headed this way about twenty minutes ago.
You two, head up, see if you can see anything.
That's weird. I used to live around here.
You do that quick and get back inside! That girl is playing musicals again!
I keep telling you, father, she's the reason we still have the building. She can sing as loud as she wants.
As long as she doesn't do Disc Two again. It's so sad.
YOU!
Oh, no.
I thought I kicked you out.

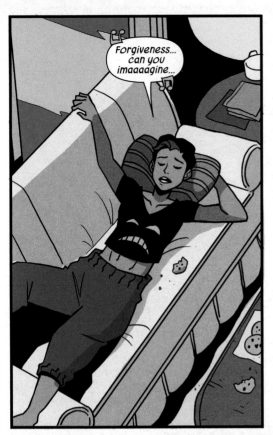

Forgiveness... can you imaaaagine...

Heeey, Ian.

It's =sniff= quiet... uptown...

Hoo boy. Disc Two, huh?

I'm...I'm sorry, Pats. I didn't mean to run off. I know I'm being weird.

It's okay. I get it. I didn't mean to push you, you know, I just...

Things were finally *good*, you know? I had the job, I met Tom, and you, and it was *nice*.

Life wasn't great before, and then it was okay, but it all went to *hell*.

I get *scared*, Pats. I don't want to lose this. Any of it.

Hey, hey. It's all right. I'm not going anywhere. Nobody's making you fight.

Are you sure?

Of course. *I'm* the muscle, remember?

CHK

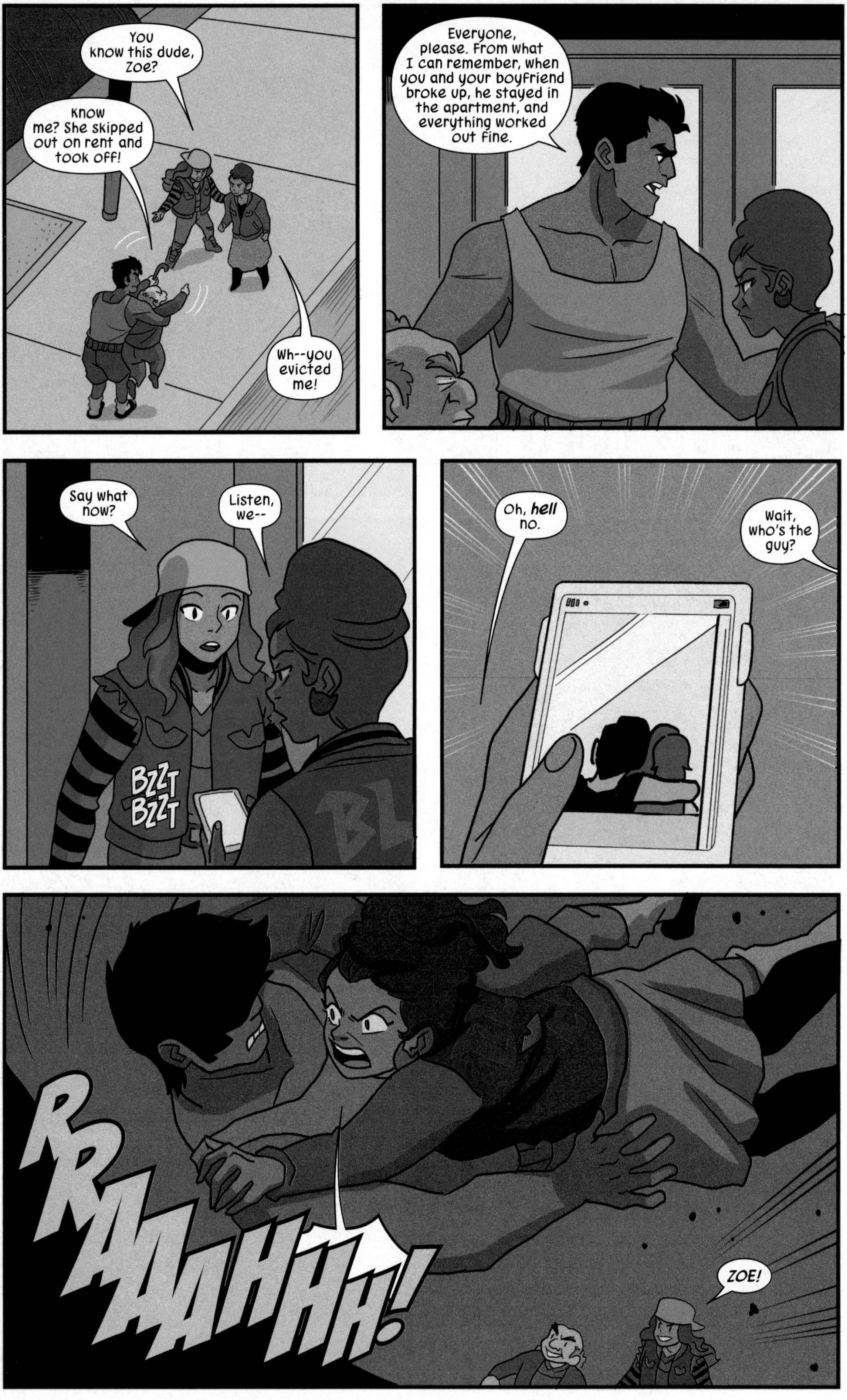

You know this dude, Zoe?
Know me? She skipped out on rent and took off!
Wh--you evicted me!
Everyone, please. From what I can remember, when you and your boyfriend broke up, he stayed in the apartment, and everything worked out fine.
Say what now?
Listen, we--
BZZT BZZT
Oh, hell no.
Wait, who's the guy?
RRAAAHHHH!
ZOE!

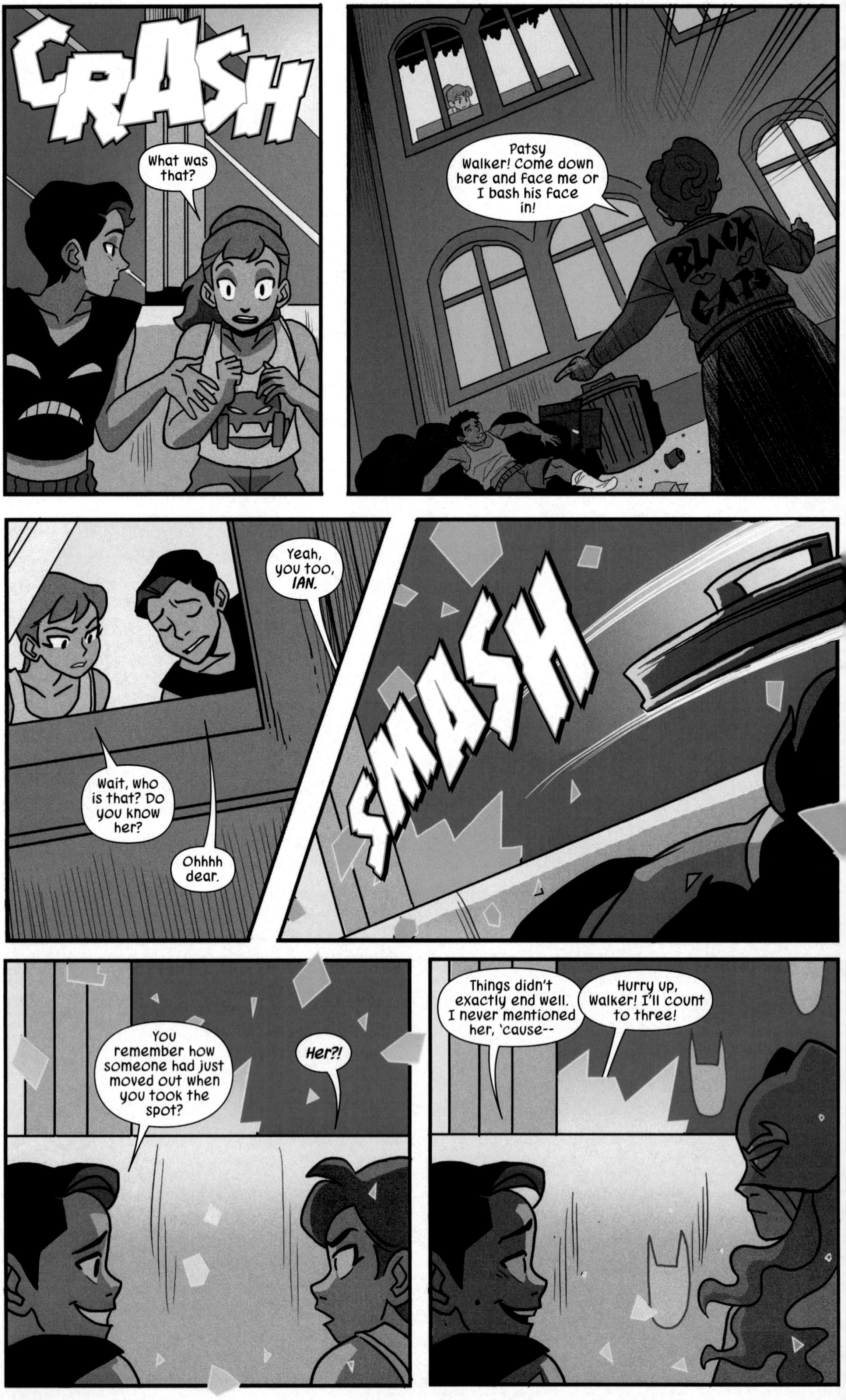
CRASH
What was that?
Patsy Walker! Come down here and face me or I bash his face in!
BLACK CATS
Yeah, you too, IAN.
Wait, who is that? Do you know her?
Ohhhh dear.
SMASH
You remember how someone had just moved out when you took the spot?
Her?!
Things didn't exactly end well. I never mentioned her, 'cause--
Hurry up, Walker! I'll count to three!

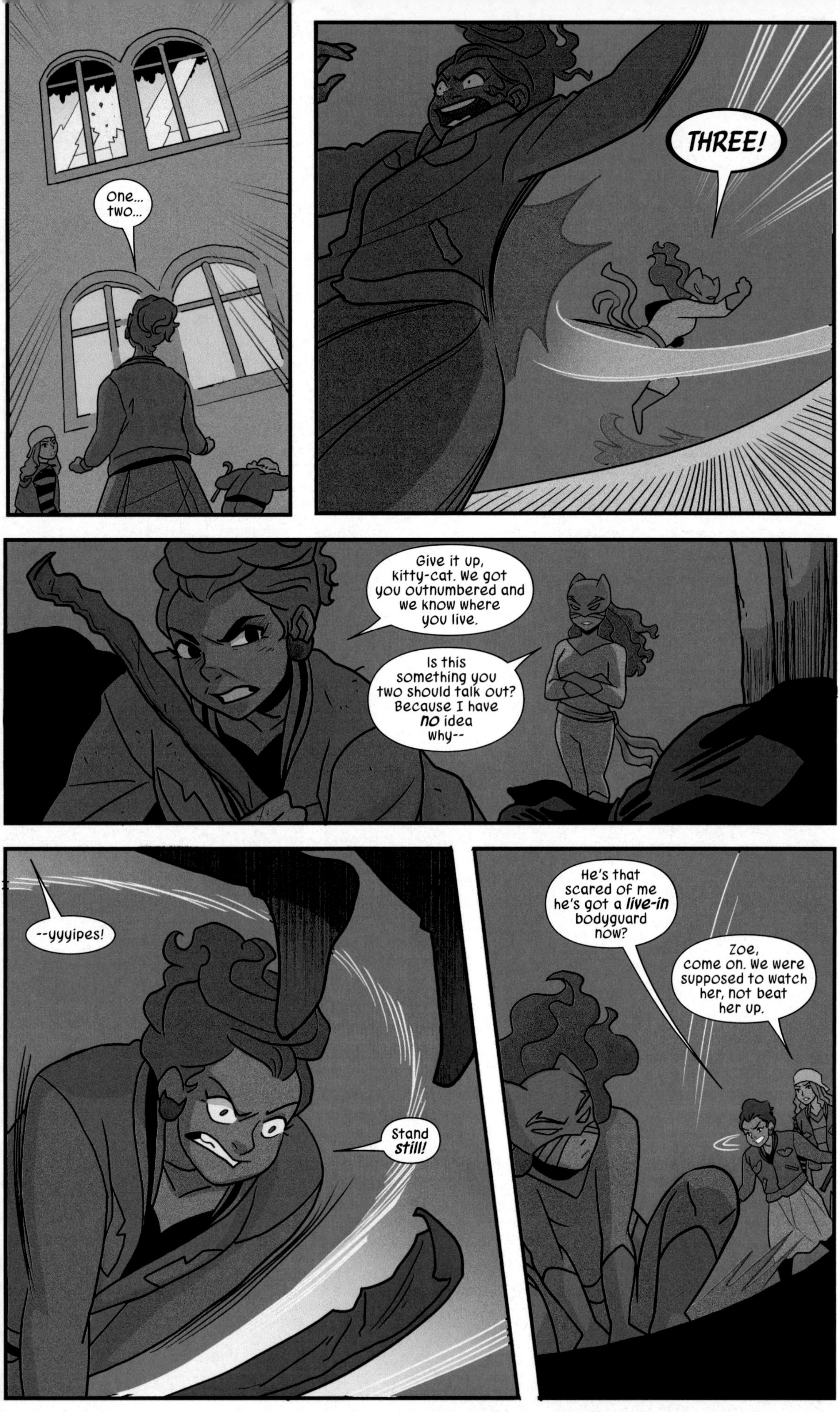
One... two...
THREE!
Give it up, kitty-cat. We got you outnumbered and we know where you live.
Is this something you two should talk out? Because I have *no* idea why--
--yyyipes!
Stand *still!*
He's that scared of me he's got a *live-in* bodyguard now?
Zoe, come on. We were supposed to watch her, not beat her up.

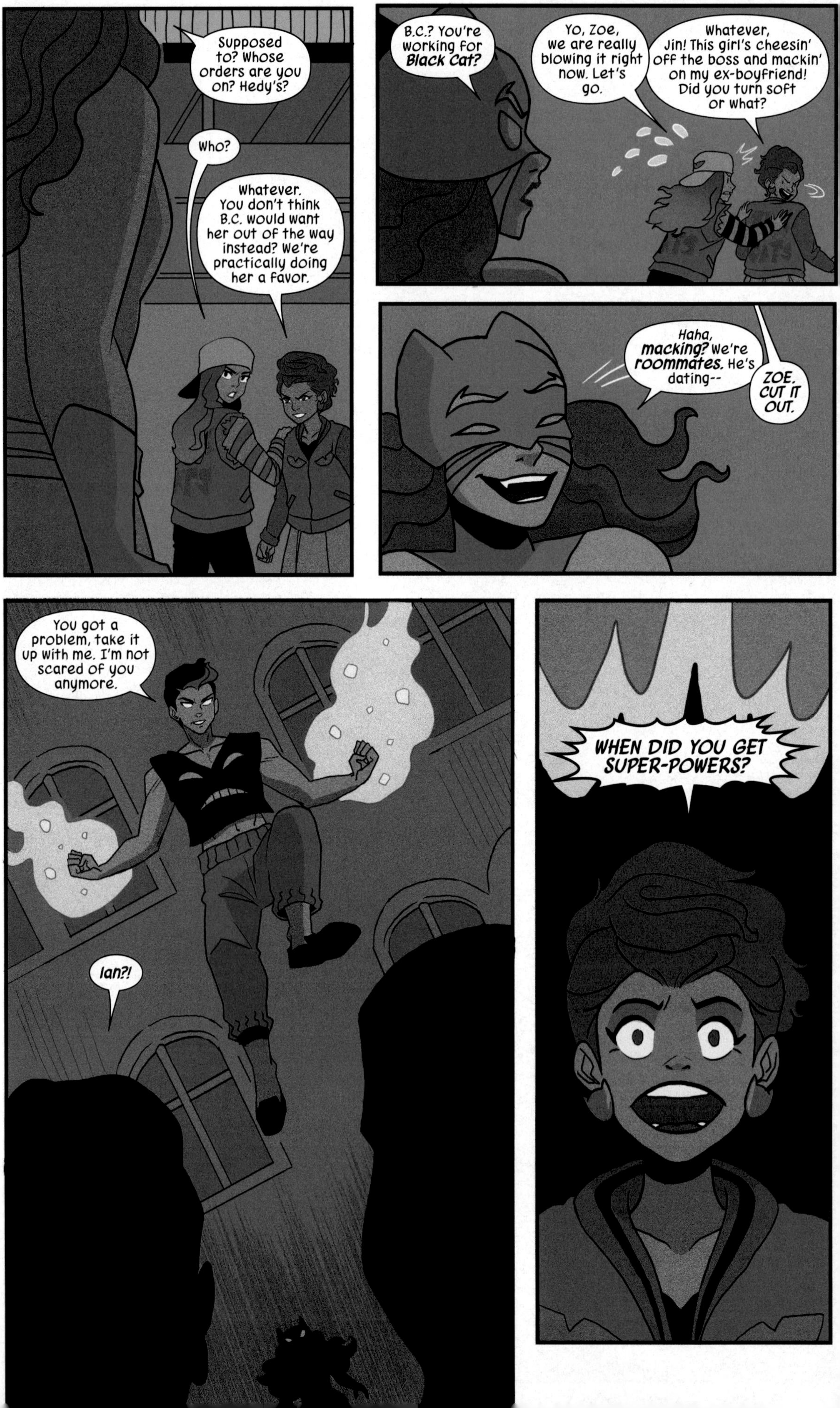
Supposed to? Whose orders are you on? Hedy's?
Who?
Whatever. You don't think B.C. would want her out of the way instead? We're practically doing her a favor.
B.C.? You're working for Black Cat?
Yo, Zoe, we are really blowing it right now. Let's go.
Whatever, Jin! This girl's cheesin' off the boss and mackin' on my ex-boyfriend! Did you turn soft or what?
Haha, macking? We're roommates. He's dating--
ZOE. CUT IT OUT.
You got a problem, take it up with me. I'm not scared of you anymore.
Ian?!
WHEN DID YOU GET SUPER-POWERS?

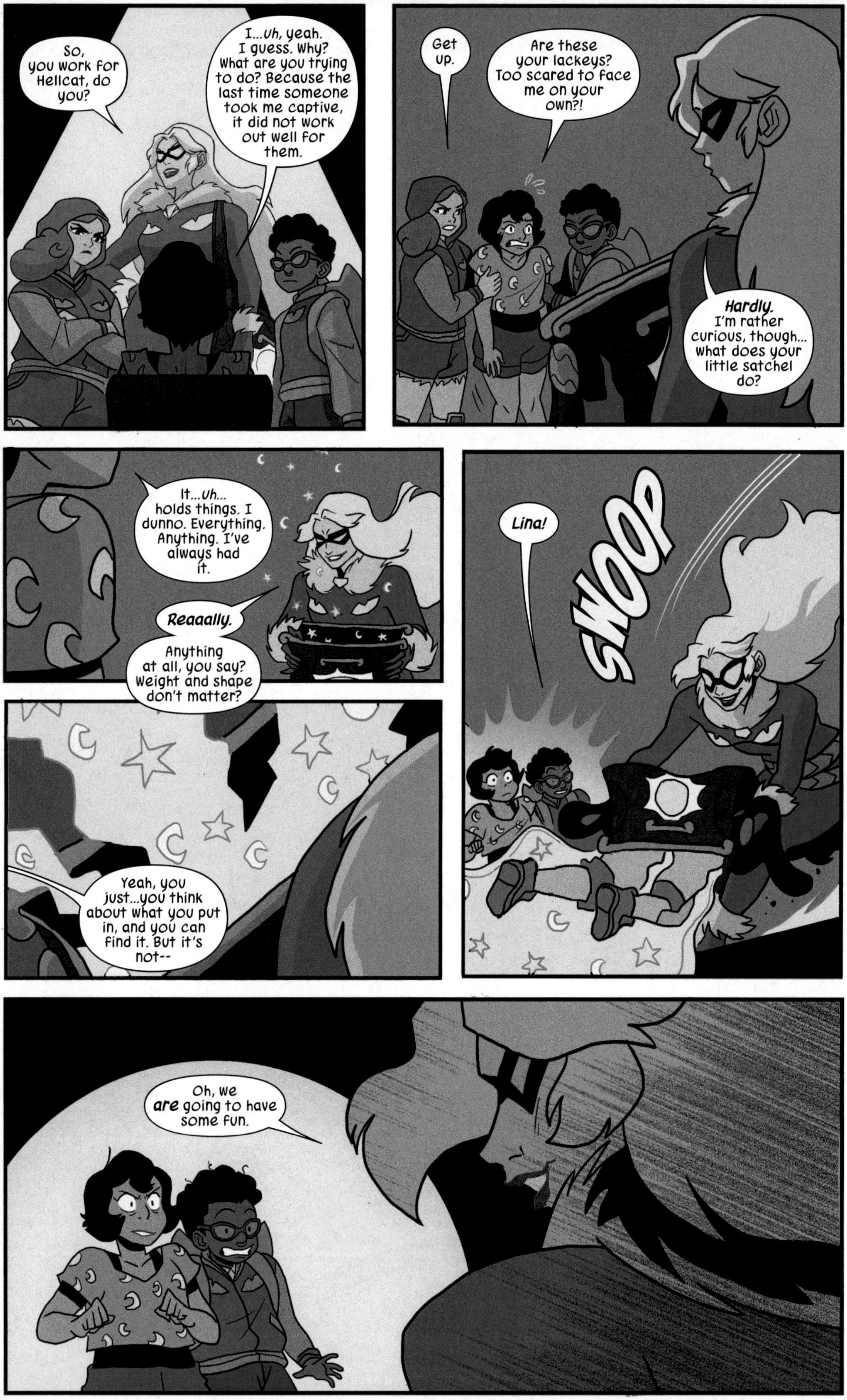
So, you work for Hellcat, do you?
I...uh, yeah. I guess. Why? What are you trying to do? Because the last time someone took me captive, it did not work out well for them.
Get up.
Are these your lackeys? Too scared to face me on your own?!
Hardly. I'm rather curious, though... what does your little satchel do?
It...uh... holds things. I dunno. Everything. Anything. I've always had it.
Reaaally.
Anything at all, you say? Weight and shape don't matter?
Yeah, you just...you think about what you put in, and you can find it. But it's not--
Lina!
SWOOP
Oh, we are going to have some fun.

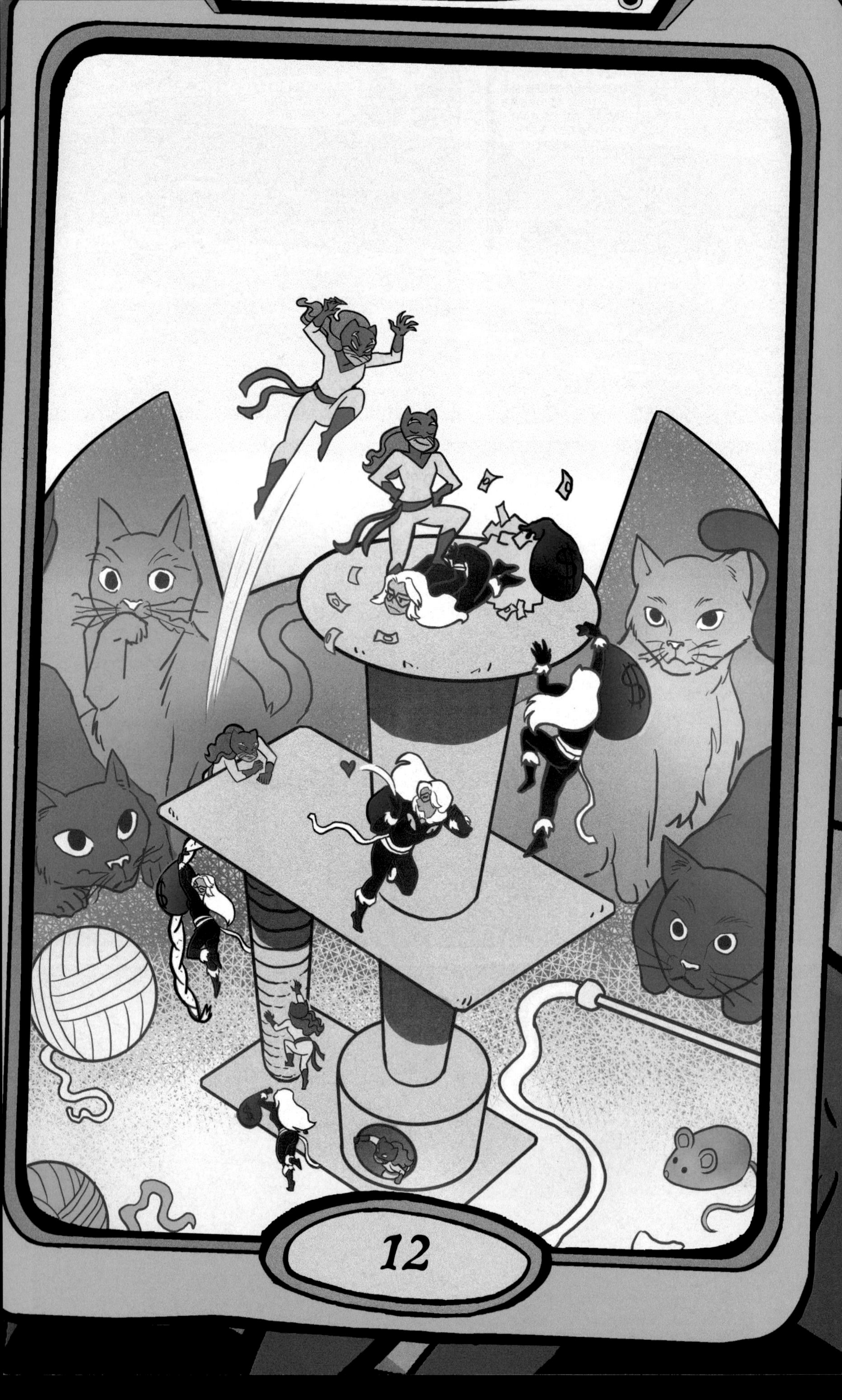
12

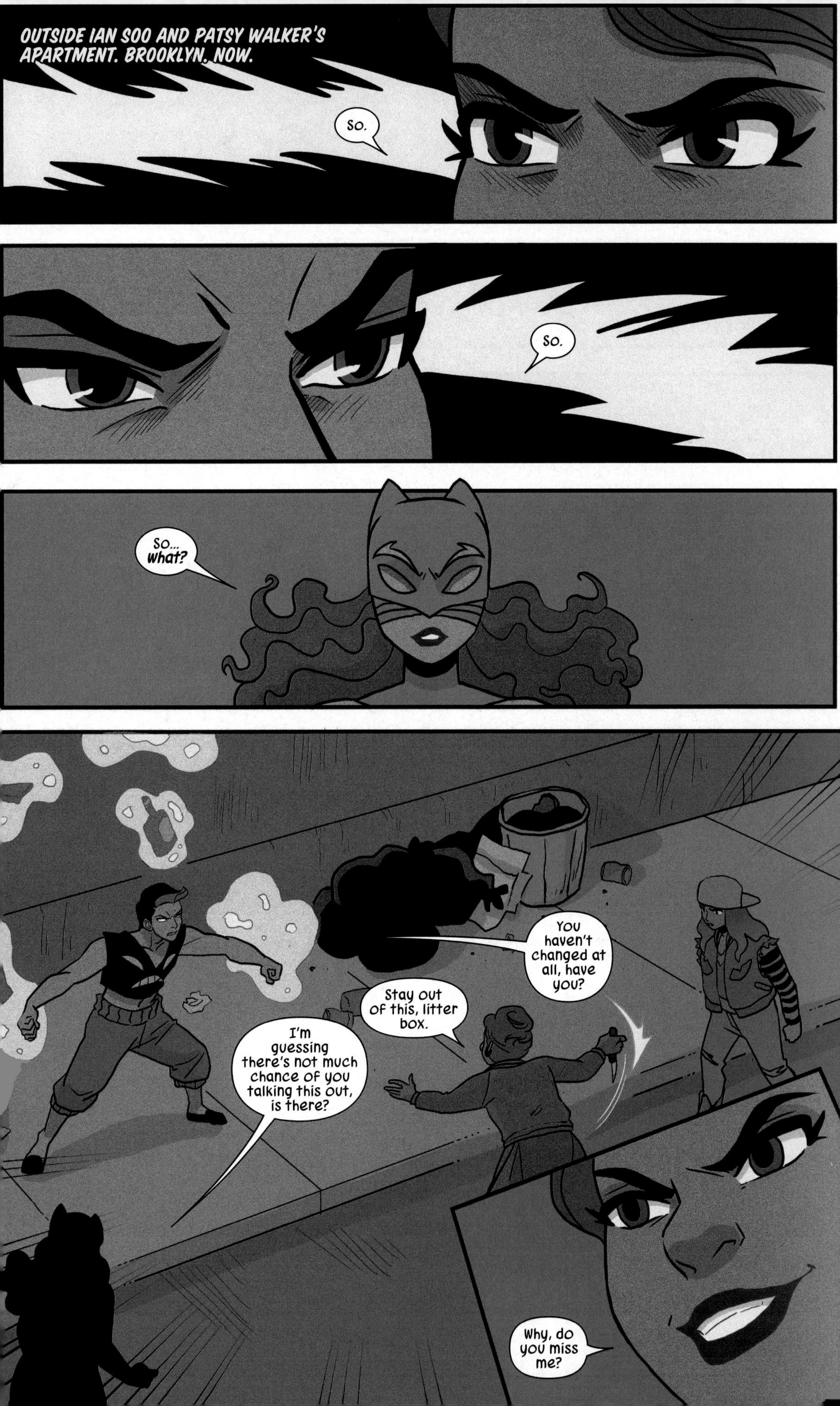
OUTSIDE IAN SOO AND PATSY WALKER'S APARTMENT. BROOKLYN. NOW.
SO.
SO.
SO... what?
You haven't changed at all, have you?
Stay out of this, litter box.
I'm guessing there's not much chance of you talking this out, is there?
Why, do you miss me?

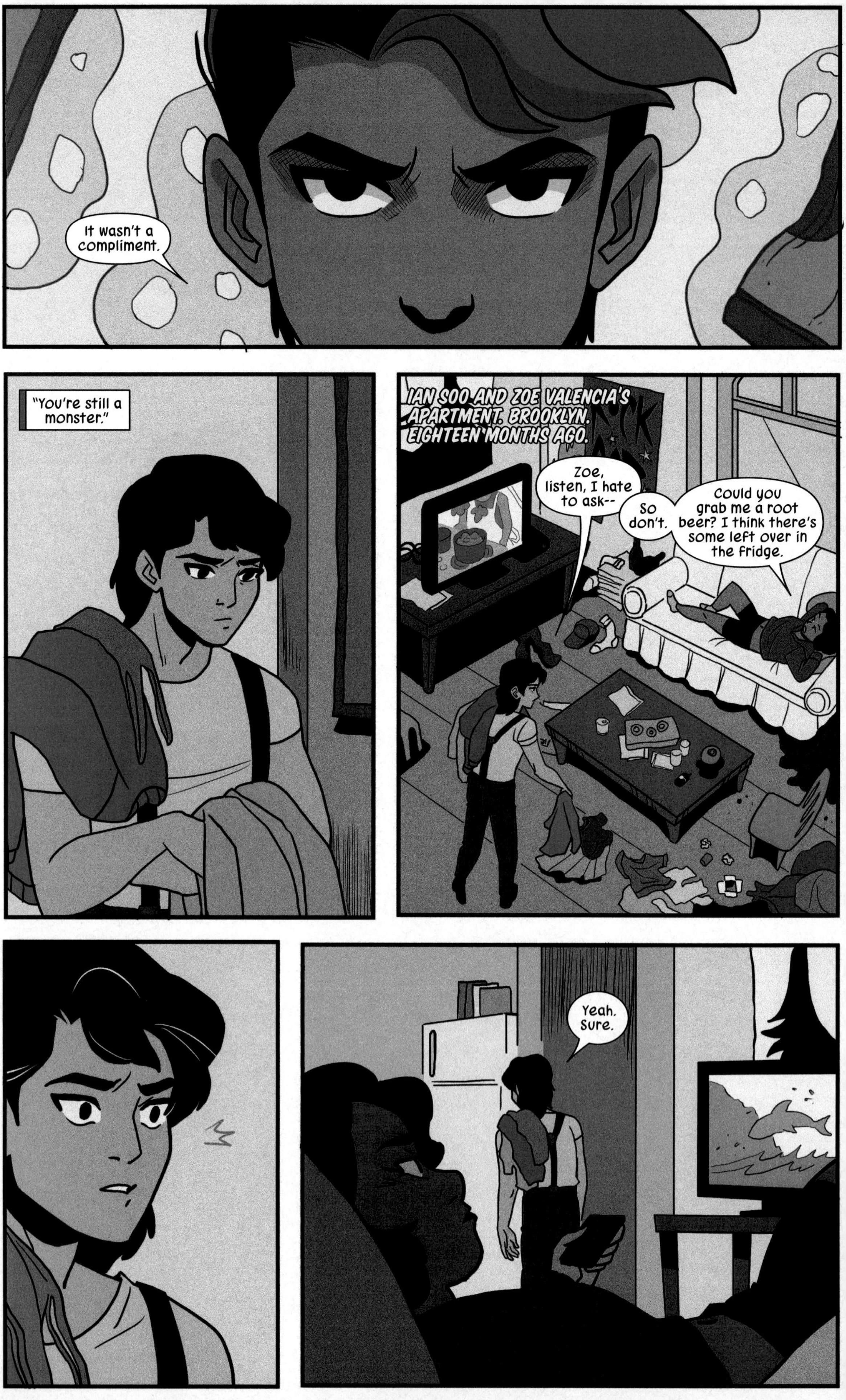
It wasn't a compliment.
"You're still a monster."
IAN SOO AND ZOE VALENCIA'S APARTMENT. BROOKLYN. EIGHTEEN MONTHS AGO.
Zoe, listen, I hate to ask--
So don't.
Could you grab me a root beer? I think there's some left over in the fridge.
Yeah. Sure.

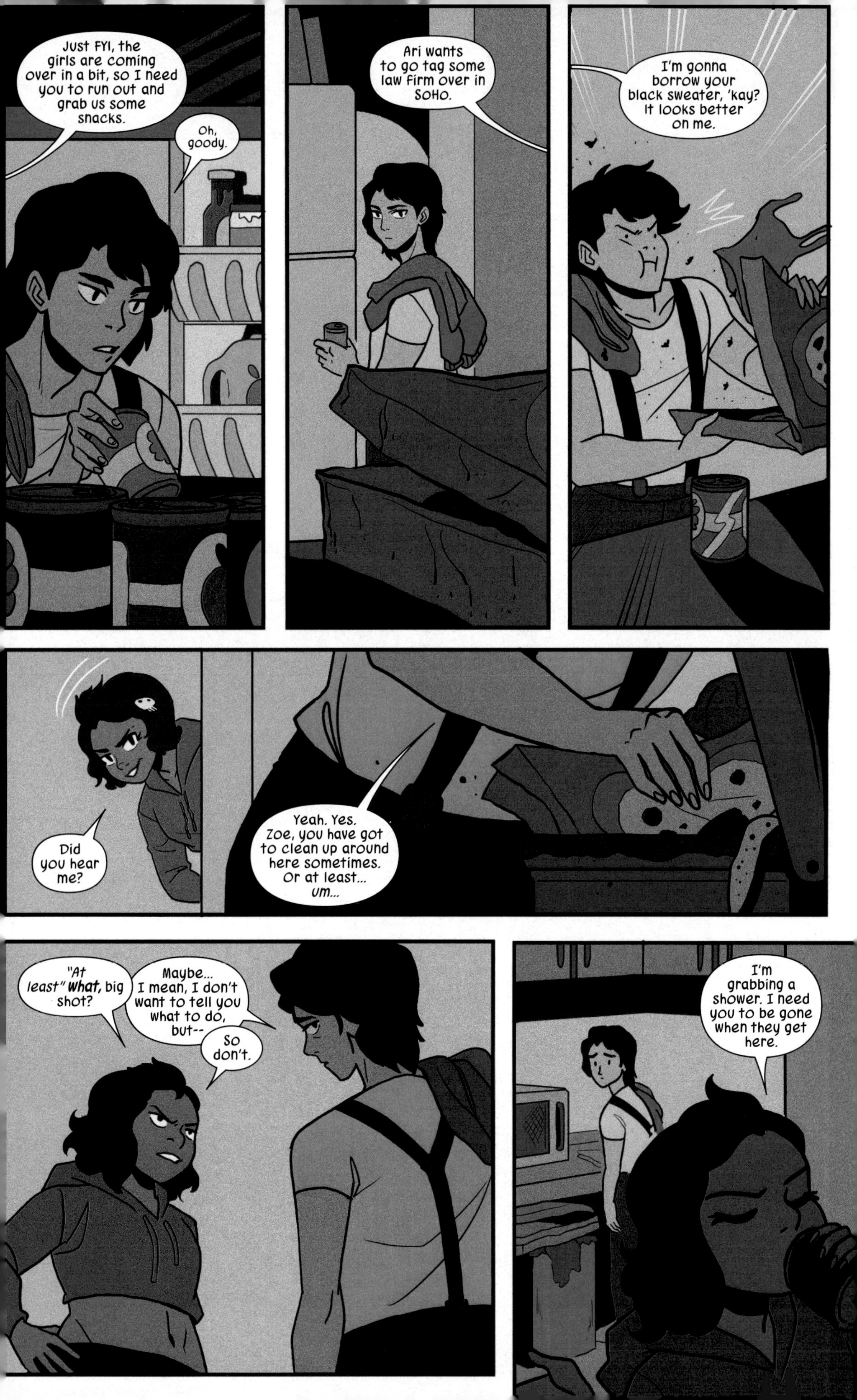
Just FYI, the girls are coming over in a bit, so I need you to run out and grab us some snacks.
Oh, goody.
Ari wants to go tag some law firm over in SOHO.
I'm gonna borrow your black sweater, 'kay? It looks better on me.
Did you hear me?
Yeah. Yes. Zoe, you have got to clean up around here sometimes. Or at least... um...
"At least" what, big shot?
Maybe... I mean, I don't want to tell you what to do, but--
So don't.
I'm grabbing a shower. I need you to be gone when they get here.

Hey! We need toilet paper, too. Chop-chop, pretty boy.

AAHCK!

Right. What was I thinking?

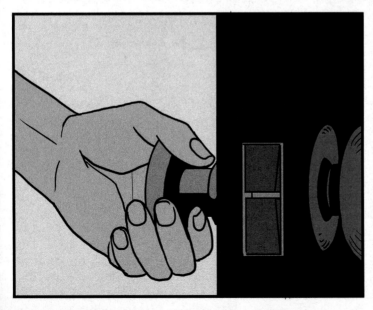

And then the Terrigen Mist happened.

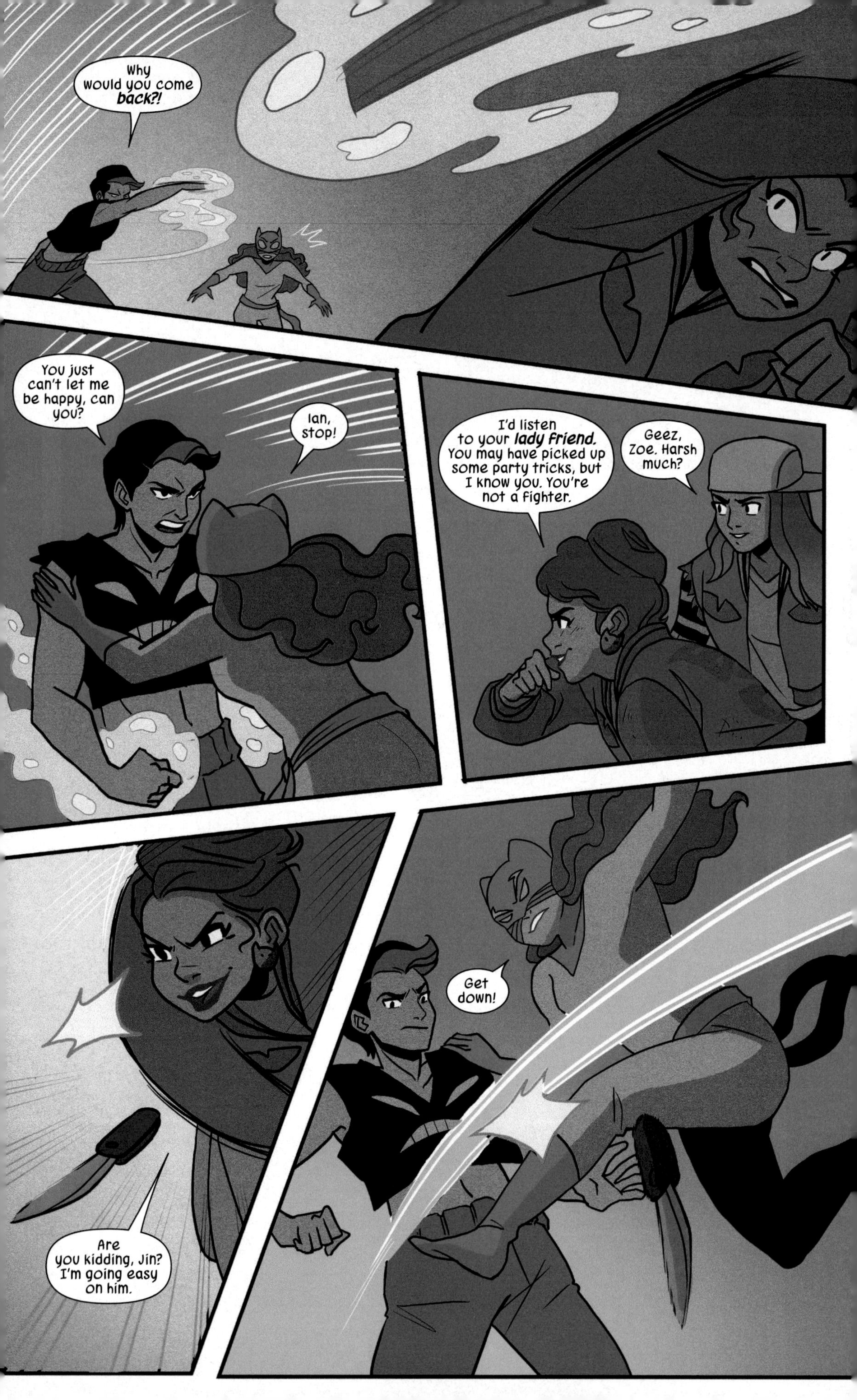
Why would you come back?!
You just can't let me be happy, can you?
Ian, stop!
I'd listen to your lady friend. You may have picked up some party tricks, but I know you. You're not a fighter.
Geez, Zoe. Harsh much?
Are you kidding, Jin? I'm going easy on him.
Get down!

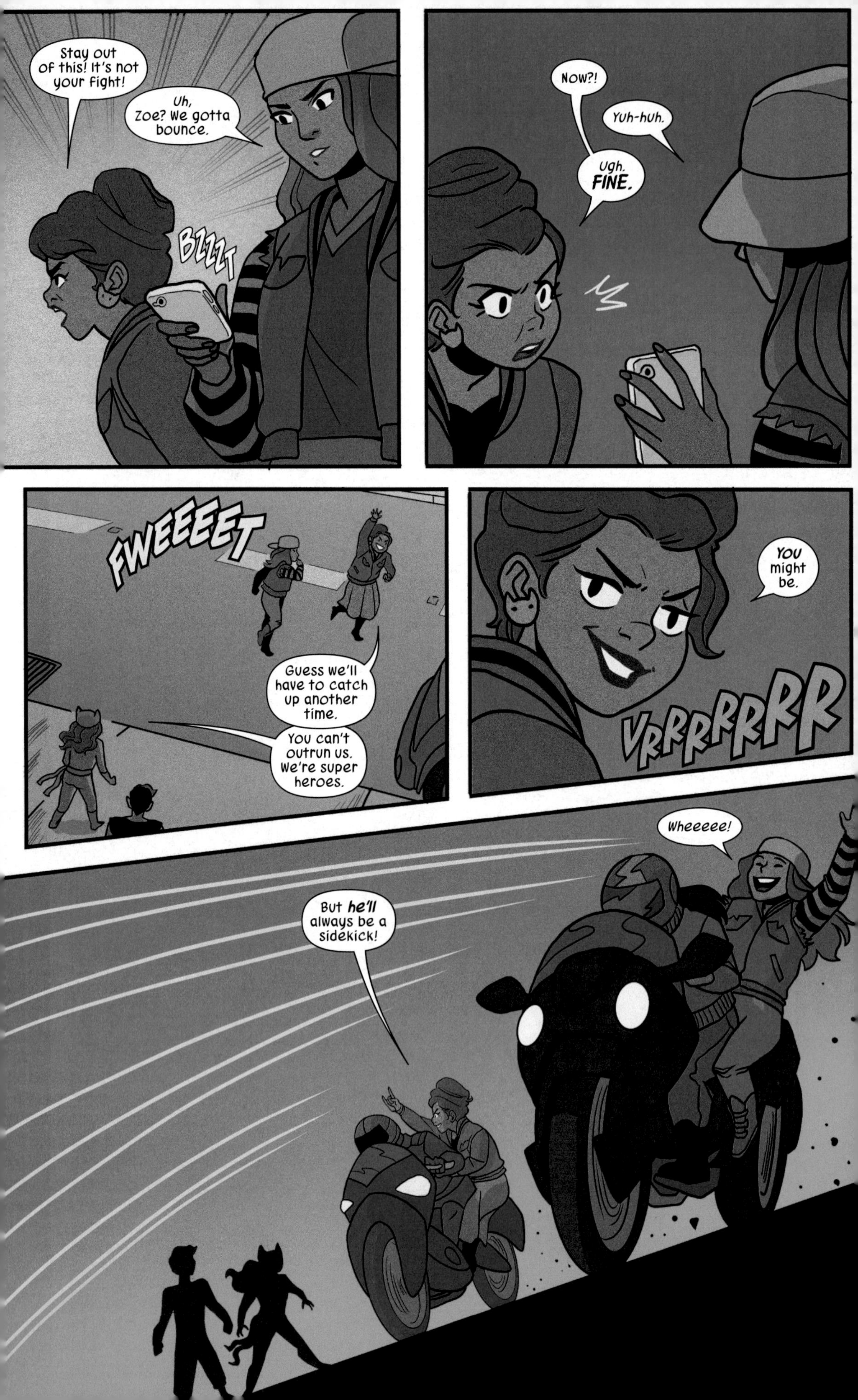
Stay out of this! It's not your fight!
Uh, Zoe? We gotta bounce.
BZZZT
NOW?!
Yuh-huh.
Ugh. FINE.
FWEEEET
Guess we'll have to catch up another time.
You can't outrun us. We're super heroes.
YOU might be.
VRRRRRRR
Wheeeee!
But he'll always be a sidekick!

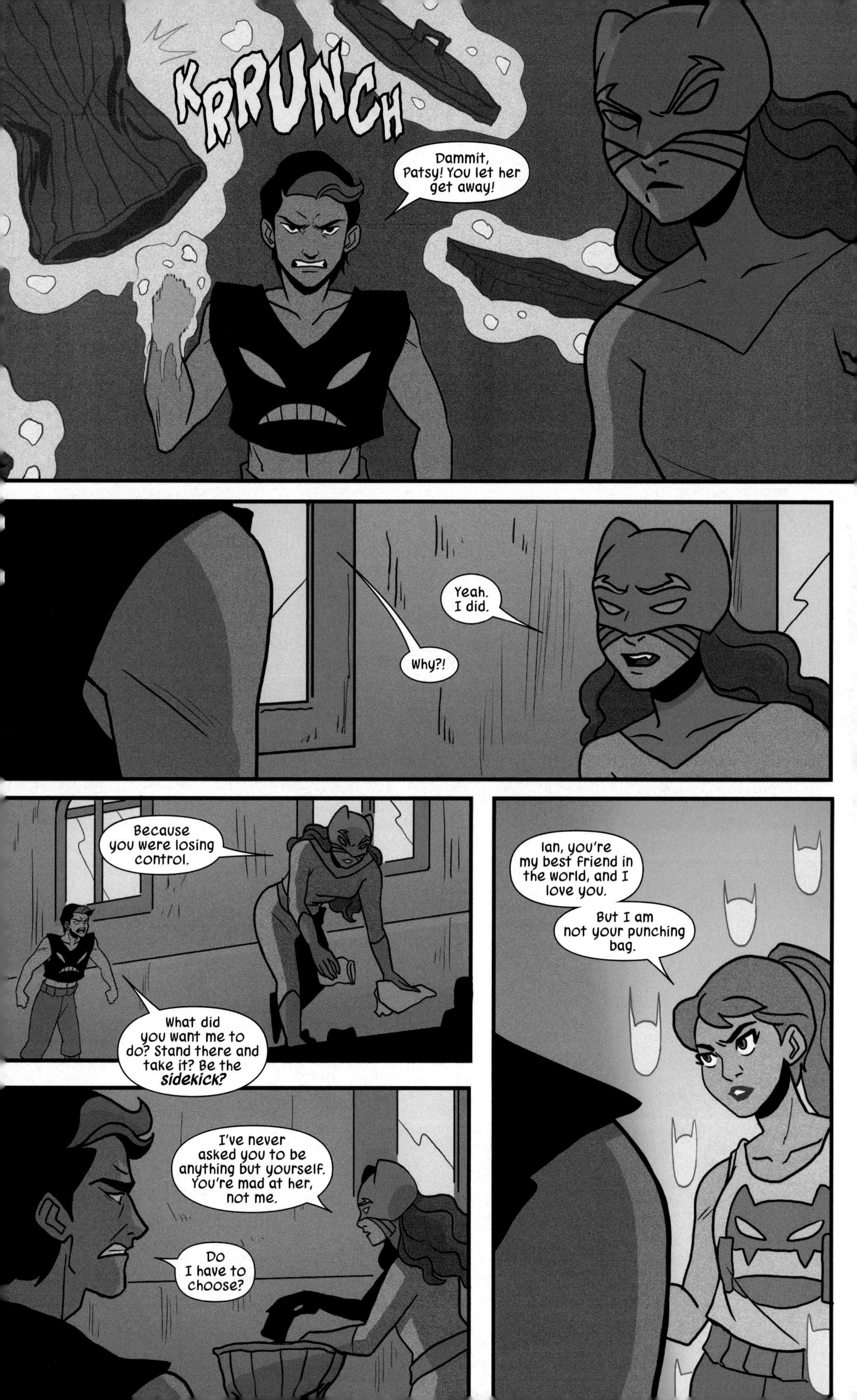
KRRUNCH
Dammit, Patsy! You let her get away!
Yeah. I did.
Why?!
Because you were losing control.
What did you want me to do? Stand there and take it? Be the *sidekick?*
I've never asked you to be anything but yourself. You're mad at her, not me.
Do I have to choose?
Ian, you're my best friend in the world, and I love you.
But I am not your punching bag.

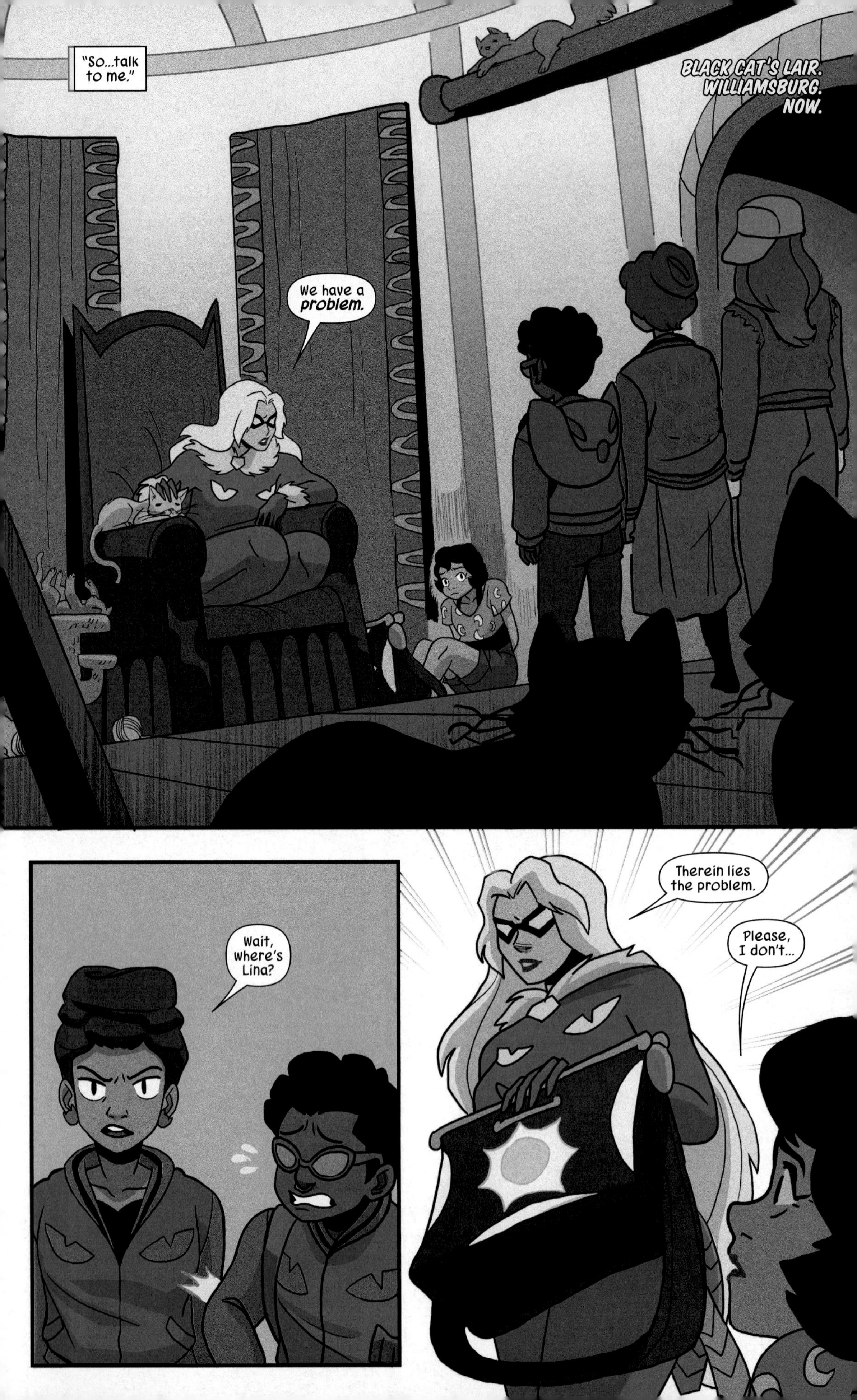
"So...talk to me."
BLACK CAT'S LAIR. WILLIAMSBURG. NOW.
We have a problem.
Wait, where's Lina?
Therein lies the problem.
Please, I don't...

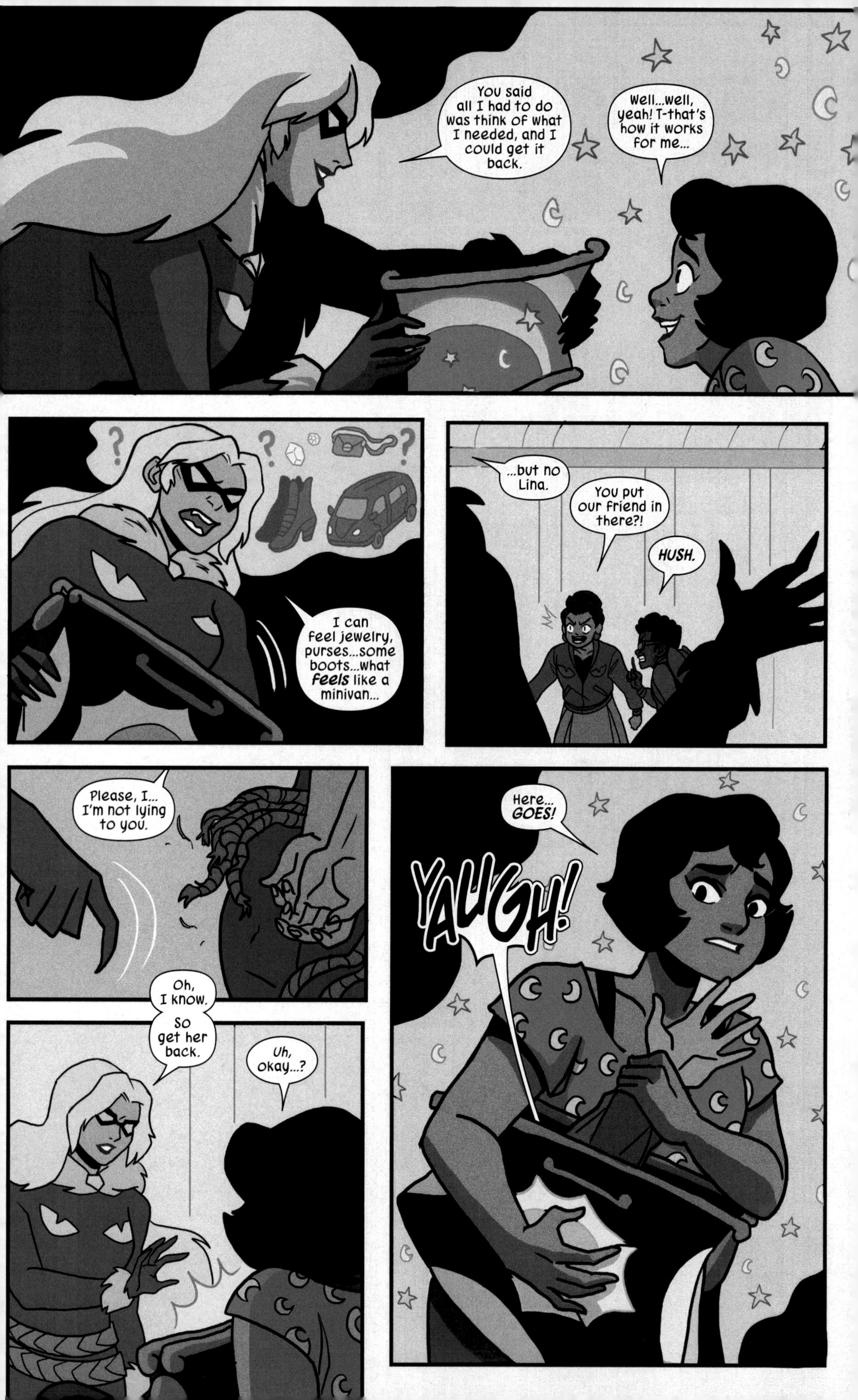
You said all I had to do was think of what I needed, and I could get it back.
Well...well, yeah! T-that's how it works for me...
I can feel jewelry, purses...some boots...what *feels* like a minivan...
...but no Lina.
You put our friend in there?!
HUSH.
Please, I... I'm not lying to you.
Oh, I know.
So get her back.
Uh, okay...?
Here... **GOES!**
YAUGH!

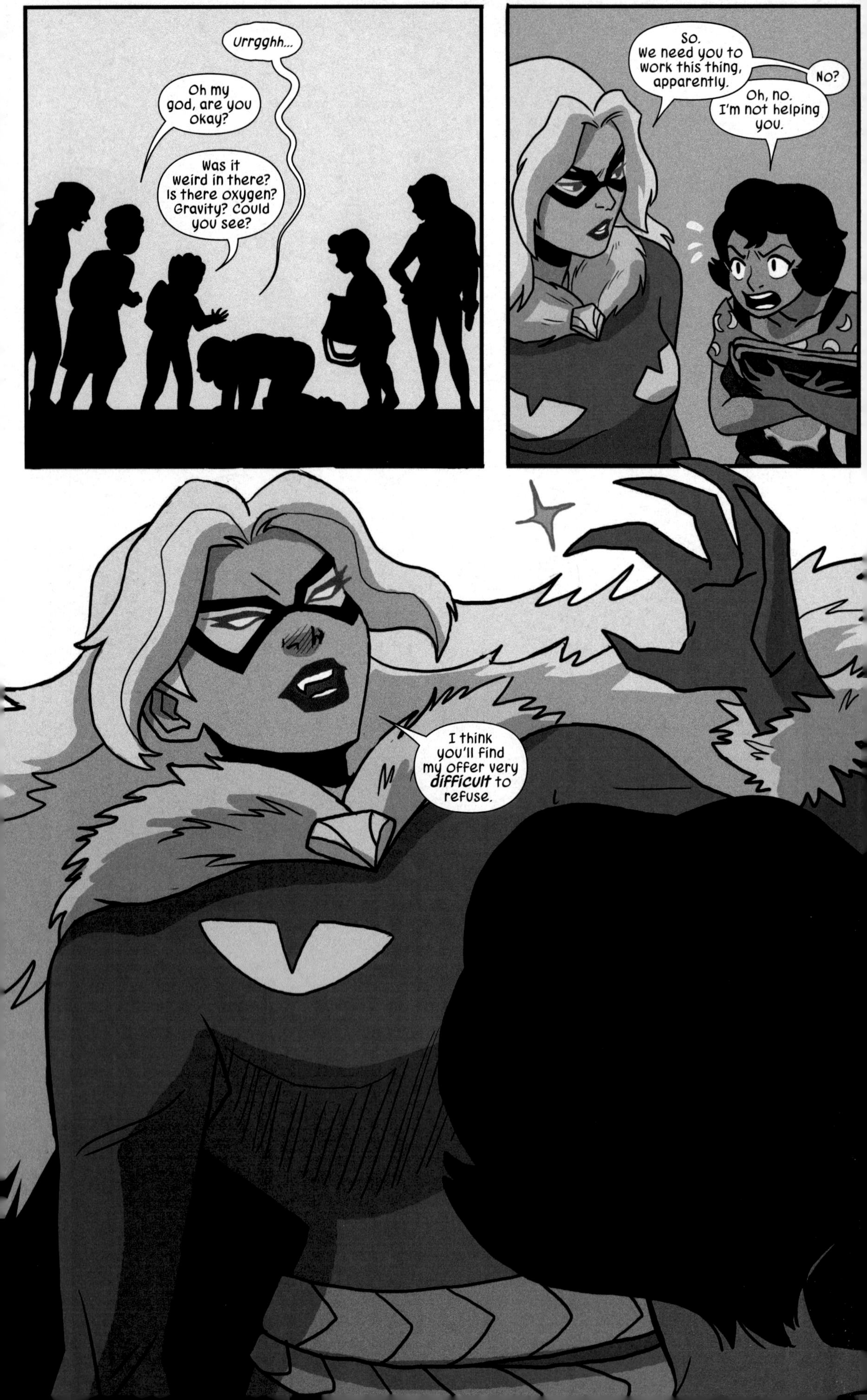
Urrgghh...
Oh my god, are you okay?
Was it weird in there? Is there oxygen? Gravity? Could you see?
So. We need you to work this thing, apparently.
No?
Oh, no. I'm not helping you.
I think you'll find my offer very *difficult* to refuse.

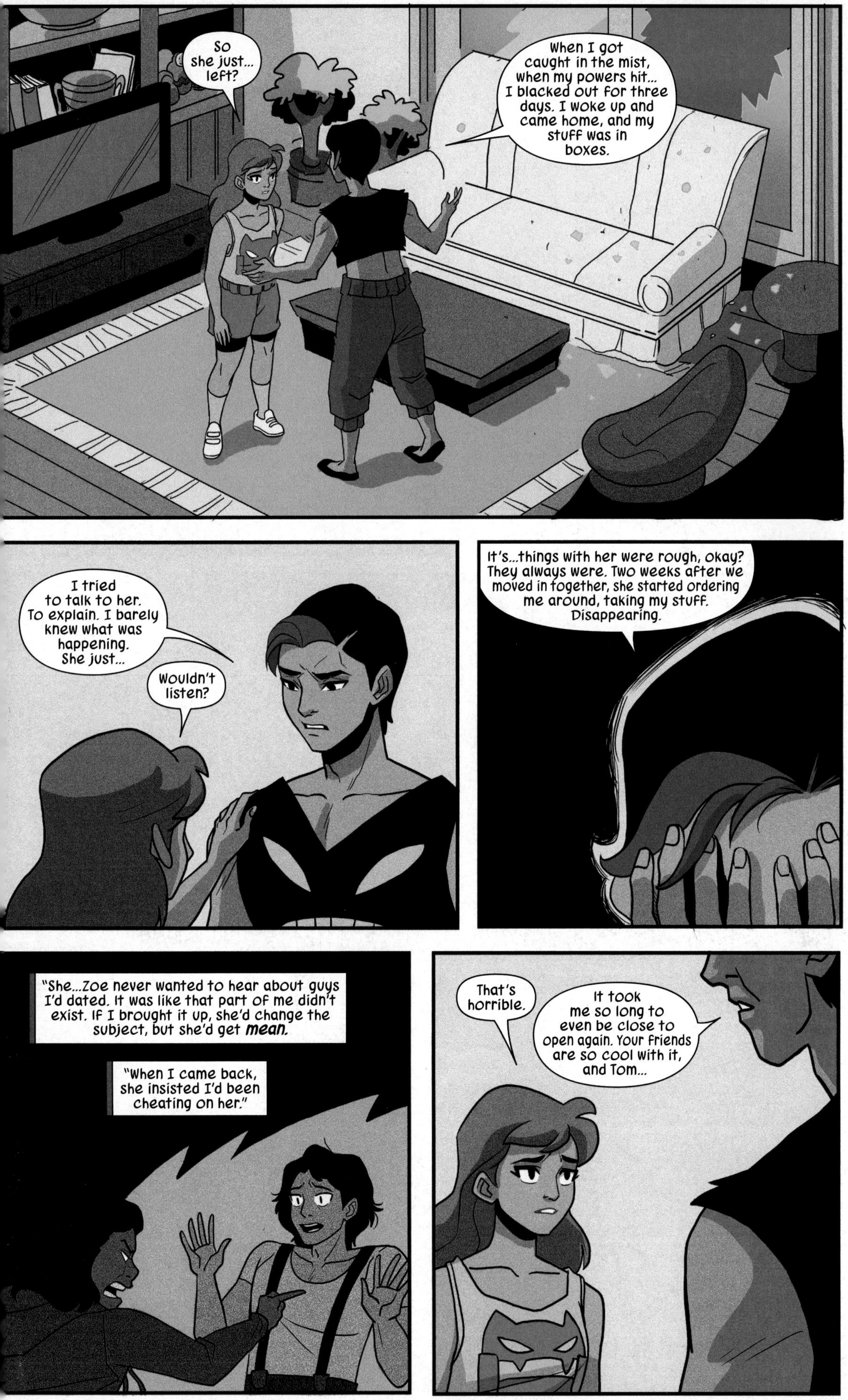
So she just... left?
When I got caught in the mist, when my powers hit... I blacked out for three days. I woke up and came home, and my stuff was in boxes.
I tried to talk to her. To explain. I barely knew what was happening. She just...
Wouldn't listen?
It's...things with her were rough, okay? They always were. Two weeks after we moved in together, she started ordering me around, taking my stuff. Disappearing.
"She...Zoe never wanted to hear about guys I'd dated. It was like that part of me didn't exist. If I brought it up, she'd change the subject, but she'd get *mean.*
"When I came back, she insisted I'd been cheating on her."
That's horrible.
It took me so long to even be close to open again. Your friends are so cool with it, and Tom...

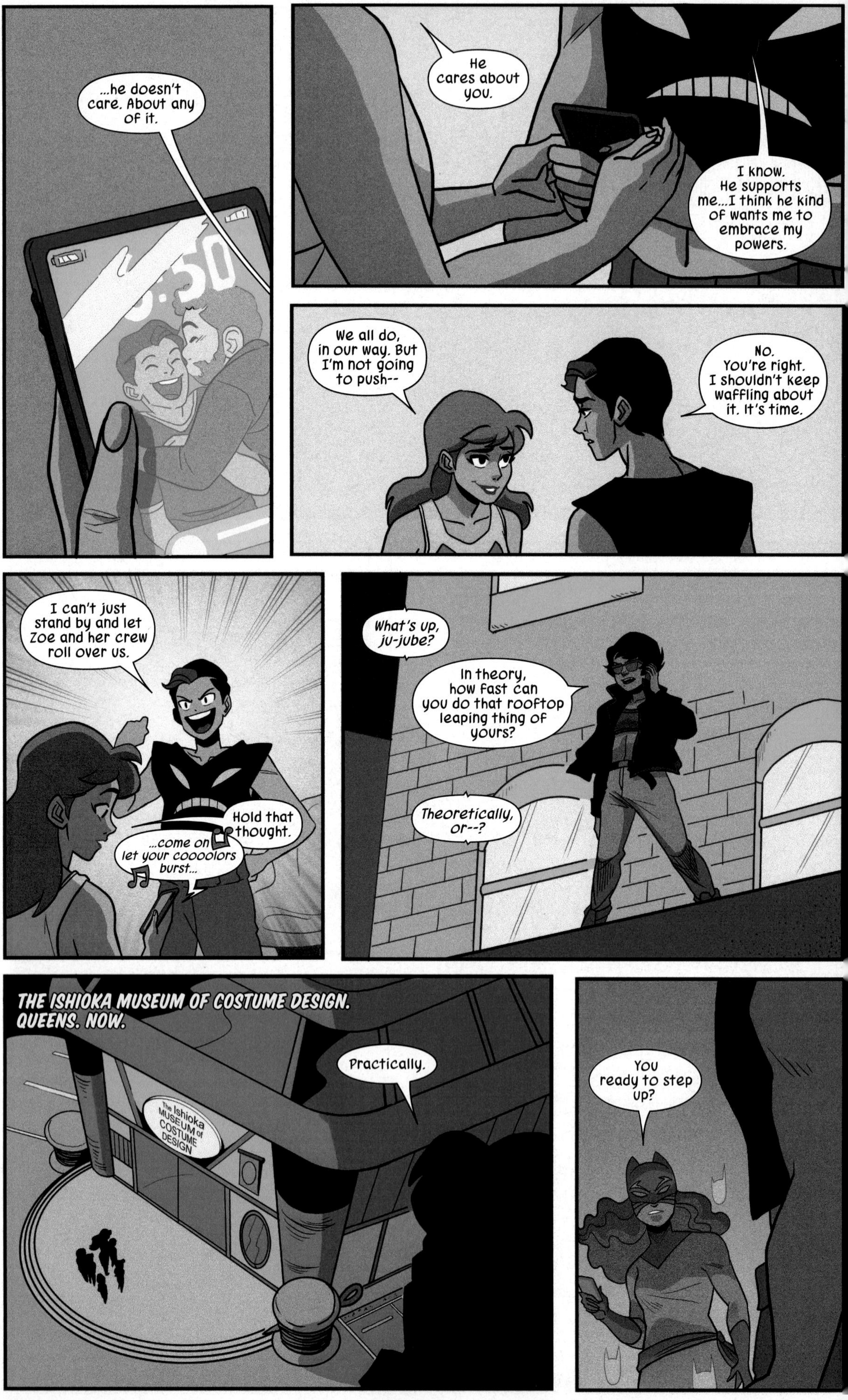
...he doesn't care. About any of it.
He cares about you.
I know. He supports me...I think he kind of wants me to embrace my powers.
We all do, in our way. But I'm not going to push--
No. You're right. I shouldn't keep waffling about it. It's time.
I can't just stand by and let Zoe and her crew roll over us.
...come on let your coooolors burst...
Hold that thought.
What's up, ju-jube?
In theory, how fast can you do that rooftop leaping thing of yours?
Theoretically, or--?
THE ISHIOKA MUSEUM OF COSTUME DESIGN. QUEENS. NOW.
The Ishioka MUSEUM of COSTUME DESIGN
Practically.
You ready to step up?

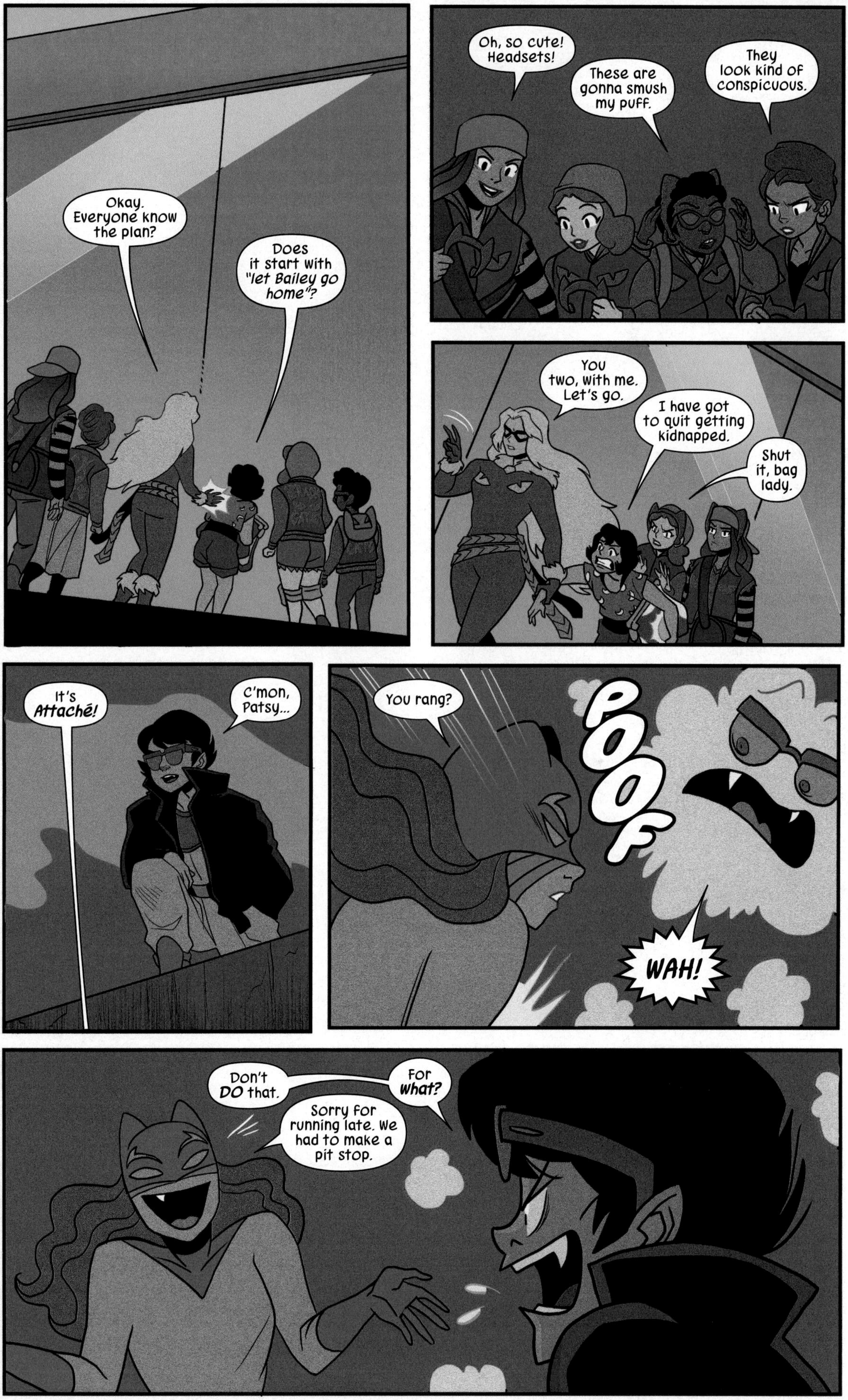
Okay. Everyone know the plan?
Does it start with "let Bailey go home"?
Oh, so cute! Headsets!
These are gonna smush my puff.
They look kind of conspicuous.
You two, with me. Let's go.
I have got to quit getting kidnapped.
Shut it, bag lady.
C'mon, Patsy...
It's Attaché!
You rang?
POOF
WAH!
Don't DO that.
For what?
Sorry for running late. We had to make a pit stop.

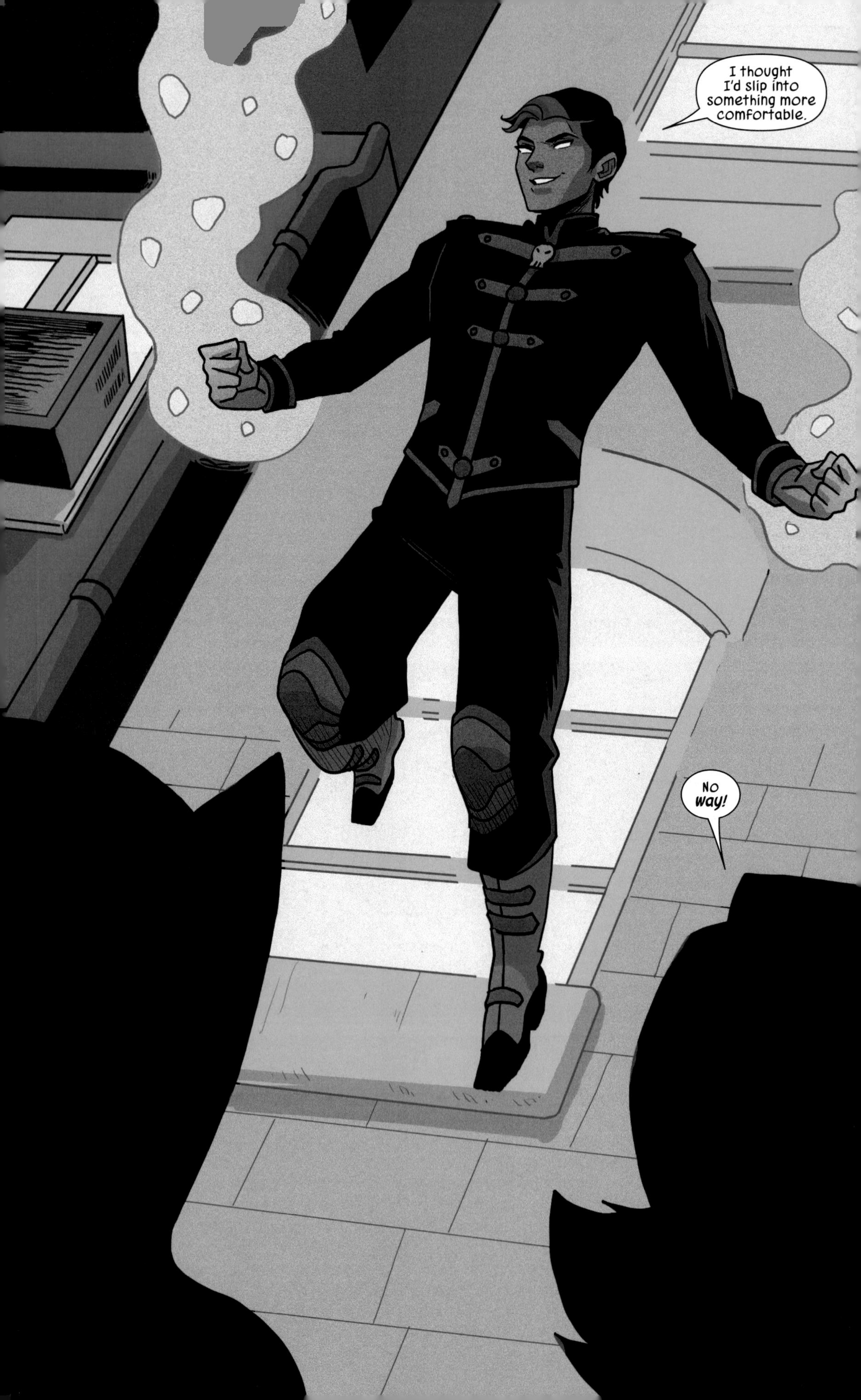
I thought I'd slip into something more comfortable.
No way!

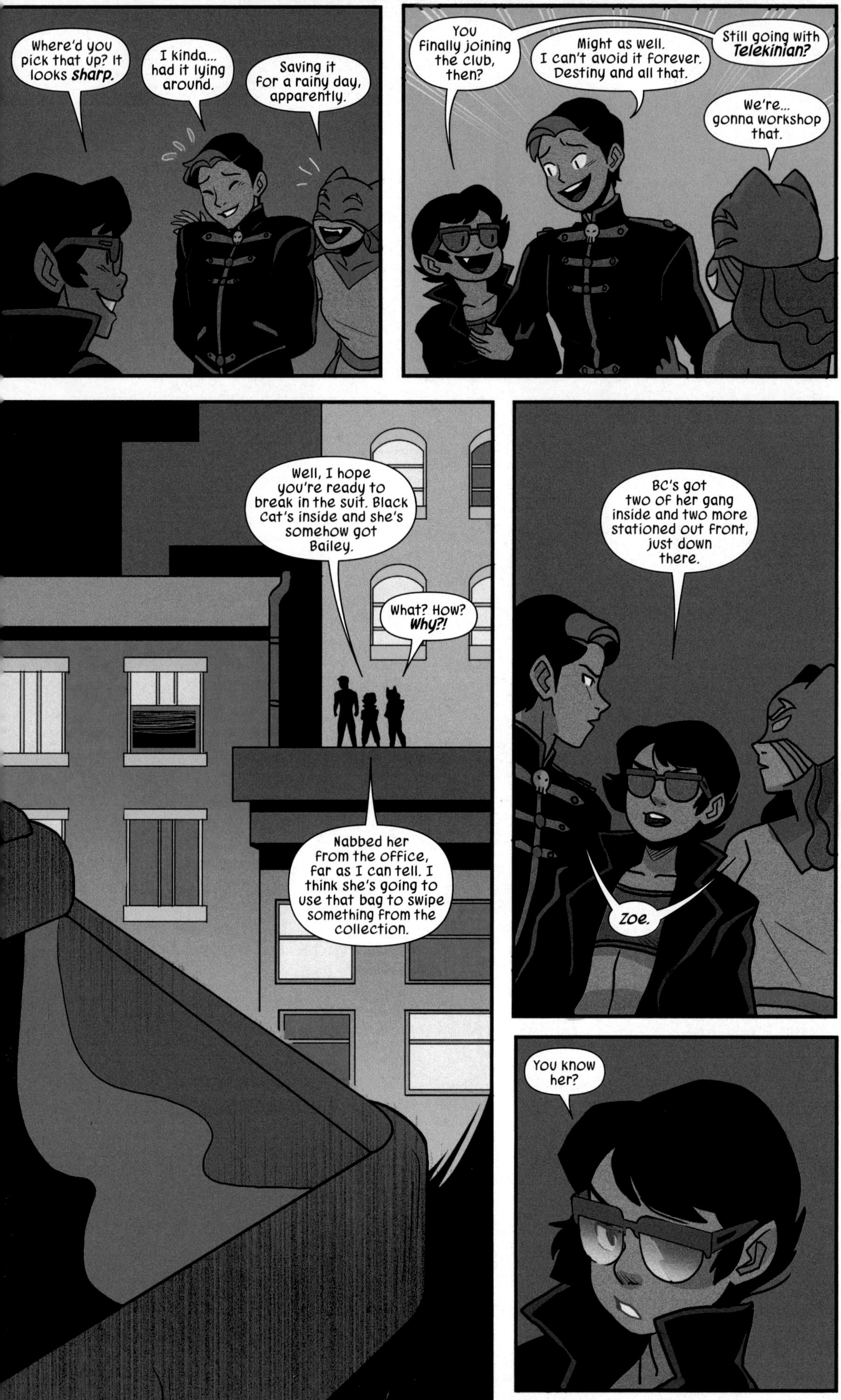

Where'd you pick that up? It looks *sharp.*
I kinda... had it lying around.
Saving it for a rainy day, apparently.
You finally joining the club, then?
Might as well. I can't avoid it forever. Destiny and all that.
Still going with *Telekinian?*
We're... gonna workshop that.
Well, I hope you're ready to break in the suit. Black Cat's inside and she's somehow got Bailey.
What? How? *Why?!*
Nabbed her from the office, far as I can tell. I think she's going to use that bag to swipe something from the collection.
BC's got two of her gang inside and two more stationed out front, just down there.
Zoe.
You know her?

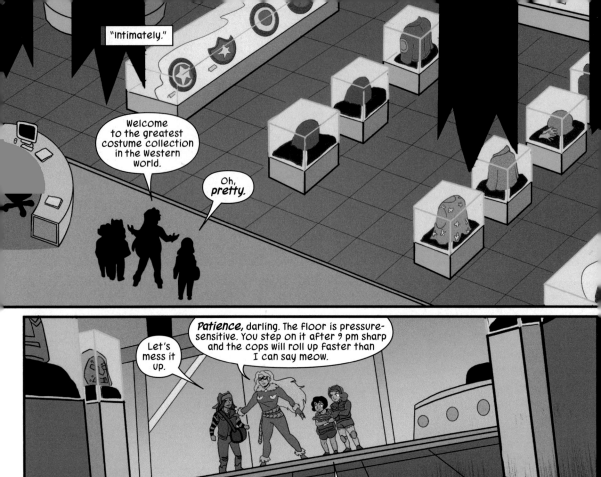

"Intimately."

Welcome to the greatest costume collection in the Western world.

Oh, pretty.

Let's mess it up.

Patience, darling. The floor is pressure-sensitive. You step on it after 9 pm sharp and the cops will roll up faster than I can say meow.

So, how exactly--

HUP!

Like so.

SCRRRRTCH

Purrrfect.

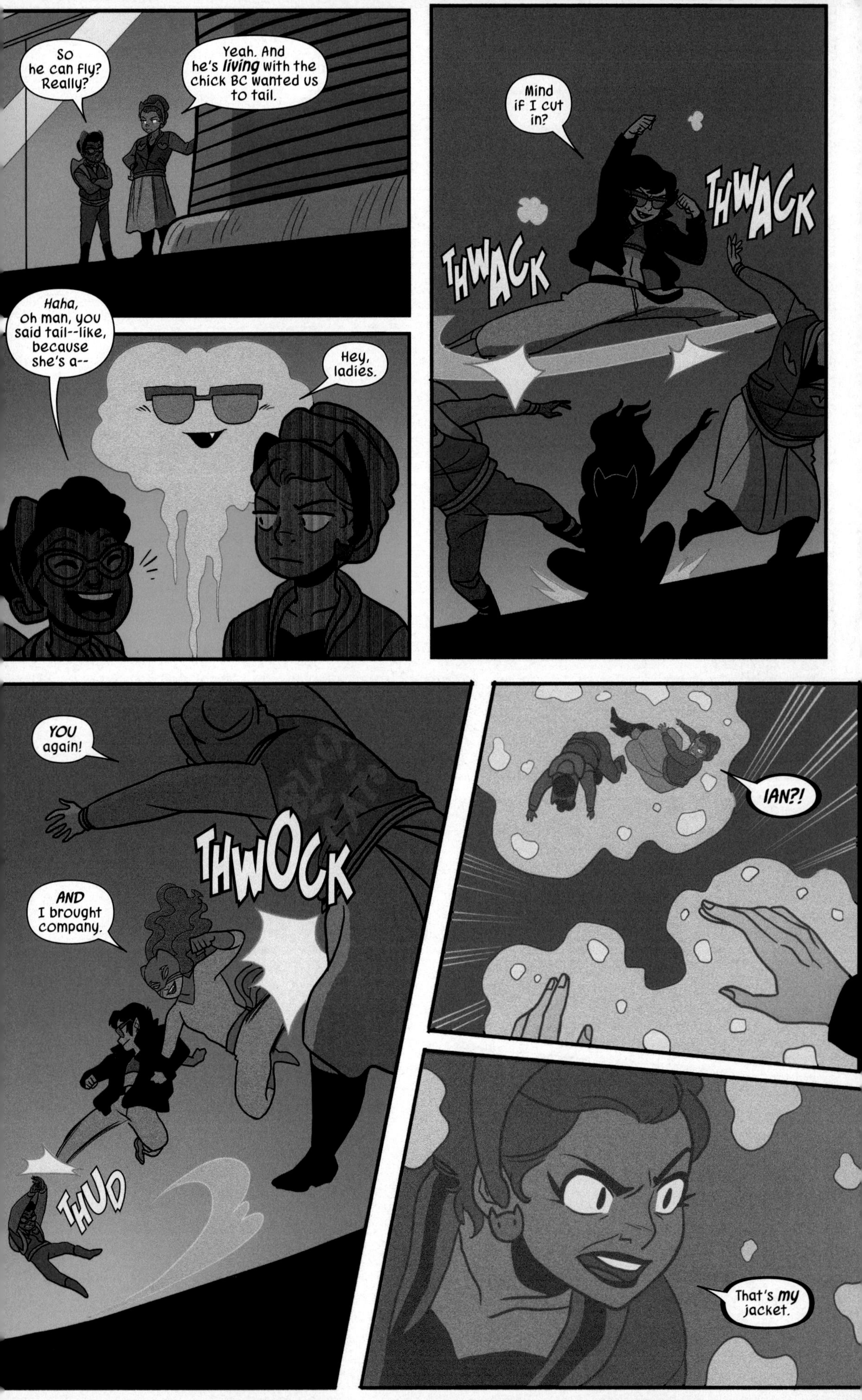
So he can fly? Really?
Yeah. And he's *living* with the chick BC wanted us to tail.
Haha, oh man, you said tail--like, because she's a--
Hey, ladies.
Mind if I cut in?
THWACK
THWACK
YOU again!
THWOCK
AND I brought company.
THUD
IAN?!
That's *my* jacket.

NOW, the trouble is finding an outfit to match.

She's taking forever. Someone's going to come.

Relax, would you? She's an *expert* thief. This is kind of her specialty.

It's weird, though...why a costume show? For that matter...why us? Doesn't she have, like, a whole bunch of goons at her disposal?

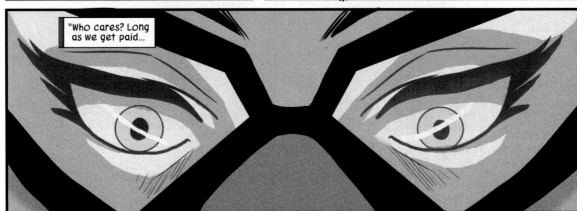

"Who cares? Long as we get paid...

"...I don't care *what* she does."

PRRRRRR

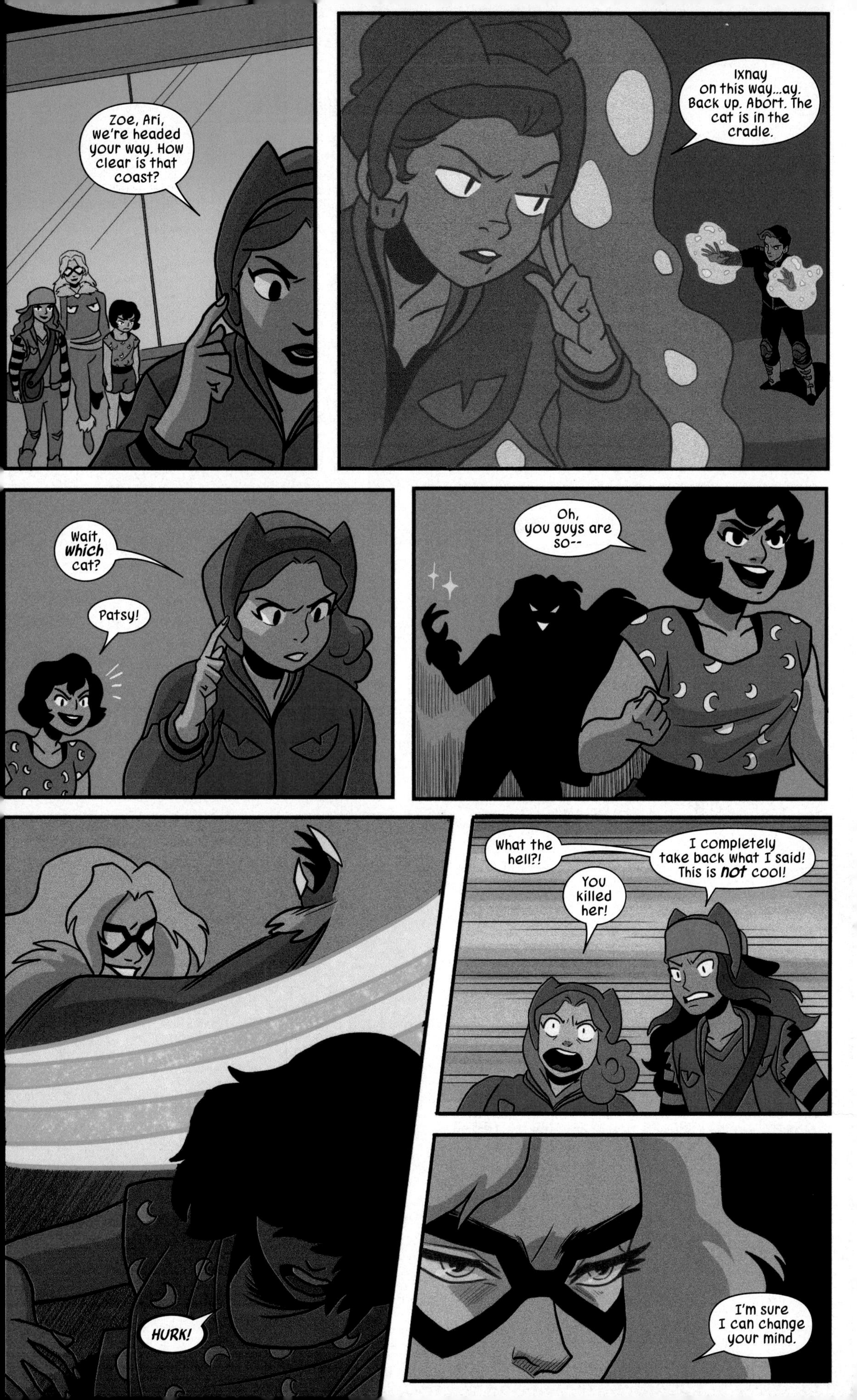
Zoe, Ari, we're headed your way. How clear is that coast?
Ixnay on this way...ay. Back up. Abort. The cat is in the cradle.
Wait, which cat?
Patsy!
Oh, you guys are so--
HURK!
What the hell?!
I completely take back what I said! This is not cool!
You killed her!
I'm sure I can change your mind.

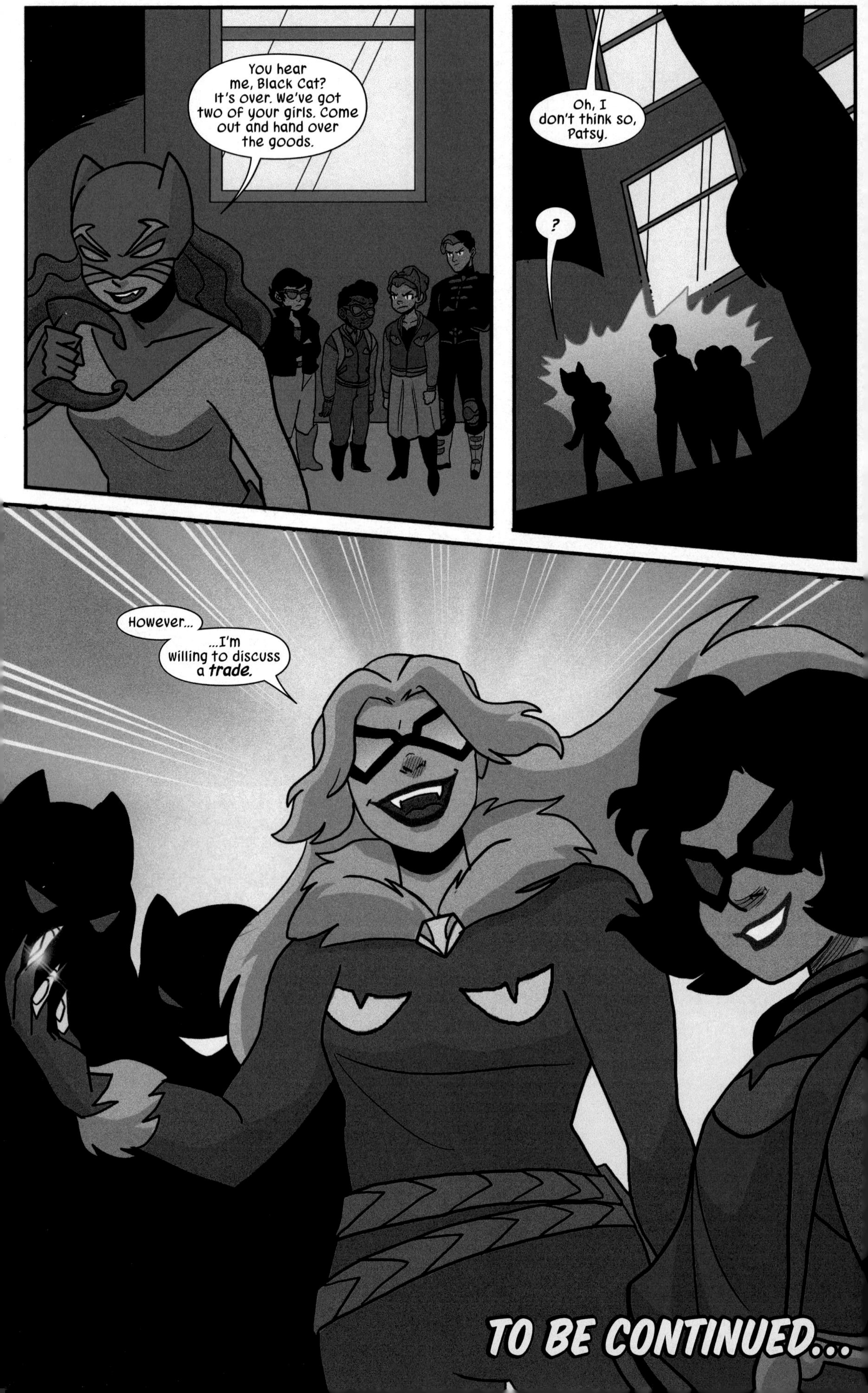
You hear me, Black Cat? It's over. We've got two of your girls. Come out and hand over the goods.
Oh, I don't think so, Patsy.
?
However...
...I'm willing to discuss a *trade.*
TO BE CONTINUED...

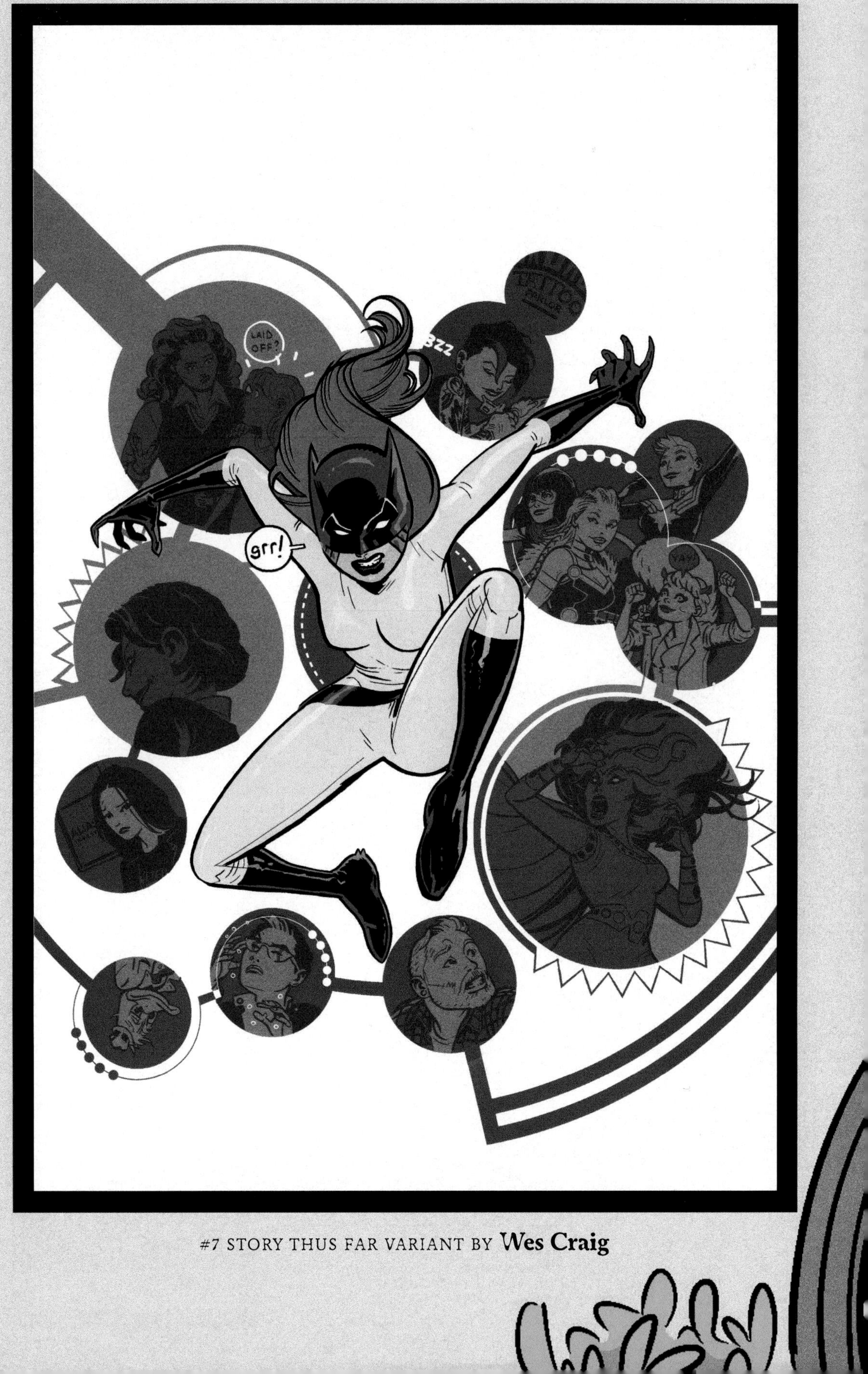
LAID OFF?
grr!

#7 STORY THUS FAR VARIANT BY **Wes Craig**

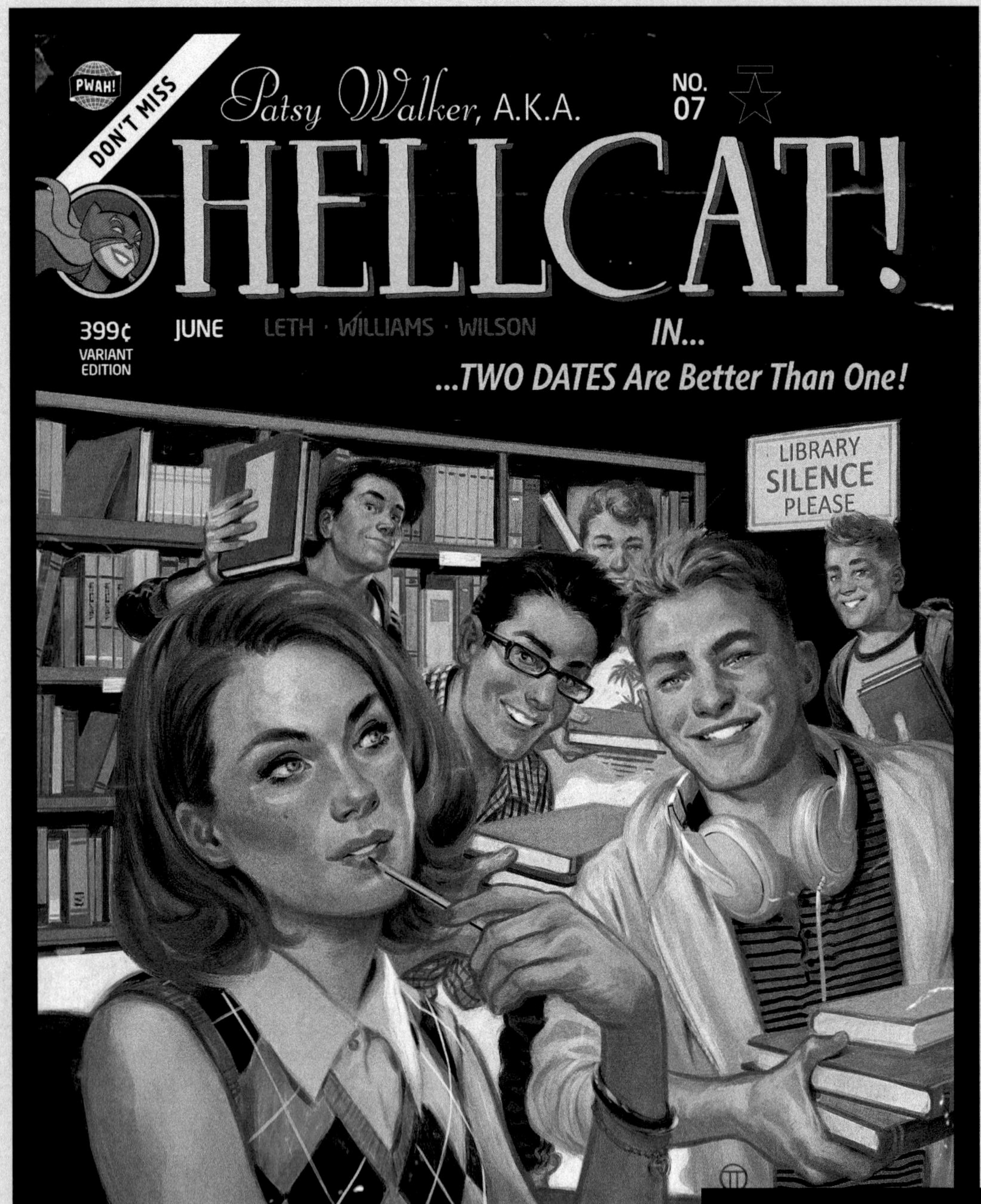
PWAH!
DON'T MISS
Patsy Walker, A.K.A.
NO. 07
HELLCAT!
399¢
VARIANT EDITION
JUNE
LETH · WILLIAMS · WILSON
IN...
...TWO DATES Are Better Than One!
LIBRARY SILENCE PLEASE

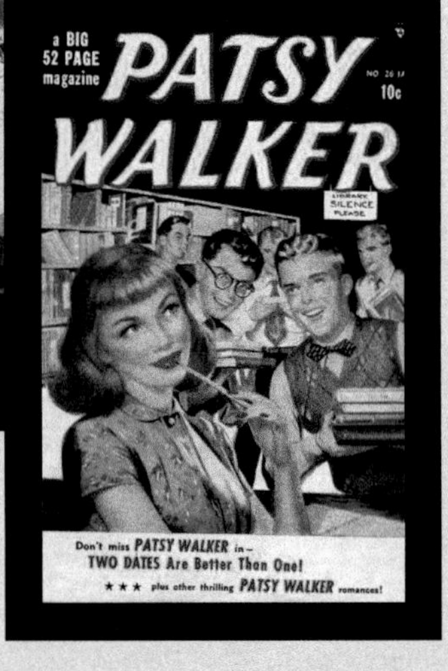
a BIG 52 PAGE magazine
PATSY WALKER
10¢
SILENCE
Don't miss PATSY WALKER in–
TWO DATES Are Better Than One!
★ ★ ★ plus other thrilling PATSY WALKER romances!

#7 VARIANT BY **Julian Totino Tedesco**

BASED ON *PATSY WALKER (1945) #26*
BY LOUISE ALTSON

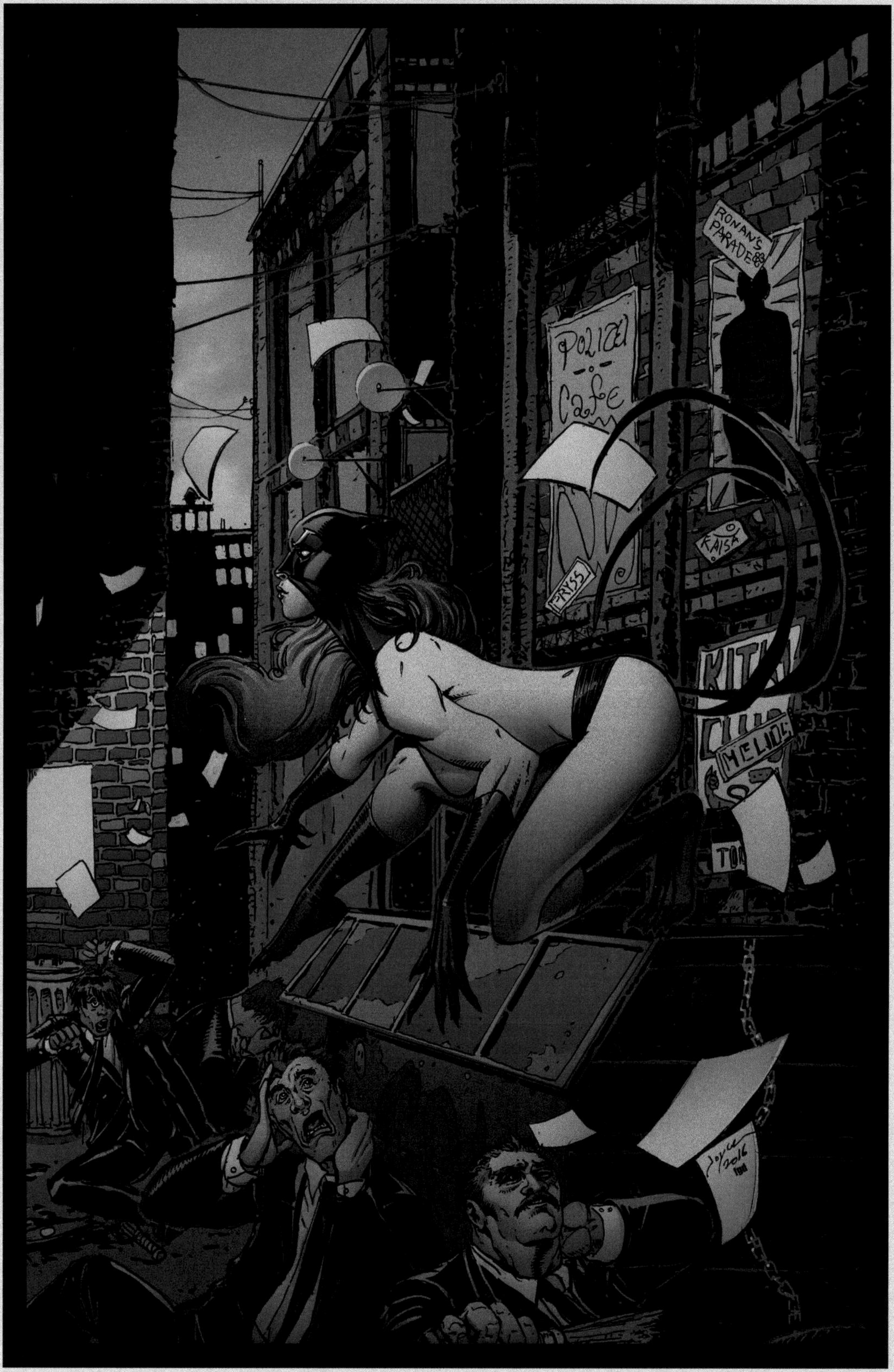
RONAN'S PARADE
POLIZEI CAFE
KAISA
FRYSS
MELIDI

#10 DEFENDERS VARIANT BY **Joyce Chin** & **Frank D'Armata**

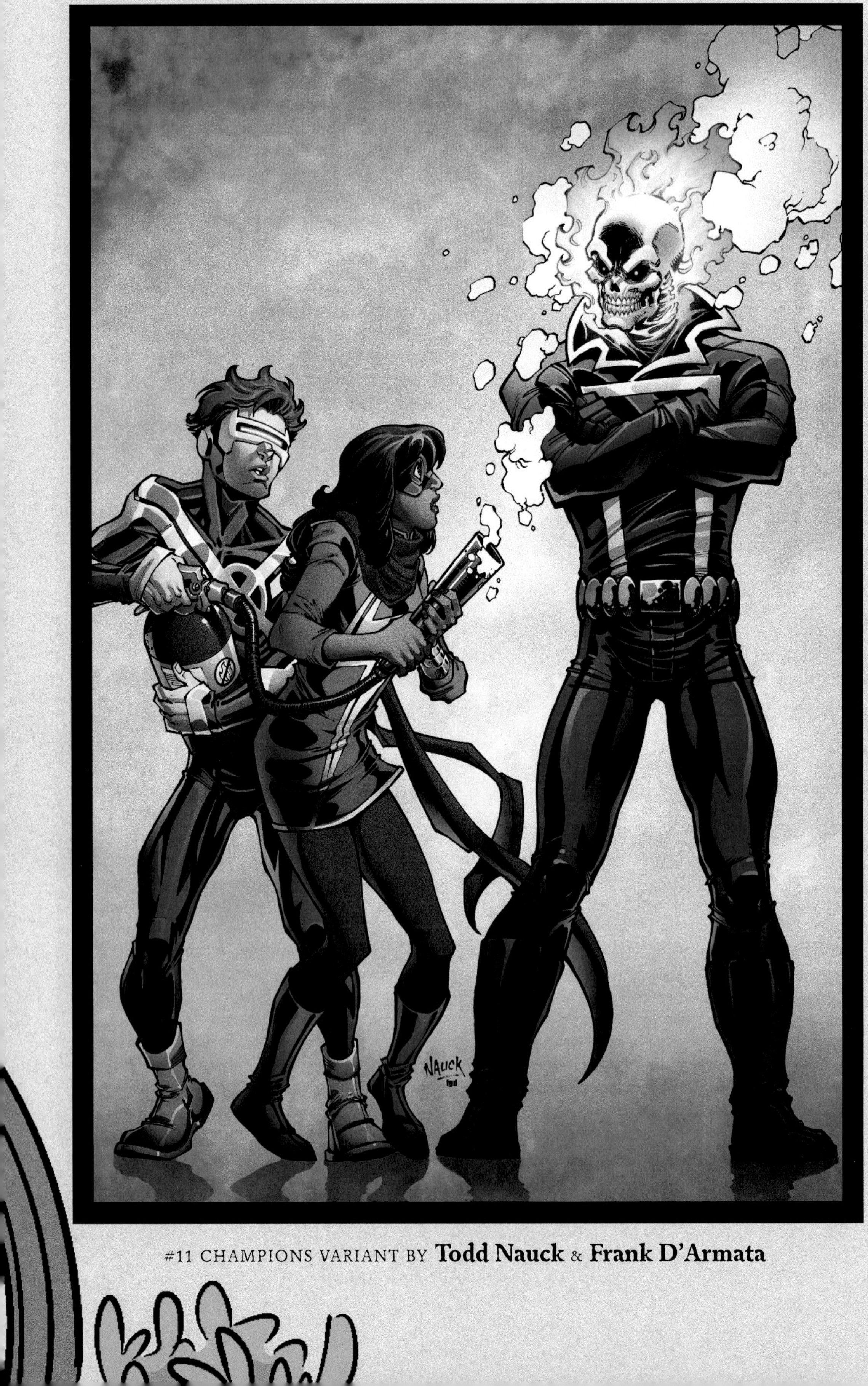
NAUCK

#11 CHAMPIONS VARIANT BY **Todd Nauck** & **Frank D'Armata**

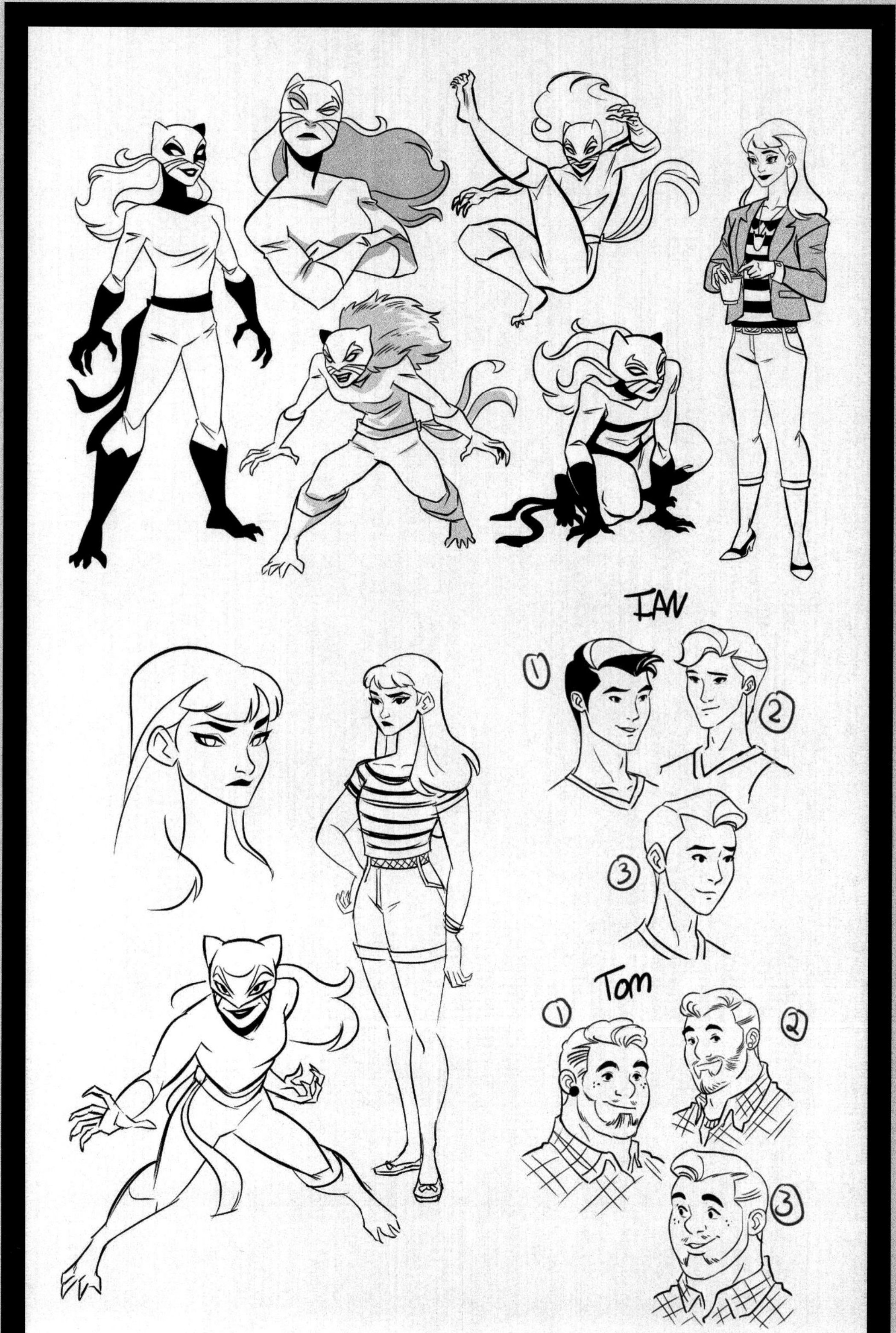
IAN
1
2
3
Tom
1
2
3

CHARACTER SKETCHES BY **Brittney L. Williams**

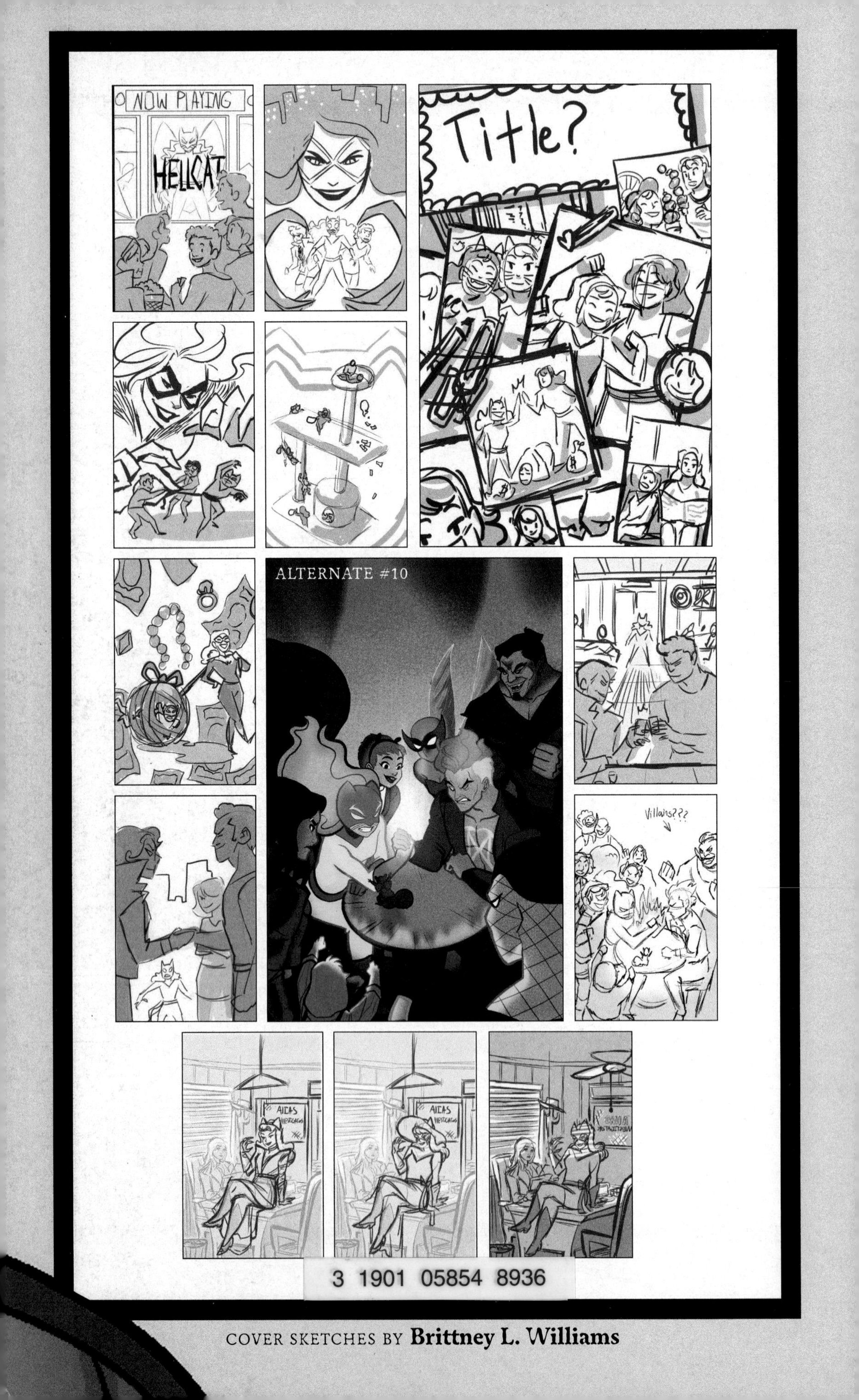
NOW PLAYING
HELLCAT
Title?
ALTERNATE #10
Villains???
ALIAS
ALIAS

COVER SKETCHES BY **Brittney L. Williams**